AN AFRICAN EDUCATION

The Social Revolution in Tanzania

AN AFRICAN EDUCATION
The Social Revolution in Tanzania

By

Laura S. Kurtz

PAGEANT-POSEIDON LTD.

Brooklyn, N.Y. 11217

370.9678

K96a

86505

Jan. 1974

Published by Pageant-Poseidon Ltd.

644 Pacific Street, Brooklyn, N. Y. 11217

Manufactured in the United States of America

To my parents, who were my first teachers, and to my friends, both Tanzanian and American, who have made my work in Tanzania so pleasant.

CONTENTS

CONTENTS

CONTENTS

Contents

LIST OF TABLES

ACKNOWLEDGMENT

I am deeply grateful to the many people who encouraged and assisted me with the preparation and writing of this study. First of all, I am deeply indebted to the chairman of my dissertation committee and my adviser throughout my doctoral studies, Dr. H. H. Giles, for his constant insight, understanding, and encouragement. Professors Brooks and Carras, the other committee members, each contributed invaluable assistance in various stages along the way. I am indeed grateful to the many other professors of New York University who shared themselves and their concerns in courses that laid the foundation for this study. To the many professors in educational institutions across the United States and in the University Dar es Salaam, who gave references for source material and persons, I also extend my gratitude.

I am obliged to the librarians of the many library branches of New York University, Columbia University, United Nations (including UNESCO), Tanzania Mission to the United Nations, and all the others who permitted me to use their facilities and provided me with master's and doctoral theses, including those writers who so generously made copies of their writings available.

Special thanks are due to Sospater Maregeri, my Tanzanian friend, who sent me the first important documents I needed from Tanzania; to Mr. E. K. Mutasa, Regional Education Officer now located at Moshi, and his colleague, Mr. N. S. Rutageruka, the Regional Education Officer of Coast Region, who bought and sent me syllabuses and volumes of the current Five-Year Plan; to my friend Gitta Komanyi for her interest and response in times of need; to Sara Ann Freed, who read the manuscript and gave valuable editorial assistance and counsel; to the typist, Marian Moss, who so graciously agreed to apply herself wholeheartedly to her task and to Julius K. Nyerere and the

1

ACKNOWLEDGEMENT

East African Publishing House for permission to quote from their works.

Last, but not least, I am particularly indebted to my family and all my friends, American and Tanzanian, for their understanding while I became less and less accessible as I concentrated on this research.

L. S. K.

Dar es Salaam, Tanzania

FOREWORD

Tanzania had been independent five years when its leaders pledged themselves to Ujamaa-ism at Arusha in early 1967. Their full-scale commitment to this Tanzanian type of socialism and self-reliance required many changes in the educational structure and curriculum content. Reforms in education during the period between 1961 and 1966 had made a few significant changes in the system. The changes since 1967, however, have been revolutionary.

This study will analyze and evaluate the significance and implications of the educational policies of post-independent Tanzania through two approaches. By abstracting the educational policies as a historical continuum, it will define the relationship between the educational policies of the postindependent Tanzania and those of colonial days. It will establish the relationship between the educational policies of postindependent Tanzania and the goals for the nation expressed by President Nyerere as a means of interconnecting education and the various facets of national development.

The main technique of research made use of documentary analysis. The researcher's experience in Tanzania's educational system since 1958 served as an additional basis for understanding. The main sources for the collection of data have included Tanzania's development plans, the many syllabuses and legislation on education, issues of the *Tanzania Education Journal*, reports of various agencies on teacher education, teacher supply and demand, books, articles of Nyerere's speeches and writings, graduate studies, and writings of scholars on various aspects of the Tanzania situation.

We will first endeavor to describe the nature of education in the colonial period, and then go on to ascertain and analyze President Nyerere's goals for the nation that are related to education, examine the educational policies of independent Tanzania in light of the expressed goals of the President, and discern the emerging patterns or trends in those educational policies. Our findings are set forth in a summary and specific conclusions have

3

been drawn in regard to the relationship between the President's goals and the educational policies since 1961. Recommendations complete the study.

Nyerere's goals were largely phrased in theoretical terminology during the first few years of the sixties, but he later emphasized greater application of the attitude of mind he upheld in earlier statements. His objectives can be capsuled as follows (the main goals to which he addressed himself specifically are included in the summary).

President Nyerere proposed:

1) that each individual be physically healthy and morally sound and contribute to his own well-being and to society by exercising his ability to communicate, to read, to inquire, and to provide for the necessities of life (objectives of self-realization);

2) that a nonracial democratic people, part of a united Africa, interact in the spirit of service rather than of self (objectives of human relationships);

3) that the standard of living be raised for everyone as a measure for the development of man rather than for the acquisition of wealth (objectives of economic efficiency);

4) that each individual exercise his rights and duties of citizenship through participation and involvement and in turn enjoy social justice (objectives of civic responsibility).

Nyerere believes the teacher has great power and influence because the key to the "new Tanzanian" lies in psychological and attitudinal change. He therefore believes that schools need to take initiative and to experiment in their task of educating for community living and development.

The educational policies of 1961 to 1966 (pre-Arusha) emphasize institution building, postprimary expansion, and the establishment of an effective education-planning unit. In deference to economic development, the social and cultural aspects of education took second or third place. The crises of 1966—the primary-school-leaver problem and the refusal of university students to accept National Service legislation—exposed how education had failed to meet the people's needs.

4

Since the Arusha Declaration of 1967, the policy for educational development still emphasizes economic development, but educational needs of the rural masses take priority. African culture and selected colonial educational policies have been revived and adjusted to the current African socio-economic setting. As primary and secondary educational institutions become community educational centers, the resulting change in emphasis requires new organization and revisions in curriculum. Revolutionizing an educational system is not an easy task. It requires the joint efforts of specialists in anthropology, psychology, sociology, educational theory; and able consultants. In addition, economists are called in to help. Just one cog out of gear can present a grave problem in the implementation of new policies. For this reason, all the age groups—from childhood to manhood—have been included in some phase of educational policy and development.

What is taking place, therefore, in Tanzania is an experiment. Many social, economic, political, and physical factors are exerting pressure to further, as well as to hinder, progress toward a self-reliant, cooperative way of life. Time will reveal the real impact or significance of the new policies developed after 1967; whether or not the teaching force can replace their former attitudes with a new set, and whether the school can coordinate rather than alienate rural life, and produce a young generation that is both creative and productive.

It is the author's hope that this research will serve as a base for many "take-off" research projects. They perhaps will be more narrow in scope and study particular elements of the educational system or certain policies in depth. If this research provides an overall view of Tanzanian education and in addition inspires further research, then the author will consider her purposes for this manuscript fulfilled.

L. S. K.
Dar es Salaam, Tanzania

INTRODUCTION

THE PROBLEM

To analyze and evaluate the significance and implications of the educational policies of postindependent Tanzania in light of the goals for Tanzania as expressed by President Nyerere, 1961-69, we must consider also the educational history of the country and divide the problem into four subproblems:

I.   To describe the nature of education in preindependent Tanzania;

II. To ascertain and analyze the goals for the nation that are related to education as expressed by President Nyerere, 1961-69;

III. To examine the education policies since independence, considering the stated goals of the President to discover congruence and differences;

IV. To discern emerging patterns or trends and evaluate the the findings of subproblem III.

Subproblem I establishes a good historical perspective. Only by understanding the educational policies as they emerged in the milieu of that particular time they were introduced, can one see the significance of some of the almost identical policies that have reappeared in the changed social, economic, and political environment of today. By establishing trends and instituting a framework for comparison, subproblem I puts the study into a perspective for assessing the successes and failures of postindependent Tanzania.

It is through a study of Ujamaa-ism, the new philosophy influencing present-day governmental policy and developmental plans for the future, that the role of education can best be evaluated for its impact on contemporary and future society. For that reason, subproblems II and III are included. Subproblem II gives the study a perspective from the aspirations of its top political leader in the sociological totality of the nation. Subproblem III analyzes the educational policies of 1961 to 1966 and since 1966 and identifies the emerging patterns.

7

Through these two approaches, this study analyzes the development of education in a context of the goals of the new Tanzania. The President envisions and projects the impact of today's educational policies into the future. Will the present policies prepare Tanzanian adults, youth, and children to contribute to and live in a society such as the President and present leaders hope for? Subproblem IV analyzes the patterns and trends in the educational policy by using the most valid methodology available for prediction and evaluation from past events.

The study combines elements of historical and descriptive research. The technique used in most of the study was a documentary analysis of existing records. The investigator's observations during active involvement in Tanzania's education system from 1958 to the present added an extra dimension in external and internal criticism. The researcher used primary and secondary sources.

Tanzania is passing through a crisis in culture and education just like the United States of America and other Western countries. What the products of the school system express do not conform to the expectations of most policymakers and educators in our countries. Even though major reforms were made in the educational system in Tanzania since independence—for example, integration of four separate racial systems into one; decentralization of responsibility for elementary education to local powers; and establishment of a Unified Teaching Service for all registered teachers—the increasing primary-school-leaver problem and the university students' revolt in 1966 against the National Service Act exposed the nationwide dimension of the educational problem.

Because President Nyerere grew up in the same British type of educational system as students of postindependent times, he has been both realistic and courageous and is proving to be a real leader in identifying the problem and seeking solutions to it.

Many of the African countries profess a form of egalitarianism and speak of an African personality or culture. Tanzania, one of the poorest economically of the African countries, seems more determined than others to go beyond the verbalization stage to some practical applications of commitment to its Tanzanian brand of socialism called "Ujamaa-ism." Changes have been made in leadership requirements, in wages for high-level earners, in the

8

nationalization of industries and banks, in rural-development patterns, and in educational policies and practices. Each change was a response to Tanzania's commitment to Ujamaa-ism and self-reliance. Conversely, some factors opposing these trends are: the traditional, colonial idea that entry to high-level manpower positions is legitimately restricted to those with specified educational qualifications; the luxurious privileges guaranteed to a post-secondary graduate, the educational pyramidal structure itself; the influence of colonialism; the isolation of teachers; and the conservatism of traditional society.

Just as Tanzania led all its neighbors in independence, it is now providing leadership for the development of socialism. African neighbors are observing the changes, and in some instances adopting a few of the same measures in their own country. Kenya and Uganda, for example, followed by several years with their adoption of a one-party democratic state, and Somalia also nationalized some institutions in 1970. These East African countries continue to watch this experiment in socialist policies and mobilization in Tanzania, hoping to find some encouragement and suggestions for their own problems.

Not only are the other African countries carefully watching Tanzania's experiments, but Tanzania itself is also analyzing the effects of its policies, re-evaluating its positions, and adjusting its policies for greater relevance in contemporary situations. These processes have been more intensive and revolutionary in the past few years due to the aforementioned increasing problem of the primary-school leaver and the university students' revolt in 1966. The latter served as a catalyst in 1967 for the *Arusha Declaration*, the official document on socialism and self-reliance (and subsequent White Papers during that year on its implications in education and rural development). Education expects to play a major role in the future implementation of this historical document, the Arusha Declaration.

Julius K. Nyerere, the teacher-philosopher president of Tanzania, has been pressing the issue of Ujamaa-ism and self-reliance for a number of years. Concurrent legislation and policy revealed that TANU (Tanganyika African National Union, the sole political party) had also been formally committed to socialism since independence. It was not until January, 1967, that the Govern-

9

ment officially declared this commitment in the *Arusha Declaration*. As mentioned previously, the crises of 1966 set the stage for the necessary re-evaluation of education, a process long overdue; primary-school leavers, some parents, and university students demonstrated attitudes at variance with the attitudes President Nyerere, other political leaders, and education officers expected them to hold. President Nyerere, as head of state, head of the political party, and head of government and public service, has been the main spokesman and policymaker for the government. Tanzanian literature on the subject of socialism and self-reliance has been confined primarily to his speeches and writings. Therefore, as long as President Nyerere is in a position to direct policy, the country's development will be determined greatly by his philosophy of socialism.

Nyerere calls the *Arusha Declaration* a statement of intent and describes it as laying a policy of revolution by evolution. It is a general outline that needs interpretation in every aspect of development. Various Governmental departments are trying to apply the general principles to their specific areas of work. Education, for example, must decrease the gap between school and community through effective communication. It must also unite the literate and illiterate school-age population on projects so that the power structure in the communities will be able to accommodate and channel the abilities of educated youths profitably. In addition, education must keep a balance between social and vocational goals and determine how a school can create an elite (until universal education is possible) that is willing to serve the country.

In Nyerere's own words:

By thinking out our own problems on the basis of those principles which have universal validity, Tanzania will make its own contribution to the development of mankind. That is our opportunity and our responsibility.[1]

---

1. Julius K. Nyerere, in his Introduction to the book, *Freedom and Socialism* (Dar: Oxford University Press, 1968), p. 32.

RELATED LITERATURE

The works and authors mentioned in this section are the most pertinent sources used in this study. Complete publishing data regarding each reference can be found in the bibliography at the end of the study.

Much of the ideology of Tanzanian socialism is determined by an analysis of the statements, written and oral, of the President. The *Arusha Declaration and TANU's Policy on Socialism and Self-Reliance* defines the commitment of the Tanzania Government to socialism and self-reliance. A few political scientists, Arrighi, Burke, and Mohiddin, have offered the most comprehensive commentaries on Nyerere's Ujamaa-ism. Dumont's book, *False Start in Africa*, has had a profound effect on Tanzania and a number of Dumont's ideas have found a place in the country's policies.

Various aspects of education have been mentioned by many authors, but only a few have focused on Tanzania: William Dodd's articles and his monograph, *Education for Self-Reliance in Tanzania: A Study of Its Vocational Aspects;* John Cameron's *The Development of Education in East Africa;* Clayton M. Schindler's and Kent State's studies on teacher education; the book, *Tanzania: Education by Revolution,* edited by Idrian N. Resnick; and studies on attitudes of Tanzanian students by Joel W. Barkan, E. L. Klinglehofer, David Koff, George von der Muhll and Kenneth Prewitt.

The graduate studies found to be most helpful are the following:

1) Ellen George's 1968 qualifying paper on " 'Education for Self-Reliance' in Tanzania: An Evaluation of Nyerere's Approach" in which she examines his approach to primary education.

2) Henry J. Hector's 1967 M.A. thesis, "The Government's Role in African Post-Primary Education in Tanganyika 1919-1939," which provides information on educational history.

3) Rodney James Hinkle's 1969 Ed.D. document, "Educational Problems and Policies in Post-Independent Tan-

11

zania," which focuses on several outstanding problems and the Government's response to these problems from 1958 to 1967.

4) Eliud Ikusa Maluki's 1965 Ph.D. dissertation on "The Influence of Traditionalism upon Nyerere's 'Ujamaa-ism' " in which he concludes that Nyerere's conceptions of government, discussion, election, and socio-economic values are principally based on the traditional values.

5) Matthew Salim Mamuya's 1965 M.A. thesis, "Religion and Society in Tanganyika: An Encounter of Western Civilization with Traditional Culture," inquiring into the impact of Western civilization on traditional culture.

6) Robert M. Martin's 1966 M.A. thesis, "An Analytic Survey of Tanganyikan Educational System During 1961-64 Period," which provides survey material and recommendations for that time.

7) Anthony Hubert Rweyemamu's 1966 Ph.D. dissertation, "Nation-Building and the Planning Processes of Tanzania," expressing the belief that the success or failure of nation building will be determined in the rural areas of Tanzania because here is where 96 per cent of the population is located; and advocating awareness and involvement on the part of citizens.

BACKGROUND TO THE STUDY

Tanzania, a country located at a sensitive place near the heart of Africa, has gone through vast social, economic, and political changes in the past twenty-five years and taken enormous strides in the past decade. Mainland Tanzania, the area covered by this study, is approximately six hundred miles square and has 11.9 million people with a range in density from 3 to eight hundred people per square mile.

There are three distinct regions: the coastal plain with a hot, humid climate; the large, semi-arid plateau about four thousand feet in altitude with a more temperate climate; and the cool, well-watered uplands in the north around Mt. Kilimanjaro and in the south. The environment is a poor and harsh one. Only one-third of Tanzania has potential for an unintensive type of pastoralism. About two-thirds of the total area is infested by the tsetse fly.

Due to a shortage of water, soil erosion, and unreliable rainfall, the population is concentrated in the periphery of the country. Nearly 99 per cent of the people are Africans, one per cent are Arabs and Asians, and 0.1 per cent are Europeans.[2] Only 4.8 per cent live in urban areas, which figure exceeds eight thousand people. Life expectancy is between thirty-five and forty years of age. With half the total population under sixteen years of age, the adult population carries a much greater burden of young than adults in developed countries. Of the 120 tribes, the largest single tribe has less than 10 per cent of the population. There are more than one hundred thousand refugees from neighboring lands in Tanzania. The majority of the population adheres to traditional religious beliefs, one-fourth are Moslem, and another one-fourth are Christians.

Swahili has been the lingua franca of the people, and is the only official language of the nation since 1967; English remains the language of commerce and higher education. Literacy in Swahili is estimated at 10 to 15 per cent for those over fifteen years of age and 1 per cent in English. About 50 per cent of the respective age groups are in primary school, 3 per cent in secondary school, and about two thousand students in university.

The majority of the people follow the traditional ways of life, which tend to be conservative and village centered. Tanzania does not have a marked elite; few are wealthy. Again, one cannot generalize in East Africa as in the Western world. No poverty line can be drawn since, for example, a man may live in poor conditions according to our standards, but his cattle are his family's hoofed trust fund. Social differences are educational differences and occupational specialization, which result in a variation of wealth and status. Consequently, one of the major aims of the Arusha Declaration is to reduce the gap between the elite and peasant.

---

2. The figures in this section are taken from the 1967 census estimates. SEE Alfison Butler Herrick, et al., *Area Handbook for Tanzania—1968*, DA Pam. No. 550-62 (Washington: U.S. Government Printing Office, 1968); and *Tanzania Today*, the Ministry of Information and Tourism's book (Nairobi: University Press of Africa, 1968).

Tanzania has few resources, but it can still develop its land, and its greatest asset, the people, by using their potentials to a greater degree. Agriculture and cattle raising are the principal occupations. Many agriculturalists keep cattle, and pastoralists dabble around in agriculture. The national income fluctuates with climatic conditions and export earnings. Industrial production exists on a modest scale. Along with the Arusha Declaration, the major industries and banks have been nationalized. Other industries remain private enterprises.

Arabs dominated the coastline for years and their influence has spread along the old inland slave routes. The Germans ruled for over thirty years and then the British administered Tanganyika until 1961 under a mandate and later the trusteeship system. TANU, the political party, was born in 1954 and in seven years' time the country had its independence. In December, 1962, it became a republic and remained in the British Commonwealth. The state was born of tribal entities; the problem was then to build a nation.

Since independence, the great task of the nation has been to develop a national ethic, to discard the repugnant, and to retain the desirable forms established under the colonial regime. For years Africans have tended to be ambivalent about their own culture. Now there has been an awakening and they can look without shame and even with pride upon their own culture. The one-party democracy seems to have been handed down from African traditional society.

Self-reliance was first introduced on the national level around 1964 and has changed many of the nation's policies in regard to economics. Self-reliance means relying on resources within the nation instead of waiting for some external aid. Self-reliance demands also that resources be used for the benefit of the people and implies an end to privileges. Along with the commitment to socialism, self-reliance has been a part of the influential force that has brought a great mobilization among the population of Tanzania.

Tanzania's commitments go beyond the verbal stage; they have reached into actions and behavior. Whether or not attitudes have really been changed will be determined at a later time than the present.

KIMYA KINGI KINA MSHINDO MKUU.

A long silence is followed by a mighty noise.

CHAPTER ONE

WESTERN INFLUENCES ENTER TANZANIA: THE GERMAN PERIOD, 1885-1916

BACKGROUND TO THE PERIOD

To understand the radical changes that have taken place in Tanzania's education since independence and especially since 1967, it is necessary to both carefully analyze the past and envision the future. As Tom Mboya has warned: "A vision of Africa—present and to come—is impossible without being armed with a background and history of colonial Africa—its impacts, effects, and the problems it has generated for the future of Africa." [1] This is the purpose of looking carefully at education during the colonial periods of the Germans and the English.

Let us begin with the Germans in East Africa, since formal education on a state level was established during the German period. This does not, however, minimize the formal traditional educational practices of the many tribes in Tanganyika; they are not within the scope of this study except through interrelationship with the state educational system.

The Industrial Revolution, having taken effect in Germany by the mid-1880's, was one of the influential factors leading to German interest in Africa. In 1885, one year after Karl Peters had negotiated treaties with chiefs in the interior of Tanganyika, Germany officially annexed the territory. The Anglo-German and the German-Portuguese agreements of 1886 and the Helgoland Treaty of 1890 set the boundaries for German East Africa. The Imperial German Government took over the right to rule from the German East Africa Company in 1891.

This was not Tanganyika's first contact with the outer world. During the medieval years, a widespread trade flourished along

---

1. Tom Mboya, "Vision of Africa" in James Duffy and Robert A. Manners (eds.), *Africa Speaks* (Princeton: D. Van Nostrand, 1961), p. 21.

17

the coast with the Arabs, Persians, Chinese, and Indians. The Portuguese intrusion of the late fifteenth and sixteenth centuries was followed by European traders, explorers, and missionaries. The German missionary Rebmann arrived in 1848, and in 1859 the German explorer Roscher was killed near Lake Nyasa after he ventured beyond Kilwa.

The Swahili language probably developed into its present structure around the thirteenth century. It was the common language of the coast and the *lingua franca* for trade transactions. It maintained a Bantu base and derived its vocabulary from the languages of the traders on the coast—Arab, Persian, Portuguese, Turkish, and Indian. The search for ivory and slaves extended the trade inland in the mid-nineteenth century. It was partly in response to this inhumane treatment of Africans that many of the English, French, and German missionaries came to Tanganyika.

The Germans encountered considerable rebellion to their rules, notably the Bushiri rebellion of 1888-89, the Mkwawa revolt from 1891 until his death in 1898, and the Maji Maji rebellion of 1905-07. Although it is generally accepted that they spent most of their time pacifying the country, a survey of some of the accomplishments during this period reveals that the Germans served greater functions than just "keeping the peace." If the period of 1891 to 1898 was largely filled with consolidating the German hold, the remaining period was one of greater growth in economic and educational development. They unified the people through the introduction of a money economy and various other facets of Westernization to a small degree. They brought a new brand of coffee to Tanganyika, introduced tea, sisal and cotton, provided a road and railway system, and trained semi-skilled workers.

Mamuya points out in his thesis the negative effect of German colonization. He believes that the Germans, convinced of their superiority, acted accordingly and damaged the people psychologically. From conversations with Tanzanians who remember the days of the Germans, this researcher would conclude that the Germans are remembered most for their harsh measures of discipline to restrain the Africans during their servitude. As a result, the Africans lost their freedom, developed an inferiority complex, and succumbed to passivity. President Nyerere would support Mamuya's idea also, for he speaks of the degradation and evils of the colonial system and lists as the number-one crime the attempt to "make us believe we had no indigenous culture of our own; of that what we did have was worthless—something of which we should be ashamed, instead of a source of pride."[2]

THE BIRTH OF A STATE EDUCATIONAL SYSTEM

The first educational efforts in addition to the local traditional education were conducted by the religious mission socieites that entered Tanganyika in the mid-nineteenth century. Their original purpose, to acquire applicants for baptism, expanded as the need for teachers and preachers arose. The Government found it necessary to set up its own education system because it viewed the mission schools inadequate on two points. The best products of the mission schools were employed by the missions in their own service, leaving "the rubbish" for governmental service; and secondly, Christianity was becoming a source of friction in the Muslim areas.

Government officials assumed that the Swahili-speaking peoples represented a culturally advanced element. The Government hired a Moslem to teach the Koran in their coastal schools and justified this decision on the grounds that the Koran was being translated from Arabic to Swahili medium. This inclusion and justification somewhat pacified Moslems and Christians, the former happy that they were allotted a place in the Government schools and the latter hoping that Swahilization of the Koran would have the effect of secularizing it, thus reducing its sphere of influence. The Germans produced the transliteration of Swahili from the Arabic to the Roman alphabet, the real core of the conflict. To answer the Christian critics, they said that Roman script would facilitate the introduction of German culture and Christianity. The use of Swahili was threatening to some missions, and as late as 1906, the home board of the Moravians prohibited its use in their schools at Tabora, claiming that Swahili would facilitate the spread of Islam.

Tanga School was begun in 1890 by a missionary and taken over by the Government in 1892. Had it not been financed from

2. Julius K. Nyerere, *Freedom and Unity/Uhuru na Umoja* (Dar: Oxford University Press, 1967), p. 186.

1892 to 1894 by an outside source, the German Colonial Society, the Government might never have established a direct, state education when strong criticism was raised by German missionaries in Tanganyika and officials in Germany. Tanga School became the main source for the recruitment of workers—clerks, interpreters, customs officials, teachers, and akidas (lower government officers). Swahili was established as a medium of instruction, with German introduced only on the advanced level. Part of the course was the memorization of law books with a corresponding course in Swahili.

Secular schooling was first included in the official budget in 1895 after Tanga School had already existed for several years and missionary objections had not dislodged it. By this time Bagamoyo and Dar es Salaam also opened schools under the state system, and a state curriculum was set up. Berlin had designated the use of the German language, but the officials in Dar rationalized a change to Swahili. Swahili was also adopted as the language of the administration. Still another policy of crucial importance at the time was the flexibility of the system of state education through the medium of Swahili, which could incorporate tribal and coastal elites.

In the succeeding years, the state system gained in precedence as the Koranic schools declined and mission schools gradually compromised with Government standards. In 1898 a subsidy was granted to any mission school on two conditions: 1) that it adopt a Swahili curriculum; and 2) allow the district officer to conduct examinations.

The main interest the Africans held for the German administrators was economic, spurred on by the Industrial Revolution in Europe. The climate of Tanganyika was not found suitable for much European settlement, so the African had to be developed to help in administration, and to exploit the resources within Tanganyika for the profit of the ruling country. German educational policies dealt with improving the physical status of the African by controlling disease, increasing his economic capacity either as a plantation laborer or semi-skilled worker, and stimulating his moral and intellectual progress through the activities of the missions. The continuing course beyond village schools was designed to last four years, but was reduced to two only when the demand for civil servants became so great.

Although the main interest of the administration was economic, development was gained at some cost to the Africans, there was some concern expressed about the welfare of the individual African: It was considered an injustice to alienate him from the land and his national life.

The official German record reads: "To alienate the Negro from farming his native soil without giving him an occupation that is in harmony with his new level of education would mean to inflict a wrong on him."

Under the civilian governors, Rechenberg and Schnee (1906-16), some new policies included an end to forced labor except for public works, protection of laborers and African ownership of land, and encouragement of African agricultural production. The Government not only emphasized the development of practical skills needed in agriculture and in administration, but also aimed at developing the character traits essential to such service—obedience, tidiness, punctuality, conscientiousness, and a sense of duty. A description of the German period cannot omit the role of the bands in the schools. There were in 1913 eighteen hundred bands in the schools, a booster start for an educational activity that has continued throughout all the years since and has added an atmosphere of dignity and creativity to the schools.

Even though education was free for all during the German era, there was no lack of problems. The Government was forced to offer free education as the missions were doing because fees were impossible to collect. They also subscribed to a compulsory system, but were powerless to keep anyone in school who wished to leave. There were other problems: Schools met with hostility; attendance was poor; and teachers became discouraged and neglected their schools. Corporal punishment of students and African teachers changed with the death of a child in 1911.

The German Colonial Institute reported in 1911 that there were 1,001 schools: 953 for elementary education; 31 for higher education; and 17 for industrial education. There were 287 European teachers, 1,256 native teachers, and 66,647 pupils. Only 83 of these schools were operated by the Government, the rest were

maintained by Roman Catholics and Protestants. A juxtaposi-
tion of the enrollment figures given by Wright for 1910 with those
of the 1911 report reveals that conflict still existed between Gov-
ernment-supported Swahili education and mission education.
She lists 3,494 elementary and 681 middle or upper students in
the state secular schools and an estimate of only 1,196 students
in mission schools following the standard Swahili curriculum.[3]
The balance of approximately fifty or sixty thousand pupils in
1910 must have attended schools that formed their own, independent curricula.

The Government schools were located mostly in the eastern
and northern parts of Tanganyika. The Anglicans, Lutherans,
Catholics, and other sects worked farther inland. Their efforts
provided education for Europeans and Africans, but not for the
Indians in that area. An estimated ten thousand Indians occupied it by 1914. They were employed as artisans, mechanics,
and Government personnel and in commerce. There were separate kindergartens for German children in Dar and three others
for South African Dutch settlers in the Arusha District. The great
increase in the number of schools and the enrollment in the early
1900's is shown on the following chart.

TABLE I

TANGANYIKA'S SCHOOLS AND THEIR ENROLLMENT
IN SELECTED YEARS
1903-14

Year	Number of schools		Pupils	
	Government	Mission	Government Schools	Mission Schools
1903	8	15	—	—
1911	83	918	3,192	63,455
1914	99	1,852	6,100	155,287

A variety of trades were taught in the artisan schools. Boys
with promise were selected and removed from the village schools

    ³   Marcia Wright, "Local Roots of Policy in German East Africa"
The Journal of African History, IX: n.4 (1968), p. 629.

and sent to the nearest schools with European headmasters. After three or four years of study there, they were sent on to Tanga, where the school had been upgraded to secondary level in 1906, for teacher training and advanced studies. A few Africans were also sent to Germany for study at this time.

The German education, with its emphasis on practical education, teacher education, and health improvement, was called to a halt by World War 1 and for four years most of the schools were closed. When the British took over the schools from the Germans in 1916, they were impressed with the standard of literacy reached in Tanganyika. Truly, Tanganyikans had reached a higher level than any of their neighboring countries, but it was still very low. The British had not yet developed a state system for a native educational policy in Kenya at this time.

SUMMARY

The Germans had succeeded in developing a state education system. The flexibility of their administration is evidenced in their ability to build a system with emphasis on the practical education required to meet the demands of the Government for semi-skilled workers in administration and in the economy. A far cry from the gymnasiums in Germany, with their Latin and classical learning, they were more similar in objectives to the *Volksschule*, the school geared to the general public. A second aspect of their flexibility is seen in their policy of subsidizing mission schools. It was more than mere recognition of these schools; it demonstrated an expression of partnership and a certain degree of cooperation (and control) in the efforts against illiteracy. Government schools, which left the education of girls to the missions, were open to all boys—Moslems, pagans, and Christians. It was no small task to form a system that met the needs of both the coastal and tribal elites.

One of the major contributions that bridged this gap and one for which the Germans will always be appreciated is the status they gave to Swahili; it has been crucial in the development of Tanganyika toward independence and in its national growth since.

In the process of expanding Tanganyika's economy and establishing a system of government for the whole territory through education, Westerners quite successfully impressed upon the natives the superiority of the Western culture.[4] The African who became educated in the schools gradually lost identity with, and the freedom of, his own tribal environment. The British continued this process until independence, when the African finally woke up to the consequences of imitation and focused attention on his heritage.

---

4. "The teaching they sought was a literary education in English, for in a European-style education in a European language, they believe, lay the source of European power and the road to equality," John Iliffe, *Tanganyika Under German Rule*, 1905-1912 (Cambridge: University Press, 1969), p. 178.

CHAPTER TWO

THE FORMATION OF BRITISH COLONIAL POLICIES BETWEEN THE WARS:

THE BRITISH MANDATE PERIOD, 1917-1945

THE MILITARY ADMINISTRATION, 1917-1919

On December 2, 1916, the British appointed Sir Horace Byatt military governor of Tanganyika, effective January 1, 1917. Very little was attempted beyond alleviating misery and suffering during this period in which World War I was being fought. Widespread influenza left its toll here as elsewhere; an estimated fifty to eighty thousand died from this disease between 1917 and 1919. Famine claimed another thirty thousand. Appalling conditions are cited in the records.

British doctrine required the colonies to be self-sufficient. Although the finances of the Tanganyika Government (received from exports sold on unstable markets) were low, the revenue exceeded the expenditures during these years. This was possible only because the administration did not spend money on pressing needs. No attempt was made to continue education until December, 1919, when the European district officers were officially permitted to re-open Government schools.

THE PERIOD OF CONSOLIDATION AND EXPANSION, 1920-31

Byatt became civil governor of Tanganyika Territory upon the declaration of the mandate in 1920. A "spirit of indecision" best describes the policy of the British, who had assumed control to prevent the territory from reverting to the Germans. The uncertainty surrounding the country's status as a mandated territory under the supervision of the League of Nations, and the lack of purpose in the British administration were the main factors in the slow development that characterized this period.

25

A director of education was appointed in 1920. He was given the responsibility to establish an educational system with goals similar to those of the German period: 1) to fill the administrative needs of the country; and 2) to supply artisans for active involvement in the economic development of the country. No clear statement was issued as to the extent of the director's responsibilities, and he was occupied mostly with picking up the pieces from the Germans until Cameron's arrival as governor in 1925. It appears that the British administration at this time thought of developing a white man's land with the natives providing for their needs. They would introduce changes into the social organization of the African only inasmuch as they were necessary to benefit the European community economically. Anthony H. Rweyemamu on pp. 61 and 63 of his unpublished Ph.D. dissertation for Syracuse University in 1966 entitled "Nation-Building and the Planning Processes of Tanzania" says: "It was planning in a way that was primarily geared to make Tanganyika a better place for the white man to live . . . The British, as a colonial power, imposed their will upon the people of Tanganyika, and never intended to build a Tanganyikan nation for the Tanganyikans." Meister in *East Africa: The Past in Chains, the Future in Pawn*, claims that policy was directed by the conservative postulate— ". . . transform traditional society only to the extent required by the economic development of modern European society."

The Director of Education aimed at reopening Government schools under the district officers on the German school sites. Central schools were also opened at Dar and Tanga. By the end of 1920 £174 had been spent on education and twenty schools had been reopened with five hundred boys attending. The Education Department realized they could accomplish only a small beginning toward formal education, and urged the Agriculture and Veterinary departments to assist them.

The educational policies of the 1920's were greatly influenced by changes in the policy of the British administration. The Native Authority Ordinance of 1923 was the first step in what was later developed and referred to as "indirect rule." The akidas, the lower government officials of Arabic or Swahili origin, who were often considered as foreign by the tribesmen as the Europeans, were to be replaced with local chiefs and headmen. Sir Donald Cameron, on his appointment as governor in 1925 succeeding Byatt, found no overall policy and administrative units. He proved to be the man for "such a time as this" in changing policy formation, especially the establishment of indirect rule, a technique proposed by Lugard, one of Britain's greatest African administrators in the early 1900's. Cameron presented his policy of indirect rule to his staff in this manner:

> We must not destroy the African atmosphere, the African mind, the whole foundations of his race, and we shall certainly do this if we sweep away all his tribal organizations, and in doing so tear up all the roots that bind him to the people from whom he has sprung. . . . It is clearly, I submit, the duty of the Mandatory Power to train the people and make its dispositions in such a manner that, when the time arrives, a full place in the political structure shall be found for the native population.[1]

The cause was good. It was seen as the only way to reach the people in a dynamic way. The local heads were the agents of the British administration and directly in contact with the people. Some of the criticisms leveled at the implementation of this system speak of the consequences of drafting local men who were not traditional leaders when a locality claimed no tribal leader. Others criticized the separation of the religious and political functions in the leadership, and of the "puppets" in leadership helping to maintain the status quo. The policy, in the long run, had the effect of mitigating against social change, and paradoxically, of breaking down the tribal practices and patterns.

The 1920's saw a tremendous growth in the economy of the country. With the discovery of gold in the northern area in 1922, the return to production of the old German sisal estates, and the white settlement led by Lord Delemere near Iringa, the economy of 1924 equaled that of pre-war years under the Germans. The revenue reached the £1 million mark. By 1929 it had almost

---

1. To his staff in July, 1925, and quoted in Alexander MacDonald, *Tanzania: Young Nation in a Hurry* (N. Y.: Hawthorn Books, Inc., 1966) p. 37.

doubled the 1924 figure, mainly through exports of sisal, gold, and coffee.

The rapid growth in the revenue permitted a greater provision of social services in the fields of health and education. From the £174 spent on education in 1920 to £18,000 in 1925, the annual education expenditures continued to rise steadily until 1931. In that year it reached a high of £122,000, a figure not realized again until after 1945. The staff in the education department grew from one in 1920 to six in 1924, doubled between 1926 and 1927, and doubled again before 1931 when the number totaled 62. Schools were established and enrollment figures increased. Concern about the dangers of overproduction from educational activities other than those with a strong agricultural bias had been expressed as early as the Annual Report of 1923 and voiced recurrently since then. It was not an idle worry since the purpose of education for the early graduate was to fill an administrative position or to become an artisan in the European community. There would be a limit to the creation of administrative positions on the one hand, and on the other, the European community was not expanding at any significant rate.

The rapid development and growth of the educational system was not without its problems on the part of teachers, parents, and students. Teachers were hard to find and in addition many of those from the German period had forgotten their training. In general, Africans were not interested in education. Parents, as a group, were indifferent to punctuality and regular attendance. Some entire areas were actively hostile to European education. The most remarkable examples are the Moslems along the coast and the Iraqu of Mbulu. Others felt that when they handed over their sons to the school authorities, they were discharged from any more duties in the upbringing of their children. The school would assume a complete role of responsibility. Innocent youth faced new confrontations in the urban centers in the areas of moral training, agricultural education, more refined eating habits, language, and night school. Unanticipated problems arose from this setting.

The educational system of the 1920's was largely a foreign import to the African continent. In general, there were few attempts to build on African traditions. Protestant and Roman Catholic missions had to provide for the well-being of their Christians. Having rejected pagan practices, they needed to find security in an alternative community that also provided for satisfaction within agriculture, construction work, commerce, or a legitimate trade. Thus the mission schools expanded their curriculum beyond religious instruction to include training in skills and improvement in agriculture. The more academic courses were included for the purpose of training leaders.

Mission schools were expanding even more rapidly than Government schools. In 1925 the school-age population was estimated at eight hundred thousand and of these, one hundred fifteen thousand were reported attending mission schools. About five thousand attended Government schools at the time. With the recommendations from the 1924 visit of the Phelps-Stokes Commission to East Africa, followed by a White Paper in 1925 from the Advisory Committee on Native Education in British East Africa, the stage was set for a profitable discussion on overall policies. An Education Conference between Government and missions was held from October 5 to 12 of the same year.

THE FORMATION OF BRITISH COLONIAL EDUCATIONAL POLICY

The dubiety of the status of the Mandated Territory and the British doctrine of self-reliance for her colonies contributed heavily to the delay in educational planning and efforts in Tanganyika. In order to assess this situation properly, it is necessary to remember that educational facilities in Britain and other European countries were quite inadequate at this time and remained so until recently.

A controversy arose in 1921 over the question of continuance of the German policy that confined the opening of schools by a missionary society to the particular area allotted to it. The practice was eventually discontinued.

The Phelps-Stokes Commission, which visited East and Central Africa in 1924 with the express purpose of investigating the educational needs of the African peoples and to suggest recommendations, was mission inspired and Government backed. The Phelps-Stokes Commission of 1924, composed of experts in American and British education, stirred up many ideas that lay dormant until this time, emphasizing what was to be later known as the philosophy of "adaptation." They stated a "view of education as a life-long process far exceeding, but including, the formal elements of schooling as the only kind of teaching and learning process likely to effect cultural change." Some of their recommendations carry the flavor of American policies for Negro education in the South of the same time. Three important ideas are found in their report in regard to adaptation for the individual, the community, and the objectives of education:

1) *School curriculum*: Normal school subjects were to be linked more closely to a study of the community and augmented radically. The study of health was included, the use of the environment in agriculture and industry, preparation for improved home life, and better use of leisure time. Above all, character development was to be related to concrete conditions and daily experiences.

2) *School-community adaptation*: School activities were to be organized to help bridge the gap between the new world to which the pupil would be introduced through his studies and the old world from which he came. He was to return better equipped to play his part in the progress of the community.

3 *Adult education*:   Adult education was to be carried on simultaneously with formal education so that the adult community should not be left behind by the increasing numbers of young people who would be privileged to attend schools. Suggestions included the Farm Demonstration Movement, home-demonstration measures for women, moveable agriculture schools, and rural farmers' clubs under the Department of Education and extension services operated by other departments, e.g., Health, Public Works, Agriculture.

The commission's suggestions were much like the UNESCO proposals, and some have not even yet found their complete fulfillment. They suggested:

1) that Government and missions cooperate by respecting each other's functions—

a) Government caring for the primary education of Moslem children and missions responsible for Christian children.

      b) Government and mission schools reducing competition and expenses by not locating their schools too close to each other;

2) that Government:
      a) aid in financing mission schools;
      b) appoint an advisory committee of both Government and mission representatives to counsel the Government on African education;
      c) increase its staff in both teaching and supervisory posts, maintaining a strong supervisory staff to improve the quality of all schools;
      d) maintain few schools at first as model schools;
      e) provide practical education in their schools, e.g., teacher training, health and hygiene, agriculture, industry, mothercrafts, and handicrafts;
      f) provide education for African girls and women, and higher institutions for qualified Africans;

3) that religious education be given equal status with other subjects, for it was essential in all the schools;

4) that the vernacular language be used in the village schools as the beginner's language.

The one recommendation that met with the least agreement in government was the place the commission gave to the vernacular languages as a medium of instruction for several years until Swahili was to be used before switching to English at a higher level.

One of the greatest accomplishments of the Phelps-Stokes Commission was that it inspired the 1925 White Paper issued by the Advisory Committee on *Education Policy in British Tropical Africa*,[2] which—even though it was amplified and redefined in later years—remained the foundation of educational policy in Tanganyika until independence. The key statement of the policy was:

Education should be adapted to the mentality, aptitudes, occupations, and traditions of the various peoples, conserving as far as possible all sound and healthy elements in

---

2.   Great Britain, Cmd. 2374 (London: HMSO, 1925).

the fabric of their social life, adapting them where necessary to changed circumstances and progressive ideas, as an agent of natural growth and evolution.[3]

This memorandum laid down the principles of adaptation, reflecting most of the opinions of the Phelps-Stokes Commission. Three aims were defined:

1) to render the individual more efficient in his or her condition of life;
2) to promote the advancement of the community as a whole through the improvement of agriculture, the development of native industries, the improvement of health, the training of the people in the management of their own affairs, and the inculcation of true ideals of citizenship and service;
3) the raising up of capable, trustworthy, public-spirited leaders of the people, belonging to their own race.

The ideal was to achieve progress on all levels of the community, an ideal based on the conviction that education should cement and strengthen those elements in the African society that would permit it to adjust to the twentieth century without the loss of basic values. The first task was to "raise the standard alike of character and efficiency of the bulk of the people," but emphasis was given to provision for the advancement, through higher education, to leadership by those with qualifying character, ability, and temperament. In practice, the balance between these two aspects became impossible to maintain as pressures weighed heavily on the production of an elite who moved out of the community.

With the initial step of educational-policy formation taken by the Phelps-Stokes Commission and the response of the colonial government in the memorandum of 1925, Governor Cameron was able to summon an early conference of educators shortly after his arrival in 1925. In his opening speech to the conference, he declared the 1925 memorandum to be the "charter of education" and it was his desire that the conference examine the implications of those policies for the territory.

---

3.   *Ibid.*, p. 4.

Several statements from the speech of the Director of Education, S. Rivers-Smith, reveal some of the policies he held dearly:

> [Africa needs] a social system suited to Africa and African psychology, in which the individual will be guided to develop on lines suitable to his natural environment, with only such Western influences as may be necessary to replace abuses which civilization demands must be abolished. . . .
>
> The basic needs of a positive policy of education would include peace, which connotes a happy and contented peasantry; increased population, which requires enlightened motherhood; and an improved social system which could be attained by the right appreciation of hygiene and the duties of citizenship generally. . . .
>
> If we are to solve the problem of a happy, peaceful, and contented Africa, we must first solve the problem of the education of women, believe me, no light task. . . . [4]

Another policy voiced at the conference argued that the chief factor in the training of the citizen was the development of character rather than vocational training. The policies developed were good, but the philosophy underlying these policies was questionable, i.e., Africans are degraded, therefore morals must be built up first.

A policy between Government and missions sprang out of the agreements reached at this conference. A system of grants-in-aid linked the schools of all agencies into one official system holding a coherent educational policy.

Following these documents and the discussions at the conference, the Government drafted a bill and a code of regulations that served the 1926 and 1927 period. The Educational Ordinance of 1927 became effective on January 1, 1928. Its main points follow:

1) All schools must be registered where secular instruction was given (theological schools and colleges exempt);

---

4. Tanganyika Government, "Report of Education Conference 1925 . . ." (Dar: Government Printer, 1925), pp. 6, 7.

2) Registration of teachers was not compulsory, but no assistance would be given unless a teacher was on the Register of Teachers or enrolled on the Provincial List;

3) Five years were allotted for a teacher to pass from the Provincial List to the Register of Teachers;

4) Old men who were efficient but unable to pass to the Register would be given an honorable certificate while others failing to be listed would not be eligible for grants-in-aid;

5) Freedom of conscience was guaranteed;

6) Registration of a Grade I teacher was required at a school before English could be taught there;

7) Grants-in-aid would be granted to mission schools only on the basis of fulfilling Government requirements.

EDUCATIONAL STRUCTURE, 1920-31

Government adopted a policy of directing primary education and leading the way in post-primary education. Government schools on the primary level consisted of Native Authority Schools (village schools under the direct responsibility of the district officer, better known as NA schools) and Central Schools (Government-controlled schools in the urban centers that offered more than lower elementary education). Missions also operated a few Central Schools, but provided many more bush and village schools.

The Phelps-Stokes Commission of 1924 reported sixty-five Government schools with five thousand pupils enrolled, thirteen missionary societies operating seven teacher-training centers, and about two thousand two hundred village schools in which seventy thousand boys and forty-five thousand girls were enrolled. Most of the instruction was catechetical in nature. Possibly the town government and main-station schools achieved a literacy level, but it is questionable whether those attending the other schools left with much religious or secular knowledge. Bush schools ranged from a high academic standard to nonproductive. The staff of the educational department took on the responsibility of supervision of all schools, and the head of the Central School was usually held responsible for the district or regional primary supervision.

The period from 1926 to 1931 saw many rapid advances in African, European, and Indian education but especially in the former, to which the Government was more committed.

For some reason, the structure of education during this period is confused with the strange jargon of "substandard" for the first two of the years spent in village schools and Government schools in which the vernacular was taught. The last two years in these schools were called Standards I and II, the equivalents of Grades 3 and 4. Since the aim of the primary school was to produce literate and enlightened farmers, pupils showing exceptional ability in village schools were removed to a Central School so that they were under a European head.

Post-elementary education began in the fifth year at a Central School. Three streams ran side by side: the Grade II (Vernacular) teachers'-training course, the industrial-education course and the English course. The three streams were located in one institution in order to offset the possibility of priggishness developing among the candidates of the English course. This also gave Grade II candidates the additional advantage of learning about the workings of a Central School while they were taught, and presented an opportunity to impress upon all the boys the importance of each of their jobs. Transfers were made from the English course to the vocational section without loss in education. The boys in the English course were viewed as potential troublemakers and political agitators. The Director of Education tried to limit the number of boys in the English course from exceeding those in vocational sections. By 1929 the Tanga School alone was training over four hundred boys, but in Dar that year they decided to close down their English course of post-elementary level because there were too few students to warrant running the course.

In an attempt to implement the principles of the 1925 memorandum, a number of interesting developments and experiments appeared in the latter part of the 1920's. We shall explore some of them in the next few paragraphs. The majority of schools possessed their own farms and gardens, at first under the Department of Agriculture and later under the Department of Education.

Teacher training was important in the Government and mission Central Schools. UMCA opened Minaki in 1925 and a number of other missions also expanded in teacher training at this time. The courses ran for three months to one year in duration. On the Grade I level, in addition to the mission Minaki school, the Mpwapwa

Teacher Training Institute was opened in 1925 by the Government. Its earlier opening a year before in Dar met with criticisms about the lack of boarding facilities and irrelevancy of the training environment to the actual teacher situations. The school was moved to a rural setting following the suggestion of the Advisory Committee, but it made slight progress due to a number of obstacles. The products of the teacher-training institutions of the mission schools were able to keep on par with their Government counterparts; they even outshined the government graduates on examinations.

An experiment in adult education in 1924 at Bagamoyo, Dar, and Tanga was short-lived. The enthusiasm of the African adult civil servants (who attended the night classes) waned quickly, and Tanga classes alone ran longer than three months.

With the introduction of indirect rule, in which traditional leaders became local Government agents, the need for the education and training of future chiefs became acute. Many chiefs were wary about entrusting their sons to mission schools, fearful that traditional practices would be undermined. But future chiefs needed a special education, so Government decided to open a school at Tabora for the express purpose of fitting the son of a chief "to fulfill efficiently his duty to the State and towards his own people as their leader and educator." Schools for training sons of minor chiefs and headmen in an elementary course were opened at Kizigo and Ibadakuli. Instead of preparing the sons of chiefs for cooperation in community life, however, the schools' effect was to isolate the young men from their communities. This consequence was early recognized as counter to the intentions of the 1925 memorandum and was left to die. And again the son sent to be educated was not always the one who was to become chief.

One of the most interesting of the East African experiments, Malangali, was built by Mumford in 1927 on the theory that building a school just ahead of the African way of life would make the transition easier for its pupils. Rather than beginning with something modified from European practices, the base had genuine African foundations. The school buildings, organization, curriculum, and way of life were developed from the tribal environment, and instruction was shared by European teachers, African teachers, and the tribal elders from the home areas of the boys. Many of the boys came from tribes with styles of life different from that of the Hehe at Malangali. The endeavor was controversial and expired upon the departure of Mumford in 1931. Mumford, with the backing of the Director of Education, is an example of the educators in Government and mission service who attempted to provide an education that would serve the local community and stimulate progress without a sharp break in social patterns.

One of the highlights of the period between 1926 and 1931 was the establishment in most provinces of rather costly boarding schools for boys. These boarding schools, which the Central Schools became in accommodating their pupils drawn from a large area, widened instead of narrowing the gap between the educated and the community. Secondary education, as such, was not considered by the Director his responsibility. He did accede that it would possibly become a duty of the Director during a later generation. He promoted postprimary vocational courses aimed at avoiding the pitfalls of overproduction, which India and Ceylon had experienced and which had led to their major social problems.

There were 120 European children in the country in 1925, and most of them were sent back to Europe for study. That year Government made arrangements for them to be admitted into Government schools in Kenya, but only two parents responded with applications. The same years the Capuchin Sisters opened the St. Joseph's Convent in Dar for the Goans and extended an invitation to Europeans to attend. In the next several years private schools were opened in Dar and Arusha by the English, German, and Greek communities.

The twenty-four private schools for Indians run by the local traders in 1928 had a total enrollment of 1,731. Government founded its own Indian schools in 1929. The code of 1929 provided grants-in-aid to Indian schools with the payment of staff in block grants based upon average attendance and capital grants for permanent building and equipment.

METHODS AND CONTENT, 1920-31

The Phelps-Stokes Commission report revealed a great need for expert advice in the educational department, for a professional inspectorate, and financial aid to make possible the upgrading of

African teachers. The Advisory Committee report of 1925, in attempting to implement the policies, suggested several ways of improving the quality of instruction. It recommended that refresher courses be held periodically, and that a team of teachers should visit each school and stay several weeks to observe the operation. All types of vocational and technical training were recommended to be handled through the departments concerned, provided there were academic instructors.

Government emphasized primary education with its stress on the rudiments of literacy, hygiene, and agriculture, and put relatively little effort into postprimary and higher education. Village schools offered a four-year terminal course in the vernacular and Swahili. The curriculum was solidly built on vocational lines in accordance with the policy of teaching the child the three R's and, at the same time, keeping him closely in touch with traditional life. The industrial influence dealt with ordinary work the student would do at home, but improved methods were taught with the hope of the availability of better implements later. Agriculture was the keynote of the educational program. Even teacher-training centers included a heavy dose of agriculture in their curricula.

Health education and practices were given a significant place in the educational system; hygiene was a separate subject. The textbook, *Afya*, was first printed in 1924. Boys were treated for illness and disease at school. At Dar es Salaam, quinine was given regularly to the students and a midday meal was served.

Central Schools led to employment in commercial or Government service or an independent trade. English courses were more than balanced with industrial and vocational courses. Courses were given in carpentry, tailoring, weaving, printing, welding, and bootmaking. No skilled artisans should be illiterate was the rationale behind artisan training efforts with a grounding in the three R's.

Central Schools were encouraged to develop African character. The most significant feature developed was a system of tribal villages and a school court where senior pupils administered customary law. The "prefect system," introduced as a correlate of indirect rule, was developed because it was thought that boys would be happier in a tribal-like environment and would offer better aid to the home community later. It has since been criticized for its view of the society as static. The purpose of the prefect system, and of education as a whole, was to prepare Africans to improve their condition in life without transcending the tribal environment.

Another criticism was that "no one tried to find out what is best in African society." Hector shows that the syllabus lacked the healthy aspects of music, art, tribal and family organization, native law, and a collection of practical uses of natural resources by the Africans.

Although the officers agreed that direct teaching was not the answer to the moral problem rising in the urban centers, educators held various opinions regarding a solution to this problem. Teachers were asked to set a good example. Religious teachers were asked to come to the school to teach religion, and Mumford stressed the Boy Scout movement as the answer. According to page 29 of the 1924 Annual Report, he felt the positive character traits encouraged by the Boy Scout Charter would "counteract two of Africa's most pressing problems, namely, the immigration to the towns and the growth of the overdressed and self-opinionated clerical type."

Thus the period of consolidation, expansion, and experimentation ended in 1931 with the effects of the slump in the world market. Educational policies and practices developed during the 1920's were destined to a slowdown in implementation during the 1930's and cutbacks in finances. Ultimately, experimentation was effected. It is interesting to note, however, that some of the policies suggested during this period were not subscribed to by Tanganyikans at that time, but came to the fore again during the 1960's when the social, economic, and political milieu had changed.

THE PERIOD OF UNCERTAINTY CULMINATING
IN NEW PURPOSE, 1932-45
BACKGROUND TO THE PERIOD

The Depression did not affect the subsistent farmer in Tanganyika in his daily life, but a retrenchment took place in development projects. In addition to faltering economic conditions, there was an underlying fear that Germany might require a return of her colony. This affected settlement and investments. When the slump in world-market prices affected Tanganyika in 1931, various economical measures were taken by the Government. The number of provinces was reduced from eleven to eight, the civil-servant list fell from 950 to 795, and Government suspended the eight posts of Superintendents of Education, two industrial instructors, and two European headmasters.

The recommendations of the Sir Armitage-Smith Report of 1932 smelled of a squeeze in the budget, suggesting ways of curtailing programs to save money. Some of the main points were:

1) Continue the grants-in-aid to missions;
2) Keep Native Authority Schools because they cost Government little (for more information on NA schools, see Structure, 1932-45);
3) Divide the duties of the Superintendent into the job of teacher and inspector;
4) Reduce teachers' salaries. (It was not necessary for them to be the same as administrators'; teachers' responsibilities and qualifications are different for their vocation.);
5) Government should hand over the Central Schools of Malangali, Bukoba, and Mwanza to NAs and revise Tanga and Dar Central Schools on a more economical basis; and
6) Abolish examination grants and the giving of tools to the industrial graduates.

The Education Department claimed that the loudest cries for cuts in expenditures in 1932 came from those who later decried the lag in 1937. Dividing the job of superintendent into administrative, inspection, and teaching in 1933 made little difference since few Europeans remained to staff Central Schools. African teachers had to carry the heavy load. The Mpwapwa Teacher Training Institute was instructed to cease training Grade I teachers in 1933 as they were not viewed as needed in the economy, and emphasis on quality was put on Grade II training.

Cutbacks crippled the economic development, but did not immobilize all organizations. The "Plant More Crops" campaign initiated by the Government was quite successful and helped to bring about a remarkable recovery. Recovery began slowly in 1935, but education had hardly reached its 1931 level when it was halted by World War II. The ranks of European education officers were thinned as men were called to war. Hit most seriously were the German Protestant Mission Schools, which lost all their expatriate staff. Arrangements were made for some American missionaries to take over, and the Government agreed to pay full teachers' wages for their work. The previous educational level would not be reached again until 1945.

Figures given during this period show that the total enrollment in both Government and VA schools in 1936 was only 3 per cent of the estimated school-age population. In 1938 there were thirty-six thousand African males in Government grant-aided schools and many more in unassisted ones, eight hundred African girls in Government schools and twenty-one thousand in grant-aided and nonassisted mission schools. The Government educational staff consisted of thirty-eight European and 428 African teachers of whom forty-nine were African females. The missions had 212 European (137 female) and 317 African (110 female) teachers.

POLICIES OF 1932-45

The general policy of the Government was one of parochial paternalism and development from below. It was designed to reinforce the status quo by training sons of the appointed chiefs in order that indirect rule be legitimatized in the next generation and become more effective. The uncertainty as to the political future of the territory explains in part why there were no long-term plans during the 1930's and why the colony was simply kept on a "care-and-maintenance basis" during this period, as the UN Visiting Mission to Tanganyika in 1948 reported. The lack of a consistent educational policy seems to be due to a blurred image of what they were attempting to do in that area. Mission societies were carrying the bulk of educational activity. This was further complicated by the fact that only a small proportion—only about 10 per cent, said the Annual Report of 1936—were British. This also explains why some of their policies ran counter to an earlier policy. Note the change in attitude toward Grade I teacher training: In 1927 it was seen as very important; in 1933 it was discontinued as they saw no demand for Grade I teachers; in 1937 it was opened again in full force to meet the emerging demands of the economic community. Only during World War II days did British policy begin to take on purpose.

As stated before, the Educational Ordinance of 1927 with its roots in the Phelps-Stokes Commission set the guidelines for the educational efforts in succeeding decades. Emerging from the Depression, the Government was forced to reconsider policies in the light of new economic demands. Better-qualified Africans were needed for service in industry and Government. More secondary schools meant better teacher training. Grade I teachers were again required.

The 1935 White Paper, *Memorandum in the Education of African Communities*, issued by the Colonial Office Advisory Committee "reiterated the policy that African interests were paramount," to the dismay of the settlers during this uncertain time. The paper stressed in clearer terms the education of the whole community through a close collaboration among agencies concerned with social development. It also placed a priority on adult education even at the expense of limiting the educational facilities for youth. The relationship of the school to the community has been summarized best by Scanlon:

> The school can make its most effective contribution only as a part of a more comprehensive programme directed to the improvement of the total life of the community. The hindrances to social advance need to be attacked simultaneously from many sides.[5]

Swahili teachers were to play a leading role in the community, using a syllabus devoted mainly to agriculture and handicrafts. The guidelines given in the memorandum for the school's function as an agent in social change were to:

1) interpret the changes taking place in the African society;
2) communicate the knowledge and skills needed for improving the community;
3) supply new motives and incentives for the old ones;
4) re-create the sense of obligation to others; and
5) foster an interest in the environment for the enjoyment of all.

Two main themes appeared in the 1925 and 1935 papers: education for all and interdependence between education and the

---

5. David Scanlon, *Traditions in African Education*, Classics in Education, 316 (New York: Bureau of Publications, Columbia University, 1964), p. 102.

forces of educational change. Progressive ideas and examples were expected to permeate the whole community.

The European developed a very narrow, but kindly, attitude toward the African, an attitude that would later be called "colonialism." The De la Warr Commission in 1938 was the first one advocating education, not for the status quo, but for social change. It spoke of two forces—the African background and the European customs—and supported an "interaction between African theory of tradition and European theory of progress." [6] The African was not to be prevented from Europeanization. The great task was to "interpret to the youth of Africa the higher values of the present world and to assist Africans in the difficult process of adjustment so they can be able to live without strain in the composite conditions which have been created.[7]

With an improved economy and growth, Government became aware of advancement and shifted away from the old attitude of "protectionism" to one of development and a more realistic view of the future. A multi-racialism concept was accepted in order to both reassure the economically important minority groups of another race and fulfill the requirements of trusteeship. Multi-racialism, as practiced, meant that the three main racial groups were to be treated as equal but separate entities. For example, the twenty-five thousand Europeans, the seventy thousand Asians, and the 8 million Africans each received £800,000 when the money from the Enemy Property was divided in 1955 to the groups.

This period is not marked by greater numbers in terms of candidates and passes in postprimary education, but by its progress in formulating and voicing opinions. Following the 1936 paper, the De la Warr Commission visited East Africa and recommended that higher education be planned and begun, even to the university level. This is the first commission to emphasize an increase without pointing to the dangers of overproduction. In 1939 Governor Cameron added yet another dimension: He stressed the need for secondary and postsecondary education with a view of Africans taking over positions then held by Europeans.[8]

---

6. *Annual Report*, 1938, p. 7.
7. *Ibid.*
8. Sir Donald Cameron, *My Tanganyika Service and Some Nigeria* (London: Allen and Unwin, 1939).

Although the British Colonial Development Act of 1929 allocated funds for developing agriculture and industry in its territories, it held a biased mercantilistic view. Its intent was to promote commerce and industry in Great Britain and reduce Britain's unemployment problem, not to develop a colony. By World War II, Britain's policies began to take on an additional dimension. In the Colonial Development and Welfare Act of 1940, Britain, for the first time, admitted that it had a moral duty to develop the colony for its own sake. The same year the Central Education Committee in Tanganyika issued a series of proposals in the belief that the larger amount of funds made available by the Colonial Act of 1940 would permit an overhaul in the educational system. This committee advocated transfer of responsibility for elementary education to the Native Authorities (hereafter NAs) and future expansion of these schools, not the Government schools nor the mission schools where 85 per cent of the educational instruction then took place.

Decentralization of authority and practical education were the main themes in their unique proposals. After four years in village schools, the most talented would go on to Junior Secondary Schools and later to Makerere. The next most capable were to join a Four-Year Rural Middle School with terminal courses, heavily loaded with rural science and practical farming activities. These four-year Rural Middle Schools were to be operated by the NAs. Teachers were to receive special training in rural teacher-training centers of the NAs. By placing control on the local level, it was hoped that the schools would be more sensitive to local needs and inculcate attitudes appropriate to rural life and occupations. There was to be more local experimentation. The intent was to build a progressive middle class.

London opposed the scheme on the grounds of prematurity, feeling most of the NAs were not financially or administratively able to carry the burden. The outcome of this ambitious report was not to be seen, for the scheme was never implemented. World War II halted the activity and postwar influences changed the situation. Skilled manpower goals took precedence over these earlier goals.

In light of the fact that ninety-two thousand soldiers from Tanganyika served abroad in Ethiopia and Burma during World

War II, the British administration anticipated the rise of political aspirations in postwar years. They recognized that forces were changing the lives of Africans and that they, the Africans, ought to be aware of and understand the forces. The third memorandum issued by the Colonial Office Advisory Committee in 1943, *Mass Education in African Society,*[9] viewed the goal of education as not only the improvement of the health and living conditions of the people and the promotion of the economic development of the country, but also "the development of political institutions and political power until the day arrives when the people can become effectively self-governing."[10] However, ex-soldiers in Tanganyika were most politically passive in the following years than expected and less active than their counterparts in neighboring countries.

The possibility of postwar inflation was one factor that led to a turning point in planning with enactment of the Colonial Development and Welfare Act, 1945. In line with Britain's desire to develop the country, the Central Development Committee in the colony was asked to submit a ten-year plan, the first time planning took place in colonial as well as colony offices. Britain now felt a moral duty to develop the country for its own sake. And, fortunately, Britain had more clearly stated goals than the French, Portuguese, or Belgians:

> . . . to develop the colonies and all their resources so as to enable their people speedily and substantially to improve their economic and social conditions, and as soon as may be practicable, to attain responsible self-government.[11]

In summary, the policies of this period were concerned with educating and developing the whole community, and administrators in the British Colonial Office backed many of them. But what chance did the educational system really have when the parents sent their children who were educated off to the urban areas to live and earn a wage? A criticism was afloat that the schools were pro-

---

9. Great Britain, Col. No. 186 (London: HMSO, 1943).
10. In forward to memorandum, *Ibid.*
11. Mr. George Hall, Br. Col. Sec'y in Labor Admin. of 1945 in Gr. Br. 5 *Parliamentary Debates (Commons).*

ducing a semi-literate boy whose sole aim was a clerical post. The demand for English was likened to a medieval father in England who wanted Latin for his son as a key to opportunity. Malinowski mentions this problem when he says that education in Africa was "planned, financed and directed by Europeans who as a rule [were] looking for definite practical ends" and thus often produced educated Africans "who have no place either in the tribal world or the European community." He claims education in Africa failed "because of a real conflict of interests, faulty planning, misunderstanding, or lack of common ground for effective joint work." [12]

EDUCATIONAL STRUCTURE, 1932-45

Administration

The early 1930s saw the reduction of a number of provinces and consequently superintendents, industrial instructors, and European headmasters. During the recovery, the education of girls and women became a greater concern, so much so that a Woman's Education Officer was appointed to organize female education throughout the territory. Inspection, first done by the European staff of Government schools when they had time, had a gradual growth during this period and by 1945 the post of Chief Inspector was created. An inspector for Indian schools in Tanganyika and Zanzibar was appointed in 1936. World War II depleted much of the European staff and even affected the African staff. Africans capably began to take over supervision of schools. In 1944 the first Local Education Authority (LEA) was inaugurated. That year the addition of four African members to the Advisory Committee on African Education brought the African representation to eight out of twenty-one.

Institutions

Elementary Education: In addition to the variety of mission-operated schools, Government had control of most Central Schools and NA schools. These NA schools were built as a

12. Bronislaw Malinowski, *The Dynamics of Culture Change* (New Haven: Yale University Press, 1958, 1945c), pp. 7-8, 17.

result of the initiative and efforts of administrative officers or chiefs and managed by them. They were generally regarded as experiments in tribal education and were free to adapt policies for organization, syllablus, and method until 1933 when an Education Ordinance set up the requirements to be met. By 1939 there were forty-one of these NA schools and the standard held in the majority was such that this type of school could be held up as an example to other countries. The *Report of the Commission on Higher Education in East Africa*, Col. No. 142 of 1937, did just that, giving a slightly overestimated report of the actual role they played in the life of the people, but really emphasizing the possibilities of these schools. They "have a large part to play in giving reality and responsibility to the system of indirect rule. . . . They are closely associated, geographically and in other ways, with health and maternity work and centres, afforestation and anti-erosion measures, agricultural demonstration and training centres, animal husbandry and veterinary work." They saw them as possible centers in the life of the rural community. To the Education Department, they were the institutions that came closest to implementing the Phelps-Stokes Commission's opinions regarding a community school. Unfortunately, drawing these NA schools into a more centralized system where they could contribute to a wider system resulted in the loss of their ability to experiment. Voluntary Agencies (mostly missions) conducted many four-year primary schools and two-year substandard schools often called"Bush Schools." The latter, numerous and not within the register of primary education of that time, increased greatly. Government, and particularly missions, were very much concerned with the education of girls in this period, but comparatively little uniformity was achieved in this area.

Secondary Education: The existing Central Schools were improved during this period and offered more advanced education. Until the conversion of Tabora Central School to a Junior Secondary School by adding Grades IX and X in 1933, no secondary-education facilities existed in the territory. Prior to this, in the hope of later joining Makerere, East Africa's higher-education institution located in Uganda, a few secondary students were sent to Uganda Junior Secondary Schools. During this period a rapid expansion took place in secondary education: From 1933 to 1938, four mission and three Government Secondary Schools added IX and X to the existing buildings; Tabora, the only Government secondary school, graduated twenty-five students a year after World War II. More Junior Secondaries were opened in 1942. The impetus for secondary education was attributed to two main factors: 1) the tremendous increase in departmental requirements; and 2) the realization that development in East Africa can only be carried out by qualified East Africans.

Vocational and Technical Education: There was little technical and vocational training at Central Schools after 1932. The 1930's saw a tendency toward centralization of the vocational training in urban areas and better coordination of technical and employment needs.

Teacher Training: In 1934 the requirements for entry to Grades I and II teacher-training courses were raised by two years— Std. X for Grade I and Std. VI for Grade II. Grade I training was ordered discontinued in 1933 and greater emphasis was placed on the Grade II Swahili course, which was extended from three to five years during the Depression to raise standards and to avoid unemployment. Women teacher candidates, until the 1950's, took an examination of lower quality than men. By 1945 small Government teacher-training centers with African staffs were operating in all but one of the eight provinces, a policy that was later reversed in 1954 for greater concentration. Because a relapse in the certification of teachers had occurred since 1928, measures were taken by 1943 to rectify this problem. Several missions formed an alliance to offer better-quality education at Kinampanda.

Indian Education increased rapidly during this time from twenty-four private schools in 1928 to sixty in 1937 (three Government, forty-six assisted, and others unassisted). The school population doubled in the 1930's.

METHODS AND CONTENT, 1932-45

The Depression hit hard on the heels of a period of expansion in African, European, and Indian education in the territory. Programs had to be curtailed, and after a comeback in the economy in the late 1930's, education was again affected by an outside force. This time it was European involvement in World War II. As is often true in times of difficulty, the consequences sometimes are beneficial. Some definite reactions to these problems were crucial to the developing educational system.

One of the views given wide publicity by the British administration during the 1930's was that education should fit pupils for rural occupations in their tribes. For that reason, handicrafts and school gardens were main subjects in the curriculum. The Government's suggestion to missions that they develop rural education even at the expense of urban education was sympathetically received. Only three of the eight Government Central Schools were retained on the grammar-school pattern. Rural Central Schools were opened near Mwanza and Moshi with the intent that NAs would open more rural boarding schools if they proved valuable.

In March, 1933, the Advisory Committee on African Education adopted the policy of training "handymen." Percival's syllabus for the course was rated "good" and was included in the syllabuses of 1947 and as late as 1952. These workshop periods were to "provide opportunity for latent talent to demonstrate itself."

The special classes at Tabora Junior Secondary School, which trained clerks for Government service and commercial firms, were in such demand that four years of operation had supplied clerks to Government and by 1933 the commercial firms had still not benefited. The Junior Secondary School graduates of Tabora were also in high demand for employment. In 1938 the place of vocational education in the primary and secondary institutions was delimited further:

1) Vocational training was to begin after a pupil has a general education;

2) Early specialization was regarded as unscientific and doomed for failure; and

3) The school could not undertake the direct preparation for a trade or profession, but could indirectly help with suitable curricular activities.

Greater cooperation was maintained with the other departments for artisan training; the Education Department tried to supply the type of pupil needed for training.

This view of the place of vocational education in primary and secondary schools was expressed at the same time that the De la

Warr Commission advised on the function of education in social change. This came one year after the Annual Report gave fundamental importance to the interrelation of health, agriculture, and education. They considered the following factors as hindrances to advancement: poverty, superstitious prejudice, malnutrition, and unhygienic conditions. They gave recognition to Frank Laubach's contribution to adult education, but decried the apathy of the older generation as the chief obstacle to combating illiteracy.

By 1938 the main problem seems to have been the task of reconciling the demand for instruction in English on the one hand with the campaigns for literacy, and on the other, raising the standard of living for the whole community. There was already evidence at this time of a desire to prolong primary education from four to six years. The demand for secondary education required quality in teacher training. New examinations were introduced: the first woman's teacher-certificate examination, in 1935; the first entrance examination to Makerere for teacher training, in 1936; and the annual entrance examination to Tabora secondary and clerical courses.

The qualifications for certification of teachers had lowered since the 1927 ordinance in a tendency to train many in short, intensive courses. It was not unusual to have over half the candidates fail the exam and sit for it the second and third times. Coinciding with the expansion in secondary education were expansion and quality controls for teacher training. Grade I courses, which had been closed for several years, opened in 1938 with higher standards. Refresher courses were provided for inservice teachers. The emphasis on teacher-community activities had had good results, and by 1938 the need was for better teaching techniques and an emphasis on the teachers' role in rural education. This was followed in 1942 with the introduction of a two-part exam for teacher training: academic and professional. A marked progress was reported in classroom management after women candidates were required to give a lesson in front of an inspector as part of the exam.

The great demand for English teachers influenced the Government in 1944 to shorten the Grade I teacher's course to one year for several consecutive terms. A significant step was taken that same year when several missions formed an alliance to offer better-quality teacher-training at Kinampanda. Missions also joined to open Dodoma Secondary School, a practice continued for secondary and TTCs of the smaller mission constituencies.

Syllabuses appeared on many topics in 1935. In 1942 a syllabus was introduced for Indian education. That same year twenty-nine headmistresses of girls' schools held a conference in which they slightly revised and amplified the girls' school syllabus. They gave as the first aim education of the majority of girls to be good home-makers and citizens, but admitted that a vocational aim would be required soon thereafter. The syllabuses mentioned in the 1944 *Annual Report* were ready at the time the Ten-Year Development Plan was published in 1947.

Physical training and moral instruction were given a great deal of consideration. One of the most noticeable activities in this area was the steady growth of the Boy Scout and Girl Guide movements.

The dual system of Government and mission schools, although necessary for financing and staffing the majority of Tanganyika's schools, was not without its problems. Table II below shows that the majority of the schools must have been assisted.

TABLE II

ENROLLMENT IN TANGANYIKAS SCHOOLS FOR SELECTED YEARS [13]

Year	Government and NA Schools	Mission Schools	Assisted Schools
1923	4,907	115,000	——
1931	7,505	159,959	——
1935	8,105	217,736	——
1941	13,370	——	26,300
1943	17,005	——	31,200

---

13. Henry J. Hector, "The Government's Role in African Post-Primary Education in Tanganyika 1919-1939" (MA thesis, Teachers College, Columbia University, 1967), pp. 51, 68; Andreas M. Kazamias and Byron G. Massiales, *Tradition and Change in Education* (New York: Praeger, 1962), pp. 11, 12; *Annual Report,* 1944.

Salary scales were not alike. Missions experienced difficulty in retaining African staff when other opportunities seemed more rewarding. During World War II, when the German- and Italian-operated schools suffered because the European staffs became involved in the war, Africans demanded that the Government and NAs be responsible for a greater number of schools so as to avoid a similar problem in the future.

In addition to greater African voice in education as the war continued, African teachers and supervisors carried greater responsibilities. Supplies were hard to get, but local experiments were successful in providing some materials. The education office boasted that even though they had operated in 1939 on a skeleton staff, they had not lowered any standards. A change was noted in African education: Whereas fifteen years earlier it had been necessary to encourage chiefs and parents, in 1942 it was a matter of providing accommodation for their enthusiasm. Two reasons were given for the spread of genuine and increasing interest in education by the African populace: 1) It was the result of fifteen years of effort; and 2) indications that where agriculture had reached above a subsistence level, people were preparing themselves for a postwar economic development in the territory.

The *Annual Report* of 1944 reveals the attitude and evaluation of the colonial administration in Tanganyika, which had the task of implementing the 1943 memorandum, *Mass Education in African Society*. It contained the additional goal of preparing the Africans politically for self-government at a later date.

> The core of the problem is to discover a suitable stimulus that will arouse the enthusiasm of the people. The more obvious reagents such as religion, a rapidly expanding industrial economy, and nationalism, are not notably present in this Territory at the moment nor is there any sign that they will become effective within the immediate future. . . .
> Without data, realistic planning is impossible.[14]

They called for new syllabuses as one response to the memorandum.

Wastage was a concern of the educators. They anticipated doing

14. Col. No. 186 (op. cit.), p. 3.

a survey when their staff was adequate for this extra undertaking. They felt some children were leaving school too early because they themselves thought they were literate and others were taking too long to master literacy in the village schools.

One might call this a transition period in the sense that it stood between the initial formation of the education system and the period of development for its own sake that followed the termination of World War II. It was an important period, one in which African attitudes and voices began to be heard and social change was creeping into the European-African milieu.

CHAPTER THREE

TOWARD DEVELOPMENT AND FREEDOM AS A TRUSTEESHIP TERRITORY 1946-1961

BACKGROUND TO THE PERIOD

British policy, which began to take on more purpose during World War II, was destined to have a significant and far-reaching effect on the future development of the colony and, subsequently, the nation. By 1945 development was wholeheartedly resumed; there were fresh advances for the education of all races. With improved financial conditions and a feeling of urgency to make up for the period of stagnation, the British administrators entered a new era of economic development in Tanganyika. The uncertainty caused by the possibility of the territory reverting to Germany had disappeared. In 1946 Tanganyika Territory was given the status of a trust territory under the United Nations in place of the former mandate. The British were instructed to prepare the colony for independence with citizens qualified to make decisions.

The colonial government was highly centralized in Tanganyika at this time and dealt with matters that are usually determined at regional and local levels in other countries, but discretionary powers of policy formulation as well as execution devolved on the District Commissioners. Upon the appointments in the 1950's of regional officers of agriculture, veterinary, education, and police, these offices became coordinators on the district and regional levels, rather than policy makers.

The period of 1946 to 1961 as a trust territory can be characterized at the national level as a time of relatively peaceful political development and constitutional change. The African political leadership that emerged was not the traditional leadership that the Phelps-Stokes Commission had visualized. Visiting committees from the United Nations every three years and English Governmental missions confirmed the Tanganyika Governmental reports and drafted recommendations that influenced the Government's policies. A Ten-Year Plan issued in 1947 and later revised in 1950 was followed by a Five-Year Plan issued in 1956.

The native's old attitudes of indifference to schooling changed to fervent demands for education. Attempts by the Government to adapt to local needs were regarded with suspicion by the Africans. Three main obstacles delayed development: 1) limited financial sources, 2) lack of qualified African staff, and 3) lack of support from the African community. Despite the upsurge of support for education, wastage—especially in Std. I and girls' education at all levels—was a problem throughout this period. The 1947 plan lists the main causes for this as detrimental educational practices, lack of interest on the part of parents and chiefs, health conditions, and environmental disruptions caused by nature. Measures were taken to make full use of the educational facilities during the period of transition. An almost visible decrease in empty places became apparent in 1958 and 1959.

In 1959 the African Parents' Association was formed. TANU handed its schools over to TAPA (Tanganyika African Parents' Association) when it was sufficiently organized.

This period is also characterized by inequalities in race, religion, sex, and geographical settings. By barring Africans from clubs and social amenities, the British indirectly caused stirrings for independence. Cameron, a former education officer in Tanganyika, claims that segregation in education was not imposed; it just happened. He explains that African education was paramount, that the others were considered fringe activities, or even nuisances.[1] The strongest argument given for segregation was one of language: Small children learn best and with greater ease in their own native language. Table III, on page 57, gives statistics for children of different races in school during selected years.

Rweyemamu points out the disparities among regions in his doctoral dissertation.[2] The early arrival of Christian missionaries in the most productive areas led to an earlier introduction of education in the Chagga, Nyakuza, and Haya districts. Koranic schools,

---

1. John Cameron, "The Integration of Education in Tanganyika," *Comparative Education Review*, XI: n. 1 (February, 1967), p. 43.
2. Anthony H. Rweyemamu, "Nation-Building and the Planning Processes of Tanzania" (unpublished Ph.D. dissertation, Syracuse University, 1966), p. 27.

with their strictly religious curriculum, did not provide equal advantages for the tribes nearer the coast, even though Moslems had arrived during a preceding age. The consequences of these differences were quite obvious in the initial formation of an independent government; many more of the leaders were Christian than Moslem and certain tribes were more highly represented than others.

TABLE III
ENROLLMENT IN TANGANYIKA'S SCHOOLS BY RACE [3]
1947-60

Year	Europeans	Asians	Africans
1947	884	10,499	119,262
1950	1,417	13,286	182,942
1952	1,757	15,353	239,642
1957	2,745	21,567	394,132
1958	2,858	23,209	406,800
1959	2,858	23,688	419,011
1960	2,837	25,031	702,896

In 1957 the UN Visiting Mission felt that education was the most pressing of all the problems connected with the emancipation of women. In that year it was estimated that only 7½ per cent of females over fifteen years of age had received any schooling. Wastage in girls' education was a problem right up to, and following, independence. The 1958 figures reveal that one-third of the total enrollment in primary schools were female. Seventeen per cent were enrolled in middle schools and 9 per cent in secondary schools. Many left after Std. X. Only twenty-four were attending XI and only 11 in XII in 1958. In 1961 there were 5,458 boys in secondary schools and only 850 girls.

Tanganyika had no reason to boast of its development in pre-independent days even though enrollment figures rose quickly. The 1959 school enrollment (approximately 420,000) more than tripled the 1949 enrollment of 130,000. Secondary-school facilities jumped the highest proportionately—from 534 boys in 1947 to 4,132 in

3. Alifeyo B. Chilivumbo, "Tanganyika Mono-Party Regime: A Study in the Problems, Conditions, and Processes of the Emergence and Development of the One-Party State on the Mainland of Tanzania" (unpublished Ph.D. dissertation, UCLA, 1968), p. 135.

1959. Tanganyika's literacy rate was estimated at 8.7 per cent in 1953 and 16 per cent in 1960. It was also estimated that one out of twenty students obtained sufficient education for literacy in 1946. The comparative figure for 1950, one out of every five, reveals a significant improvement in the quality of education. Although 36 per cent of P/S-age children entered school in 1949 and the figure rose to 44 per cent in 1960, the wastage was so great that the percentage of the school-age population attending school never rose above 16 per cent. Facilities were sufficient to provide for 55 per cent of the group to enter Std. I in 1961.

The role of the school in later colonial years was limited to manpower needs. Some of the consequences of this emphasis can be seen in the strikes of 1959 held at the trade schools. Students objected to cleaning their tools and tidying their training area and demanded that laborers be hired for those purposes. Exposure to different outlooks and associations created a gulf between the educated and the balance of the population. In addition to the demonstration of unhealthy attitudes toward work, actual skilled African manpower was lacking. In 1960 and 1961 there were only sixty-one graduates of university level, no qualified African judges, less than twenty qualified African lawyers. Moreover, Tanganyika could not fill her quota in Makerere University.

EDUCATIONAL POLICIES, 1946-61

The educational policies of the period between 1946 and 1961 are found in the Ten-Year Plan for 1947-56, the revision in 1950, and the Five-Year Plan issued to cover the period 1957-61. Several significant education ordinances and amendments were also passed during this time. The Colonial Offices in London issued memos, which were not binding on the colonial governors, but governors usually implemented the recommendations. In general, educational policy was directed towards building a community which will be well-equipped to assume full social, economic, and political responsibility.

Christopher Cox, a former education advisor to the British Secretary of State for the colonies, headed the commission bearing his name, which in 1947 drew up educational plans for the next ten years of development. The aim of the Ten-Year Plan was:

... to make the best use of available resources in expanding the school system at all stages, so as not only to ensure that the greatest possible number became literate in the shortest time ... but also to enable an increasing number of pupils to have the advantages of secondary and higher education.

This widespread literacy objective included the distribution of educational facilities fairly evenly over the territory in terms of population. Paraphrased, the list of the proposals contained in the Ten-Year Plan are:

1) double sessions in village schools;
2) an increase in Swahili publications;
3) closer supervision by African School Supervisors;
4) the development of district education committees with co-operation of all agencies;
5) an increase in the number of district schools; a transfer of V and VI from secondary to primary schools;
6) an improvement in the quality of Grade II teachers;
7) building up the number of secondary schools, a reduction of VIII wastage;
8) concentration on special staff at Senior Secondary Schools and introduction of the School Certificate examinations;
9) selection of Makerere students for scholarships overseas;
10) a rapid expansion of girls' education by an increase of European staff and women teachers to village schools and opening a full secondary school for girls;
11) the development of industrial and technical schools;
12) the incorporation of selected bush schools within the recognized education system; and
13) the development of adult literacy.

A decision was made to continue with the four-year primary course rather than to change to a six-year course. A suggestion was also made to create a Grade III teacher who had completed Std. VI and had six months of professional training at a Teacher Training Center (TTC hereafter). This type of teacher was never trained.

In 1948 the last of the four memoranda from the Colonial Office in Britain, Education for Citizenship in Africa, recognized that political freedom would become a reality to Africans.[4] It stressed that the task of education was to guide all the people toward use of this political freedom for the common good.

Due to the absence of any mention of European and Indian education in the Ten-Year Plan, it was necessary to pass the Non-Native Education Ordinance and Non-Native Tax Ordinance in 1948. The European Education Authority and the Indian Education Authority had complete control of funds and general administration of their respective schools. Later Goan education was separated from the Indian Education Authority forming a non-native education fund, mainly because they are a Catholic community. As the enrollment grew, Europeans joined correspondence courses as a measure to prevent overcrowding of the existing European schools. No European S/S was developed until 1956. Indian Education was characterized by crowded conditions, poor facilities, and employment of untrained teachers. The Tait and Riddy Report of 1955 supported the plan of the Indian Education Authority to improve and expand their schools.

The Ten-Year Plan for African Education of 1947 was revised in 1950. Its emphasis was on middle schools (hereafter M/Ss), which took the place of all other post-village P/Ss. The Grade III teacher plan was abandoned. An earlier proposal to establish a Jeanes School for chiefs, school supervisors, and wives was also to be forgotten, and in its place was proposed an addition of two or three trade schools and possibly a technical institute for ex-Std. X's. Wherever it was possible, a third teacher was to be added to P/Ss to link mass literacy work with some form of community development.

Practical education—with biases on agriculture, pastoral, commercial, and homecrafts—was stressed, especially in the M/S curriculum. The emphasis on agriculture was the outcome of an investigation made in M/S and P/S levels in February 1949 by Swynnerton. The separation of nonstarters for S/S was rejected so that agriculture would not be given secondary importance. The main aims for the M/Ss were: to provide education that would be a foundation for the student's future life of useful citizenship and immediate employment in the community or further education

---

4. Col. No. 216 (London: HMSO, 1948).

and training, and to provide sound character training and moral instruction. It was an experiment on the African continent and received mixed reception.

The Binns Study Report of 1951 was the first comprehensive survey on Tanganyika education since the Phelps-Stokes Commission Report of 1924. Like that document, it was to have a profound effect on policy formation in later years. It emphasized practical education and terminal education for each level. It was not a duplication of European education, but sought a more liberal education for Africans based on their environment and own way of life, having a strong agricultural bias. The 4-4-4 structure was accepted. The Africans argued against this system up to 1959, stating that four years were too few and eight years an impossibility, and argued for a six-year course as an alternative. The fact that non-native, European, and Indian education were on a 6-5 and 6-6 structure intensified the argument for a six-year primary course. Later the World Bank Mission sympathized with this view, but advocated that 6-4 be provided only as finances permitted. The Binns Report had supported the 4-4 structure because it felt that one who completed the six-year course was on in-between grounds. He could not return to the farm, neither had he enough education to qualify for careers. He was "likely to become unemployed, unemployable, and unsettled," [5] while an ex-VIII could move on to the community, to employment, or to a Seconday School.

The Conference at Cambridge University in 1952, composed of the Binns Study group and some representatives from Tanganyika, made one recommendation, which the Tanganyika Government did not accept. This was the suggestion to retain the use of the vernacular in primary education and to use English where no vernacular was dominant. The fact that Kenya and Uganda followed this recommendation hindered independence and the growth of nationalism in their countries. Tanganyika retained Swahili as a language of the people and attained unity more quickly because of its use.

---

5. B. G. George, *Education for Africans in Tanganyika: A Preliminary Study.* **Bulletin No. 19 (Washington: U.S. Dept. of HEW, 1960),** p. 27.

The *Annual Report* of 1953 carried a very extensive description of the aim of education:

The ultimate objective is the building up of a community well equipped, by the advancement of education in its widest sense, to assume full social, economic, and political responsibility. If education is to achieve its purpose, it must clearly encompass much more than technical or academic training; it must provide both the incentive and the means for the attainment of a full measure of mental, physical, and spiritual development; . . . however, progress towards the ultimate objective depends on the achievement of the immediate objective of the educational advancement of the more backward sections of the territory's population, and it is to this end that efforts must at this stage be mainly directed.

The *Annual Report* of 1954 considered the development of initiative and self-reliance of equal importance with progress in academic work. Discipline from within was encouraged in Senior S/Ss by the participation of students in the organization and government of the school and in the management of school activities.

The Chiefs Ordinance of 1954 provided for selected chiefs to be sent overseas or to the newly established school of local government at Mzumbe, Morogoro, for additional training and administrative experience. The Amendment to the Education (African) Ordinance in 1954 required: 1) publication of the list of schools registered in Part I; 2) a register of teachers for Part I and II; and 3) that sub-Part I schools be registered as Part II. Bush schools were allowed to remain as long as Part I schools were inadequate for the need.

The Five-Year Plan, beginning in 1957, aimed at providing more opportunities for more students to climb higher on the educational ladder beyond the primary course. The plan called for two-hundred boys' and thirty-eight girls' new M/Ss in operation by 1962 and the expansion of secondary, technical, and teacher-training facilities, "so vital to the economic, social, and political devlopment of Tanganyika."[6] The plan emphasized the quality of education pro-

---

6. *Report for the Year* 1960. Col. No. 349 (London: HMSO, 1963).

vided on all levels and the measures for improving the standard of teaching and attainment in P/Ss. The intention was to build a better base to feed into the postprimary schools. Quality was necessary, and it was the only way to expand when finances were channeled mainly into higher-level education. Double sessions were considered preferable to the hiring of untrained teachers. The suggestion of including technical and commercial subjects in School Certificate courses was a step forward, although this was not implemented until postindependence.

Other amendments to the Education (African) Ordinance appeared in the late 1950's. Some of the measures taken were:

1) The appointment of Native Authority Education Commitees (hereafter NAECs) composed mostly of Africans held responsible for P/Ss and M/Ss, advising Government on registration of schools and school management;

2) One of the main functions assigned the Department of Education was the classification and accreditation of schools, NAs and VAs, with aided and nonaided;

3) A registered and licensed teacher could teach as long as he was proficient and not suspended by the Director on certain specific grounds;

4) Special authorization from the Director of Education was required to teach English when the subject was introduced in selected schools in 1958;

5) A law set a maximum of forty-five pupils per class with a minimum of thirty in Std. I and 18 in Std. IV for a school to remain in operation. P/Ss were to be day schools and coeducational. Six years were set as a total for a child to attend P/S, with no more than two years in any grade;

6) The Director was granted greater control over non-government schools with authority to close schools and to prohibit certain textbooks if any were considered to be inferior.

More uniformity was effected among the various agency-operated schools through better supervision of the schools. Due to the fact that approximately two-thirds of the P/Ss were voluntary-agency operated, and Government officers and inspectors were too hard put to visit the schools as often as they wished, government felt a need to create a new post of inspectorate to raise the standard of P/S instruction and to train African School Supervisors in supervision. The Education Assistant office, attached to the Voluntary Agency (VA hereafter), was to be temporary and ran until the end of 1962. Eight Africans held the post of Education Assistant while the rest were degree-holding Americans, Swedes, and English. S/Ss were inspected by officers in the combined central inspectorate of the department, also responsible for inspection of non-African schools.

Partly in response to the report of the Working Party of Higher Education of 1955 and 1958, which discovered a much greater need for assistants than senior officials in the ten-year period, trade schools, a Technical Institute, and departmental-training programs were established and other courses expanded. The Government's viewpoint contended that education should develop only as rapidly as society could manage it.

Religious freedom, granted by the GT Notice No. 157 of 1943, did not make attendance at a religious service or study obligatory at Government or NA schools. VAs were not grant-aided unless they were prepared to admit children of all persuasions for enrollment. In certain areas religion became a greater issue than in others. One reason given for vacant places in Part I schools in 1959 is that some parents preferred to send their children to bush schools because there the religious instruction was of their own preference.

Although the British Government affirmed the principle of integration, it moved slowly. The UN Visiting Mission of 1957 advocated acceleration of this policy and, as a response, the Education Integration Committee was appointed in December, 1958, to investigate the possibility of integrating four separate racial educational systems into one. The Report of the Committee, submitted in 1960, was accepted almost in toto. Because these policies are generally attributed to forces of independence and were implemented after independence, they will be discussed in full with the educational policies of 1961 to 1966.

The Government's policy of financing education changed during the period between 1946 and 1961. In 1947 VAs received 85 per cent of the salary grants for teachers and those who had been unaided until 1946 became partially aided at 50 per cent salary grants. In 1955 it was raised to 95 per cent or 100 per cent African teacher-salary grants, and amended in 1957 to include aid to Education Assistants. In the late 1950's grants-in-aid to VAs usually covered the salaries and supply costs, and one-half of the building costs. Non-native education was financed separately from a tax imposed on non-natives by the 1948 Ordinance. To cite the inequality of expenditures, Government spent £25 per African and Asian child in 1959 and £250 per European child. It became Government's policy that local authorities must raise funds from local taxes to contribute heavily to P/S and M/S education. The target was 50 per cent of recurrent expenditures and 80 per cent of capital expenditures. Beginning in 1958, NAs met the cost of M/S remissions in boarding schools, which was formerly shared with Central Government. The Government's position on fees was that, until universal primary education is possible, parents should contribute to the recurrent expenditures for the education of their children. Also, the communities in which the new S/S streams of the 1957-61 plan were located were expected to contribute cash, labor, and materials to the construction of the new buildings.

As a response to a number of criticisms of the 1957-61 plan, the Director of Education prepared and issued a Three-Year Plan in 1959. He proposed that the primary course be extended to six years with double sessions from Stds. I-IV and single sessions for V and VI. Two years of intermediate schools would provide preparatory education beyond P/S for S/S. M/Ss could be converted into double-stream VII and VIIIs, be purely academic, or have an agricultural or handicraft bias. The remainder of the existing M/S facilities could be converted into S/Ss of various types. These suggestions, with the possibilities of a vertical expansion in African education, certainly met the approval of the majority of Africans. With independence approaching, however, these ideas had to wait to be incorporated in the first plan issued by the new government.

It was the African who objected most vehemently to the emphasis and amount of time spent on agriculture and practical training, especially in the M/Ss. Some of them seemed to feel that they were being given an education inferior to that of their Western counterparts. They were staunch supporters of the urban-type school. In 1959 Mason evaluated the problem of adaptation in these words:

The form and nature of African society are intricate and have so many aspects that change can only be accomplished by a change on many fronts and through many agencies. . . . A successful adaptation can be made only by Africans themselves.[7]

Perhaps his explanation points out the reasons for the disparity between the goal of education in 1960: ". . . to impart a broad general education which will equip the pupil to make his individual contribution to the life and development of the community"[8] and the actuality of a growing gulf between the educated and his home village. In general, Africans were not involved in the educational planning. Also, examination-oriented education supplemented the emphasis of Government for skilled manpower in urban centers rather than an emphasis on rural community development.

EDUCATIONAL STRUCTURE, 1946-61

Administration

With the rapid development of education during this period, it was necessary to form clear statements of duties for education officers at the regional and local levels as well as centrally. The Ministry of Social Services included in its portfolio the Department of Education. The Director or Education was given the power to administer all types of Part I schools: NA, VA, partially aided schools, and registered schools with licensed but not certified teachers. He was given power to inspect all schools and to close unsatisfactory ones.

The Provincial Education Officer (PEO) was assisted by education officers, Women's Education Officers, and African School Supervisors. It was his job to maintain a liaison with the VAs and NAECs and to disperse the payments of grants-in-aid. His duties lay mainly in the field, including the inspection of M/Ss and as many P/Ss as possible.

The Inspectorate also developed during these years. Until 1957 two inspectors of African S/Ss were centered at headquarters; then

---

7. R. J. Mason, *British Education in Africa* (London: Oxford University Press, 1959), pp. 136-37.
8. The aim of S/S given in Col. No. 349, *op. cit.*

the inspectorate was organized on a nonracial basis. African School Supervisors were required to inspect both VA and NA schools. With the expansion of upper primary education, the office of Education Assistant was created as a measure of quality control.

Decentralization took place as responsibility for the operation of P/Ss and M/Ss was placed in the hands of local authorities. NAECs met frequently with the District Commissioners to give advice on the location and management of schools.

Non-native, European, and Indian Education Authorities were organized during this period to care for their respective education systems. They had control of their non-native education tax funds.

Institutions

The Ten-Year Plan for African education (1947-56) had a 4-2-2-4 structure:

I-IV   Village schools
V-VI   District schools (two parallel types: terminal or attached to a secondary or teacher-training school)
VII-X   Provincial secondary schools (VII-VIII were preparatory)
XI-XII Senior secondary schools

Each cycle of the 4-4-4 structure, which became effective in 1952, was to be complete in itself but linked to the one above it. Tests were given at the end of Stds. IV, VIII, X, and XII, which were followed by selections of the best performers for the next level.

Bush schools were out of the category of schools during most of the 1947 plan. They were subgrade with or without religious instruction, providing secular instruction approximating Std. I and II of the primary course. Those with religion only remained outside the jurisdiction of the Ministry of Education after they were legalized in 1954. The majority were run by religious bodies, but a few were also started by TANU during the 1950's and later handed over to TAPA after independence. To demonstrate the vast network, one can cite that in 1949 it was estimated that there were 5,420 of these schools with an enrollment of some 208,000 students.[9] No estimate is available for the Koranic schools. The 1954 law gave bush schools legal existence and required registration of the Part II (bush) schools and teachers. Bush schools represented no financial obligation to the Government. Teachers were untrained ex-Std. VIII students. Members of the Department of Education held the powers of inspection for Part II schools, even though these schools were not required to follow the curriculum of a Part I school. The registration of a Part II school could be withheld if the building facilities were inadequate, staff requirements were not met, or the school was operating less than 180 days per year. Students usually transferred to a Part I school before Std. III level if there were empty places corresponding to their ability.

Primary schools (P/Ss), first called village schools, were four-year coeducational day schools. Teaching in earlier stages was first permitted in the vernacular, but later recalled. A great expansion was accomplished in the Ten-Year Plan. Double sessions were introduced and closer supervision began with the African School Supervisors. English was not introduced until 1958 in selected schools on the Std. III level. A gradual improvement in the holding power reduced the tendency for dropouts before Std. IV only near the very end of the 1950's. The Triennial Survey covering 1955 to 1957 views the most important feature of education as the rapid increase in P/S facilities. Simultaneous with the introduction of English in Std. III was the addition of a third classroom, so that Std. III and IV read one whole day each instead of half days as in a double-session schedule. Wastage was high for girls in all grades and for all students between I and II. The aim of the P/Ss was to provide basic skills of literacy and citizenship.[10]

The *district schools* were either attached to I-IV day schools or were V-VI district boarding schools. English was not introduced until this stage except for its inclusion in some Std. IIIs of P/Ss in 1958.

Middle Schools (M/Ss) replaced the district schools because they provided inadequate preparation not only for further educa-

---

9. *Annual Report,* 1949, p. 9.
10. Col. No. 349, *op. cit.,* p. 132, and the P/S syllabus, 1947.

tion or training, but also for life in a rural community. M/Ss in town were day schools. All of the girls' M/Ss and rural boys' M/Ss were boarding institutions. They were educationally advantageous but costly. The title "middle" proved to be more exact for its function than the practical aims stated for its creation.

A limiting factor in M/S development was the small number of African female teachers for Domestic Science, due to the general attitude toward girls' education prior to this time. The Ten-Year Plan stated:

> Most parents are reluctant that girls should leave their home neighborhood, and tribal tradition is at present opposed in many cases to such a practice.[11]

Girls attended the village P/Ss, which were coeducational, and were also admitted to day district schools. There were special schools also for them with Stds I-IV, I-V, III and IV of which all were boarding schools but two. In 1950, Tanganyika girls took the boys' Std. X examination for the first time, and in 1951 the first Tanganyika woman was admitted to Makerere. A significant increase in girls' enrollment was seen in the late 1950's when it reached one-third of the total enrollment in the P/Ss. This was partially due to the ruling in the Department of Education establishing one-third as a requirement. The World Bank Report gives four reasons for the great wastage in girls' education:

a) Parents with limited means preferred to educate boys;

b) Nonrecognition of the value of education of girls was a potent force;

c) The men teachers did not know how to teach girls; and

d) The curriculum of school was often unrelated to the girls' needs.[12]

The mission recommended expansion of facilities on all levels, an introduction of more practical courses for girls in M/Ss, and an increase in the number of qualified women teachers and heads

---

11. p. 14 of the plan, 1947.
12. World Bank. *The Economic Development of Tanganyika: Report of a Mission Organized by the International Bank for Reconstruction and Development.* (Baltimore: John Hopkins Press, 1963), p. 311.

of girls' M/Ss. Government TTCs were all coeducational by independence. The girls' wastage problem did not diminish until 1965. A survey taken of the girls in Tabora Secondary School in 1959 reveals that they were not university minded. It was hard to keep girls in S/S when careers as medical assistants, policewomen, clerks, and social workers attracted them.

Secondary Schools (S/Ss) were primarily academic, leading to various goals. A Territorial Examination was introduced at the completion of Std. X in 1947. An ex-Std. X student went on to Grade II teacher training, a technical institute, a Natural Resource School, departmental training, Std. XI in secondary education, or sought general employment. An ex-XII, who sat for the Cambridge Overseas School Certificate exam, went on to further education, general employment, or enrolled in a departmental training course.

The European and Indian S/Ss, which followed the 6-5 or 6-6 plan, were purely academic. In 1959 St. Michael's and St. George's S/S opened for European children, the two largest Government Indian schools offered the Higher School Certificate courses, and four assisted non-native schools offered secondary education. One of them offered School Certificate courses. The number of African S/Ss, all of which were boarding schools, grew from nineteen in 1957 (three were Senior S/Ss) to twenty-eight in 1960 (fifteen with the full S/S course). Four schools added Form V in 1959. Secondary boarding schools had some advantages: The long and close association of students from several tribes living together encouraged tolerance, respect, and firm relationships. Adequate study, recreation periods, and regular meals were other benefits.

The 1947 syllabus contended that selection for *teacher training* was done at the end of Std. VI so that "failures of Std. VIII would not be forced to enter training." Although the appointment of a Grade III teacher was recommended, it never materialized and only Grades I and II teachers were trained during this period. As District Schools and pre-teacher training VII and VIII were replaced by the M/Ss in the 1950's, candidates were selected for Grade II TTCs at the completion of Std. VIII instead of VI. It was hoped that this would lower the number of dropouts in TTCs, for a number had left at the end of the second academic year in TTCs before beginning the two years of professional training. Teacher-training feeding areas were to affect the bias of the school, determine whether it would be agricultural, fishing, industrial, etc. The Grade II candidate became a village or P/S teacher and the Grade I a M/S, senior P/S or Grade II TTC teacher. There were few candidates for Grade I training as Africans were attracted to salaries paid while in Government training courses. Grade I training efforts were concentrated in larger centers in the last half of the 1950's. An African School Supervisors' specialized-training course was opened at one TTC.

The number of TTCs rose from fourteen VAs plus two Government schools in 1946 and 1947 to twenty-four VAs and seven Government institutions in 1958. Whereas the 1957-61 plan stressed postprimary education rather than a continued rapid expansion of primary education as in the Ten-Year Plan, teacher education was obliged to change the Grade II training to one of quality rather than quantity. The Triennial Survey (1955-57) called for a reduction in the intake of Grade II candidates by 50 per cent in order to provide for normal wastage of teachers, plus additional teachers for the third classroom. Thus a more or less level output was expected. Graduate teachers were almost all expatriates, for African graduates were occupied in administration. In order to meet the need for the practical subjects offered in boys' and girls' M/Ss, in-service training was offered to Grade II teachers to prepare them for special teaching in handwork, domestic science, and agriculture. Refresher courses for teachers were held on the provincial level and supervisors' seminars were multi-provincial.

In 1947 there were five Government and four VA schools offering *vocational training* courses in carpentry, building, and tailoring, apprenticeships of three to five years' duration. These were open to ex-Std. VI students. The policy for trade training and technical education changed in 1951 when the Government formulated schemes for this branch of education. Trade training was to be provided for Africans in specially built and equipped schools, while courses in Government and VA schools of substandard secondary education level were to be phased out. The reason given for this change was that modern craftsmen must be intelligent and responsible, and work with their brains as well as with their hands.[13] No trade training was planned for Europeans or Asians at this time. There was approval for a Technical Institute in the 1950 revision of the Ten-Year Plan. This institution was to be interracial and for both sexes of all three groups.

Subprofessional and semiprofessional level courses were developed in Tanganyika. Two trade schools were opened on the post-VIII level; Ifunda's first output came in 1953 and Moshi opened in May, 1957. They offered three years of the five in subject matter and then two years of on-the-job-training with recognized firms. The building section attracted more students than the engineering courses.

Various opportunities opened for vocational training. In the early 1950's Dar offered clerical classes on the ex-X level, enrolling fifty students yearly. The Natural Resources School at Tengeru opened in 1953 and gave officers of the Junior Service training in agriculture, veterinary, and forestry. It also trained teachers in agriculture for M/Ss, TTCs, and S/Ss. Tabora Girls' Secondary School made a start with the training of African girls for clerical posts. Mzumbe Center trained Africans for provincial and central administration. Full-time residential courses for the training of engineering assistants were established in 1956.

Industrial and commercial courses were run by other departments and companies, e.g., East African Railways and Harbour, East African Post and Telecommunications, East African Power and Lighting, Gailey and Roberts, Bata Shoes, etc. Kilimanjaro Native Cooperative Union (KNCU) opened a College of Commerce in 1957 and offered some Domestic Science and Commercial courses of ex-X level on a formal basis.

The Technical Institute at Dar opened in 1958 and was a link between the trade schools and the Royal Technical College, Nairobi, which was less used by Tanzanians until 1958 than Makerere College. It offered engineering, secretarial, clerical, foremanship, and commercial courses. No secondary technical course opened until 1961.

Higher education was not offered in Tanganyika during pre-

---

13. In the Government's syllabus, *Trade Training: Technical, and Commercial Education* (Dar: Government Printer, 1954).

independent days. Students went to interterritorial institutions in
East Africa, the Royal Technical College, and Makerere College;
or received scholarships to England and Ireland, the United States,
and India. The Working Party of 1958 urged that an interterritorial university college be established in Dar, to open to students in 1965/66. In 1959 seventy Africans held degrees and
forty-four had diplomas. In 1960 it was estimated that six hundred Africans were taking postsecondary courses.

TABLE IV
NUMBER OF AFRICAN STUDENTS ENROLLED
IN EACH STANDARD FOR EACH THOUSAND STUDENTS
ENTERING STANDARD I, 1960 [14]

Standard	Enrollment as Percentage of Previous Standard	Enrollment (using a base figure of 1,000)
1	—	1,000
2	91	910
3	93	846
4	97	820
	exam	
5	18	219
6	92	196
7	85	166
8	96	160
	exam	
9	25	40
10	99	40
	exam	
11	35	13
12	100	13
	exam	
13	35	5
14	91	4

14. Arthur J. Lewis, "The Shortage of Teachers in East Africa:
The Causes, Extent, and Plans for Alleviation" (paper presented at the
Conference on the Supply and Training of Teachers for Scondary Schools
of East Africa, Entebbe, Uganda, January 21-23, 1963), p. 6; quoted by
Rodney Hinkle, "Educational Problems and Policies in Post-Independent
Tanzania" (an Ed. D. document, Columbia Teachers College, 1969), p. 111.

Table IV shows the iceberg of African opportunities and demonstrates clearly where colonial education had emphasized education on the lower levels.

In 1950 a Social Development Department was organized under the Ministry of Local Government. For the next year, it functioned well in directing adult education and literacy classes, and led to various development projects. Besides enlarging knowledge in many areas, these projects unified communities in voluntary group labor and joined them through contacts with the local government.

METHODS AND CONTENT, 1946-61

There was an unusual bustle of activity in the administrative offices of Tanganyika Government at the time of transfer from a status of mandated territory to one of trusteeship. For the first time in its history, the colony had been asked to submit a ten-year development plan with the development aim being the sake of the colony. The British Colonial Development and Welfare Act of 1945 had ushered in a new era in the colonies. With the involvement of Tanganyika administrators in development plans throughout the trusteeship period, and the appearance of successive syllabuses, laws, and regulations for education, Tanganyika was bound to witness growth and changes in its fight against ignorance. Those Education Secretaries of the VAs who had ambitiously committed themselves in 1947 to opening a generous number of schools during the ten-year period jealously guarded their promises while time threatened to run out on them in the 1950's. They refused to trade off any part of their quota to unfortunate agencies who had lacked such foresight.

The syllabuses issued by the Department of Education during these years contained helpful suggestions and encouraged certain methods of teaching, but they were not binding. They issued directions on how the subject courses should be taught, how the course work ought to be planned, and the time that should be allotted for each course. Registered authorities and school managers had the freedom to take this broad and general framework of the set curricula and to construct their own. Courses could be shifted for convenience of work and weather. Religious authorities were asked to work out their own religious instruction. As the educational system grew in size, the inspectorate developed, and in particular, the intensified competition in selection for a succeeding educational level sharpened. The syllabuses were considered more prescriptive. The young, inexperienced teachers were not very flexible in a role that taxed their abilities. The aims given for each subject in the early syllabuses were ideal in many respects, but too ideal for the times and training of the teachers. Many of the aims lay quite dormant until the late 1960's.

Rote learning and repetition were the common methods of teaching. The exams scheduled for each terminal point (at the completion of Std. IV, VIII, X, and XII) tested much factual knowledge and no one but the composers of the questions knew which facts would be required on any particular examination. Examinations became more and more influential as an end in themselves. They became instruments for a process of thinning out the ranks and selecting for more advanced courses rather than the instruments of measurement of school progress. The Territorial VIII Certificate Examination was changed in title to General Entrance Examination (G.E.E.) in 1958, and was literally a test to select pupils for entrance to secondary schools, to the Grade II teacher-training centers, to the trade schools, and to the training school for nurses and rural medical aids. With all the examinations except the one for Std. IV written in English, an additional variable confounded the results. The selective process became more like a game—those who could interpret the meaning of the questions, remember details, and perform well on this type of measurement were given the privileged places up the ladder. Undoubtedly, no one can say that only those who found themselves in those cherished positions were the most intelligent people in Tanzania, for less than 36 per cent of the age-groups entered Std. I, and many of these never reached even the first important exit point.

The Std. VIII exam has always been centrally set, but after 1953 the corrections and selection were done in the provinces. At the same time a two-hour Domestic Science test was set for girls in place of the General Science required of the boys. None of the other practical subjects of M/Ss (agriculture, carpentry, handicrafts) were ever tested. Perhaps they would have held their prestige and purpose if they had been a part of the exam, giving it the flavor of a "school-leaving exam" rather than "preparatory." The use of the Cambridge Overseas School Certificate Examination in XII tended to hold the secondary schools on purely academic standards with greater relevancy to British than East African interests.

The 1955 syllabuses for M/Ss and S/Ss both stressed the importance of the activity method over verbalization. The M/S syllabus had a very practical note and connection to daily life in each subject. One-third of the time was to be spent on practical learning—a "core of instruction," not a "chore." Apparently the activity method was never completely understood or utilized, for this was one of the areas that caused the Peace Corps staff great frustration in the early 1960's.

Swynnerton had recommended a "liberal education to stimulate thought on the problems of the country and to show the interdependence of peasant and salaried worker." [15] He suggested that a strong bias in agriculture be introduced into the curriculum to broaden secondary education because "in the near future the only outlet for many of those pupils will be agriculture." [16] His view regarding agriculture in P/S and M/S was finally accepted: Improving the three R's in P/S is better than teaching agriculture, for ex-primary pupils will be better able to read agriculture pamphlets later on. He felt that, if a few basic principles of better land use could be inculcated in P/S days, there would be a slightly better chance that the general level of peasant agriculture could be raised in time. The argument given in a report by the Department of Agriculture in 1956 was that the curriculum did not need more than minor improvements, but better-qualified teachers who were flexible and competent. This they supported by the weak explanations and reasons for methods in agriculture that were given by students. They held to their point that the M/S syllabus would not be fully implemented until properly trained teachers were available. Their suggestions for an agriculture paper in the Territorial VIII Certificate Examination was not accepted,

---

15. "Report on an Inquiry into Agricultural Extension at Primary and Middle Schools," (Dar: Government Printer, 1956), p. 2.
16. *Ibid.*

but thereafter a few agriculture questions were included and one was made mandatory.

During this period the usual variety of subjects included the language-skill subjects, general-knowledge subjects, manual skills and creative arts, and physical training. Kitchen feels that the inclusion of English in P/Ss in 1958 "changed the nature of the Primary School course." [17] Health, citizenship, manual and creative arts, and religious instruction were aimed at providing self-respect, moral well-being, and responsibility toward the tribe and community. Projects and out-of-class activities were to build character. The secondary educational course was concerned with the production of potential leaders. They were to emphasize agriculture, even though the pupils' futures lay elsewhere, but later on many would find this their only outlet. A general education was required until Std. X and then a certain amount of specialization was permissible in XI and XII.

With the great expansion in primary education in the Ten-Year and Five-Year plans, certain measures had to be taken to ensure quality as well as quantity. School broadcasts were increased after the birth of the Tanganyika Broadcasting Corporation (TBC) in 1956. Serving mostly M/Ss in Std. V to VIII, the up-to-date features negated flexibility in the scheduling of the courses involved. They provided for more uniformity in M/S teaching and supplemented classroom learning.

Provincial Education Officers found it impossible to visit and supervise the increasing numbers of M/Ss. African School Supervisors were inadequately prepared for inspection of these higher-level subjects. The Government created the post of Education Assistant to fill the gap in the mission-operated schools (which were in the majority) as well as to give assistance and training to the Mission School Supervisors while they conjointly supervised P/Ss.

TTCs also adopted quality measures. Two-week refresher courses were held for in-service teachers and supervisors periodically at various centers throughout the country. Three-year courses

17. H. Kitchen (ed.), *The Educated African: A Country-by-Country Survey of Educational Development in Africa* (New York: Praeger, 1962), p. 153.

were given to selected Grade II teachers to specialize in handi-work, agriculture, and domestic science for M/S instruction. Girls' TTCs included needlework in their syllabus and provision was made for a Grade II teacher to upgrade to Grade I if he passed the Territorial Std. X Examination and petitioned for upgrading. Although courses at TTCs included academic subjects and theory and the practice of teaching, in the final examination the practi-cal section was weighted more heavily. In 1958, the same year that English was introduced into selected Std. IIIs, the medium of instruction of the Grade II TTCs changed from Swahili to English. The number of Grade II trainees was reduced as the number of Grade Is was increased. (Grade Is were required for the last two years of the M/S course.)

During the mid-1950's trade and vocational training was de-veloped. This provided for various skills in building, engineering, and clerical careers, and was aimed at sublevel and semiskilled occupations where the need was great. In writing about the two trade schools and the series of strikes in them during 1959, Thomas concludes: "The trade school boys . . . apparently never really accepted the fact that they were being trained as working artisans." [18] A survey of 1964 showed that employers held a heavy consensus that "trade school graduates were not a desirable source of labor supply," and they "did not look to the trade schools for a significant proportion of their skilled labor needs." [19] The Technical Institute offered courses on a higher level where the student could more likely meet his aspirations of a "white-collar" job upon graduation or an entrance to university outside the coun-try.

Finances for the various educational systems were full of in-equities. In 1958 the amount spent per African child each year was about Shs. 120; per Asian child, about Shs. 180; and per Euro-pean child, more than Shs. 1,000. The 1960 figures reveal a greater disparity: £3 per African child; £15 per Asian child; and £95 per European child for P/S. In secondary education it was £162 per African child and £ 262 per European child annually.[20]

---

18. Idrian N. Resnick (ed.), *Tanzania: Revolution by Education* (Arusha: Longmans of Tanzania, 1968), p. 116.
19. *Ibid*, p. 117.
20. Col. No. 349, *op. cit.*

SUMMARY

In summary, the first formation of a native education system under the Central Government occurred during the German period. They, like the British during the decades that followed, aimed at educating Africans to help in administrative positions and in the economy. This policy found its implementation in an emphasis of health, vocational, and practical education. The adoption of Swahili for official and educational activities was one of the most significant decisions of the time.

The British held to their policy that the colony be self-reliant through the mandated era. Some aid was legislated to the colony in the 1929 Act, but it was not until the end of the mandated period that development for the colony's sake was considered.

They put a great deal of stress on literacy, health, and agriculture (the keynote) and less emphasis on postprimary education. They were very cautious to avoid an overproduction of graduates whom the socio-economic milieu could not absorb. The rise in the economy after the Depression had its impact on the system by demanding quality secondary and teacher-training courses. As the system increased in size, flexibility and experimentation on local levels decreased proportionately. It seems logical to assume that this may have been a major factor in leading to an accelerated nationalization rather than tribalized-power centers. On the other hand, one can only surmise what might have been accomplished through greater adaptation to the local community. Since projecting what might have been is not the purpose of this historical section, no further speculation is considered at this point.

Although educational policies were flavored with school-community relevancy, educational institutions were an alien feature in the community and uprooted the "successful" student, transferring him to another social setting generally outside the community. The curriculum was not spiced with genuine expressions of African culture; many of the arts were missing. Moral instruction and character training were awarded a cherished place. Again, one might bring up the question of relevancy; there seems to be little correlation between the character training given in the formal, traditional education in the tribes and the European-engineered curriculum.

The inclusion of greater purpose of development policies of the British coincided with the outbreak of World War II and the transfer of Tanganyika to a trusteeship status. The more rapid development of the economy required a highly centralized government with long-range plans. As political aspirations arose and social changes emerged, the main problem seems to have been how to maintain a balance between social and vocational goals, with the great expansion on different levels of education.

The adoption of the 4-4-4 cycle and a M/S curriculum aimed at more adequately preparing the elementary child for community life through terminal educational courses never accomplished what the educational planners had hoped. Rather, the M/S functioned as a stepping stone true to its title, preparing the few for post-primary education and serving a dysfunctional role for many of the rest. Conservative elders were not receptive to experimenting with new methods on their land. The 1964 survey mentioned earlier also showed that the trade schools were not producing what they had been created to do.

Attitudes of the African populace toward education ran the gamut from adulation to indifference, accounting for the fervent demand on one hand and the wastage problem on the other, for the suspicion that any adaptation was a means of shortchanging them, and the lists of court cases registered concerning truancy. It was a compliment rather than an insult to call a man who imitated the Europeans a "Black European." [21]

Inequalities due to sex, race, religion, and geographical settings became more noticeable as years passed and independence approached. Vocational goals took precedence over social goals in education. To many of the colonial educators and religious leaders, expansion in the number of schools and churches mean development. Quantity had to be counterchecked by quality.

The swift transition to independence was less expected and, consequently, found the British administrators and Africans less prepared than in some other African countries. The forces of independence skewed the focus to manpower goals. The rewards for the educated were many and appealing. The need for higher education increased the complexity of attempting to plan a system

---

21. Nyerere in *Freedom and Unity*, p. 186.

whereby as many people as possible could benefit from the limited finances.

The broad policy statements of pre-independence days were less specific and comprehensive than postindependence plans, and consequently could not bypass the impact of their inadequacies. Superstition and age-old social constraints were still forceful and mitigated against rational thinking. Observations of expatriate employers showed that activities that required recall in their employees were usually done well, but those that required a transfer of principles to a new situation were found difficult. Only what was examinable was considered important in the curriculum; the rest was considered frills. The emphasis on examinations fostered individual competition and careerism (necessary for progress), but lacked a counterbalance with a spirit of social service and tenderheartedness to the underprivileged. The language, textbooks, and examinations were alien to the African setting. Failure became a reality to many students who, after performing well, faced a scarcity of opportunities to advance, thus prohibiting further studies. The strongly academic and humanistic secondary education, narrowed by the specialties of the expatriate teachers and the requirements of the School Certificate examination, brought the Africans quickly into contact with the world of the European culture.

In conclusion, one can say that the colonial administrators made a contribution to education in Tanzania by providing a set of principles to serve as a guide for developing a system of education. They laid the foundations for such a system, and gradually subscribed to education as a social force through which a socially, economically, and politically healthy society could be created. They conceived of an African education having two functions: to provide the pupil with better equipment to cope with his environment, and to prepare him for the changes to which the environment would increasingly be subjected. The second function seems to have appeared latently in the first decades and to have gathered strength around the time of World War II.

CHAPTER FOUR

THE PHILOSOPHICAL BASE OF UJAMAA-ISM

As a background to the analysis that follows in the next chapter, it is necessary to outline the philosophical base from which President Nyerere has drawn his goals for the nation. This chapter, therefore, will contain the ideas and principles that underlie his thinking and hence determine his policies and actions. By reviewing briefly the assumptions and concepts of Nyerere's Ujamaa-ism, it is hoped to lay a foundation with a proper perspective for a scholarly treatment of the goals for the emerging nation. His definitions of African socialism in "Ujamaa: The Basis of African Socialism" and his statement, "National Ethic," [1] originally provided as a guide to the Commission on the Establishment of a Democratic One-Party State, most eloquently sum up his ideology. His other statements consistently build on these writings, enlarging on policies, goals, and means toward becoming a socialist state.

AFRICAN SOCIALISM AND UJAMAA-ISM

Socialism is a term that has various connotations and meanings for people around the globe. Even among African authors and statesmen, there is no complete agreement regarding the African brand of socialism. Their interpretations, however, according to sociologist Meister, do share some elements in common:

1) Reaffirmation of the values held by traditional society and its various institutions;

2) Emphasis on a type of personality apropos to this society; and

3) Proclamation of "this type of society as fundamentally different from European societies divided by class conflicts and as the model that it can and must constitute for the new African nations." [2]

---

1. Nyerere in *Freedom and Unity*, pp. 162-71, 262-64.
2. Albert Meister, *East Africa: The Past in Chains, the Future in Pawn.* Translated by Phyllis Nauts Ott. (New York: Walker & Co., 1968c), p. 159.

Nyerere's concept of socialism, referred to hereafter as *Uja-maa-ism* in order to distinguish it from the other versions, is categorized by political and social scientists as a synthesis of the African socialism of Kenya, Ghana, Mali, and others; a mixture of Christian, Fabian, and welfare Labourism; and most like Proudhon's views.[3] Another political scientiest, Geiss, calls it a "socialism of a poor society" with its egalitarianism "based on the equality of poverty." [4]

Ujamaa-ism for Tanzania is not meant to be nor can it be a reprint of another nation's socialism. Nyerere argues that the universal characteristics of socialism must be applied to each particular situation in a manner best suited to it. He further argues that "one will not recognize or define a socialist society by its institutions or its statements, but by its fundamental characteristics of equality, cooperation, and freedom." Each socialist country may then differ at any stage of development and adhere to different methods, but all aim at the same ultimate goal.

Based on two African traditions—political democracy and mutual social responsibility—Ujamaa-ism eschews both communism or doctrinaire socialism and capitalism; their differences will be further identified in the discussion of the next section. Nyerere's Ujamaa-ism did not originate in conflicting classes nor from concerted group or mass pressure, but in an attitude of mind growing out of a colonial experience.

Ujamaa-ism has not been formulated as a call to action, but as a statement of humanistic ideals. The following section, therefore, is an analysis of its principles, its socio-economic environment, and some other writings of President Nyerere that show how Ujamaa-ism is applied to the social, political, and economic organizations of society affecting the education of the country.

THE PURPOSE OF ALL SOCIAL ACTIVITIES IS MAN

The foundation and objective of Nyerere's socialism is Ujamaa. Nyerere views society as an extension of the family, ever widening to encompass the tribe, the nation, and finally, the world of man-

3. Harvey Glickman, "Monopolitics in Tanzania," *Public Administration in Israel and Abroad,* 1968, No. 9: Jerusalem (1969), p. 154.

4. Immanuel Geiss, "Nyerere's Political Philosophy—2," *Venture,* XIX: n. 6 (June 1967), pp. 11, 12.

kind.[5] The underlying purpose of the society is man and his well-being. As such, the people are supreme; individual man and family precede the state. The people exert their will peacefully and initiate changes in the law and in personnel serving in roles of leadership. The glorification of the nation or increased production is not the foremost goal. These elements are relevant inasmuch as they address themselves to the well-being of man. For example, government as the instrument of the party, and not vice versa, serves the people, and goods must be produced that are useful to and make life better for man. In Nyerere's philosophy, man's life in society is a whole; the spiritual and temporal are wedded and form a total way of life. Religious beliefs become a concern of socialism only when religious practices interfere with socialistic principles of equality, mutual respect, and harmony.

"The people" are not an abstraction in this form of society. In Nyerere's Ujamaa-ism, society consists of workers, and only workers who contribute to, and receive from, each other. The tools of production and mechanisms of exchange are in the hands of the people. Society is so organized that "all individual needs and all co-operative social values are considered, with priority being given to those which are most urgent—but without any being destroyed." [6] Ujamaa-ism is an ideology that seeks to establish a balance between group solidarity and personal freedom, a balance not achieved in capitalism or communism. This point is discussed in more detail under the second principle in the following section.

THE PRINCIPLES OF UJAMAA-ISM

There are three major principles of Ujamaa-ism that are continuously recurring either simultaneously or singularly in Nyerere's statements, thus providing reason or logic for his innovations.

The first principle is based on an acceptance of human equality. All men are brothers. Therefore, some cannot be included and others excluded. There is no room for racism, for doctrines of aristocracy, for arrogance. It is not the equality of one man, but of

---

5. One of the goals for the nation is "to build an attitude of mind which [will] enable us to live together with our fellow citizens of Tanzania, and of the whole world, in mutual friendliness and cooperation," *Nyerere, Freedom and Unity*, p. 178; also see *Ibid.*, p. 171.
6. *Nyerere, Freedom and Socialism*, p. 12.

everyone equally, i.e., utilizing the diversities of men for the benefit of all. Nyerere recognizes differences in men—in physique, in intelligence, and in skills—and conflicts between man's selfish and social instincts. In Nyerere's thinking, it is essential that the organization of society allow for "man's inequalities [to be] put to the service of his equalities." In other words, it should be difficult or almost impossible for individuals to pursue their desires at the expense of others or that individual strength be exploited by others, but rather that the special abilities of any man could be put to use for the profit of all. Human dignity and mutual respect are the keywords in the exposition of this principle.

The second principle, sharing cooperatively, requires the element of equality. As mentioned earlier, man is the reason for the existence of society in the Ujamaa-ism of Nyerere. It is the individual man, his growth, his health, his security, his dignity, and his happiness of which Nyerere speakes. Man must have freedom to pursue his interests and inclinations. And there are also certain freedoms he obtains by being a part of society: freedom from the fear of personal attack, from natural dangers requiring assistance from others; and the freedom to gain rewards from nature that he could not acquire single-handedly. Thus, in striving for a medium between emphasis on group solidarity and individual freedom:

> ... neither the good of the individual as such, nor the group as such, can always be the determining factor in society's decisions. Both have constantly to be served.[7]

A member of such a society, then, thinks of himself and of others in the framework of his membership in the group. In a given society the individual can fulfill himself while society gives him shape, form, and cohesion. This is the crucial point that differentiates Ujamaa-ism from communism and capitalism. The personal freedoms that would be lost to an individual in a communistic society, allow him in Ujamaa-ism to participate in democratic processes, to discuss with the group until an agreement is reached.

---

7. Nyerere, *Freedom and Unity*. For a discussion on individual versus group, see all of pp. 7-14 in Introduction and page 121. "His concept of individualism is one where individuals are not identified by and with their own interests. That would be selfishness": Henry Bienen, *Tanzania: Party Transformation and Economic Development*. (*Princeton*: Princeton University Press, 1965), p. 231.

Neither are personal freedoms lost in demands of "efficiency" and "production," overriding his needs for a good and full life, "making him less of a man and less free." [8] Cooperation would then be supplanted by ruthless competition, positing the individual in a world by himself. Acquisitiveness is not inherent in Ujamaa; the accumulation of property and wealth opposes the spirit of sharing and distribution. As Nyerere says:

> [Ujamaa] is opposed to capitalism, which seeks to build a happy society on the exploitation of man by man; and it is equally opposed to doctrinaire socialism which seeks to build its happy society on a philosophy of inevitable conflict between man and man.[9]

The third principle is one of unity and harmony, which includes an obligation to work.

The other two principles, of sharing and a practical recognition of equality, serve to maintain and strengthen the social unit. There is reciprocity; each individual cares for the community and, in turn, is cared for by the community. Each person and age group has different obligations to fulfill. In this sense, society is classless because "all members employ their special skills, various resources and talents to promote the fortunes of the national community," as Fred B. Burke puts it in his commentary on Ujamaa. It may be well to add also that, speaking of university students, Nyerere said they must have "an attitude of wanting to work, in whatever work there is to do, alongside and within the rest of the community, until finally there is no more distinction between a graduate and an illiterate than there is between a man who works as a carpenter and his fellow who works as a bricklayer." [10] Parasitism and idleness are considered social sins. There is a common ownership of land and wealth. A man holds the privilege to cultivate the area allocated to him as long as he wishes, but loses this privilege as soon as he allows the land to lay untouched. Opposition is acceptable on a personal basis, but never on a factional one; man can be at odds with his fellow-man, but never at odds with society as a whole.

---

8.   Ahmed Mohiddin, "Ujamaa: A Commentary on President Nyerere's Vision of Tanzania Society," *African Affairs*, LXVII: n. 267 (April 1968), p. 135.

9.   In *Freedom and Unity*, p. 164.

10.   In *Freedom and Socialism*, p. 186.

These three basic principles of Ujamaa-ism are overlapping and interdependent. Together they suggest that there cannot be true harmony and freedom without cooperation and an acceptance of human equality. Freedom for both the individual and group is crucial to mutual respect and peaceful, democratic processes.

Expanding on these basic three tenets, Nyerere has offered eight ethical principles in his "National Ethic," which are reprinted in full because of their clarity in representing the normative values and ideals expected to form the base for the new society in Tanzania.

1. The fundamental equality of all human beings and the right of every individual to dignity and respect.

2. Every Tanganyika citizen is an integral part of the nation and has the right to take an equal part in government at local, regional, and national level.

3. Every individual citizen has the right to freedom of expression, of movement, of religious belief, of association within the context of the law, subject in all cases only to the maintenance of equal freedom for all other citizens.

4. Every individual has the right to receive from society protection of his life, and of property held according to law, and to freedom from arbitrary arrest. Every citizen has the corresponding duty to uphold the law, constitutionally arrived at, and to assist those responsible for law enforcement.

5. Every individual citizen has the right to receive a just return for his labor, whether by hand or brain.

6. All the citizens of the country together possess all the natural resources of the country in trust for their descendants, and those resources may therefore not be surrendered in perpetuity to any individual, family, group, or association.

7. It is the responsibility of the state, which is the people, to intervene actively in the economic life of the nation so as to ensure the well-being of all citizens of Tanganyika, and so as to prevent the exploitation of any person, or the accumulation of wealth, which is inconsistent with the existence of a classless society.

8. The nation of Tanganyika is unalterably opposed to the exploitation of one man by another, of one nation by another, or one group by another. It is the responsibility of the state,

therefore, to take an active role in the fight against colonialism wherever it may exist, and to work for African unity, and for human equality and freedom.

UJAMAA IS ROOTED IN TRADITIONAL SOCIETY

"Traditional society" in this study refers to the historical social unit that evolved in Tanganyika to suit and meet ecological and social demands of the people living there. This is the meaning that Nyerere also gives to it in his analysis of the past.

Nyerere argues that Ujamaa is no foreign ideology; it is this socialism that their forefathers believed and practiced, although they did not label it as such. Traditional society, in fact, could serve as a guide for the present, because 1) it has demonstrated that it can be a self-contained unit, providing the essentials for both material and psychological needs, and 2) it is intrinsically good. Traditional society was a total way of life: familial, egalitarian, democratic, and based on mutual aid. Religious codes of conduct provided the moral code.

The dynamics of traditional African society as presented by Onuoha were operating in Tanganyika's traditional societies. Onuoha's chart follows:

TABLE V

DYNAMICS OF TRADITIONAL AFRICAN SOCIETY [11]

Social Units	Social Processes	Social Negatives
1. The extended family	Work	No loiterers
2. The village	Discussion	No loneliness
3. The tribe	Co-operation	No classes
4. The chief	Leadership	No commune
5. The elders	Public service	No individualism
6. The people	Common ownership	No capitalism
7. The priest	Common worship	No atheism

Other scholars find these dynamics even currently at work in this nation, to some degree in the urban areas and to a greater degree in the rural areas. This fact should make Ujamaa-ism, based on traditional society, more acceptable.

---

11. Father Bede Onuoha. *The Elements of African Socialism.* (London: Andre Deutsch, 1965), p. 31.

The principles mentioned in the foregoing section found their application in traditional society in communal ownership of land, a low degree of stratification, democratic decision making where the leader never gave the final word until the elders (those who acted as guardians of the society and its wealth) had agreed by consensus, mutual concern, universal hospitality, and respect for age and service—all practices and attitudes that together meant basic equality, freedom, and unity.

No system is perfect, not even one in a "primitive" society. Accordingly, Nyerere lists two main inadequacies in Tanganyika's traditional way of life: Women were not given their rightful respect, a fact that reveals an acceptance of inequality, and there was poverty due to both ignorance and the small scale of operations. In the latter case, the economy was not geared to a surplus; there was no felt need for abundance in this egalitarian and sharing group.

TRADITIONAL SOCIETY AND CHANGE

Not only does Nyerere recognize that change is taking place, but he views it as pre-eminent. He sees it as a transformation process rather than mere improvement. Change must be planned, he warns, to avoid chaos and extreme social stress. All the different aspects of change are interconnected: Agricultural change brings social change; social change is prerequisite to agricultural change; and the social ethic must be altered to befit the national society.

The society that Nyerere sees in change is not the "pure" traditional society with its pristine values. Rather, it is a society of traditional values mutated by a Western impact through colonialism. Colonialism subverted egalitarianism, set up stratified structure on racial inequalities, exploited the many by the few, and laid waste the country through private and national rapacity. The "privileged" native became class conscious and alienated from his people through the individual acquisitiveness and economic competition of capitalism.

Tanganyika, a colony of a Western power, was on the fringe of the capitalist world that colonialism introduced. As a result, it inherited some of the worst and best parts of this Western legacy. A positive influence was the British system of Parliament, which embued members with a sense of responsibility to the public. But for those citizens who tried to adapt to the ways of the capitalist world, the result was deleterious. Some citizens who tried to be capitalists failed when they could not actually imbibe the economic principles and attitudes of a capitalist. For others, the resulting oppression came not so much from the failure of being able to work in that system as from the overall psychological impact of it.

Nyerere sums up the Western impact well in the following excerpt:

> Our whole existence has been controlled by people with an alien attitude to life, people with different customs and beliefs. They have determined the forms of government, the type of economic activity—if any—and the schooling which our children have had. They have shaped the present generation of Tanganyikans, more than any other influence.[12]

Mohiddin explains the results of shifting "the center of political, social, and economic gravity from the African's own environment to the colonial metropole":

> All his actions and aspirations had to be appraised and facilitated by the metropolitan power. He was left with no judgment or initiative of his own, save those permitted by the colonial power. This was a catastrophe to the African psyche: it engendered an acute inferiority complex.[13]

Nyerere's emphasis on the virtues of traditional society is aimed at establishing a sense of pride and dignity, which was weakened by colonialism.

His defense for founding TANU as an "African-only" party at first was on this very point; he argued that, by refusing entrance to Europeans and Asians, Africans would be able to hold the positions of responsibility, and thus combat the feelings of inferiority created during colonialism by replacing them with confidence.

The alteration in attitudes is one of kind, not in degree. Rediscovering and revitalizing pristine values is not enough, nor depriving Tanzanians of incentives of selfishness through a rejection of capitalism. The required attitudes for Ujamaa-ism would and could not spring out of traditional customs; traditional attitudes

---

12. *Freedom and Unity*, p. 133.
13. Mohiddin, *op. cit.*, p. 134.

must be changed to extend beyond the family and to all of mankind so they can embrace the possibilities of modern technology. Some institutions of traditional society are, in fact, irrelevant for modern Tanzania. Instead of fighting against nature and sometimes man, such institutions are to be brought into the service of man in the new society. There must be teaching and guiding, effective social incentives offered, but no coercion.

Throughout his writings Nyerere inserts proverbs, illustrations, and a fictitious character, Baba Kabwela (a typical Tanganyikan farmer) to fortify the ideology of Ujamaa and to clarify its complexities. Baba Kabwela's "attitude of mind" and behavior are crucial for change; his realization of the social and economic goals depend ultimately on his comprehension of Ujamaa.

INTERPRETATIONS OF UJAMAA-ISM OF A
GENERAL NATURE

It is only logical to expect that changes have already taken place in Tanzania's political, economic, and social life since independence, and that many more will occur in the future. On examination, however, few or no major changes may have taken place. As late as August, 1969, Nyerere summed up the situation:

> We have decided to be, but are not yet, socialists. For instance, there is no equality in our country. The truth is that the life of the majority of our people is disgusting.[14]

In the President's opinion, the majority, the "have nots," still need to better their condition, raising themselves to a position more in congruence with the "haves."

Burke, Arrighi and Saul, and Mohiddin have written the most comprehensive commentaries on Ujamaa-ism. Burke mentions the granting of eighty-acre holdings to individual farmers in 1962 by Tanganyika Agriculture Corporation (TAC) with the intention of developing large-scale African commercial agriculture. This program was later shelved because it was contrary to the principles of Ujamaa-ism. He concludes that later government policies flow directly from its philosophy, and that there are a number of basic consistencies in the practices of Ujamaa.

---

14. In *African Diary*, IX: n.31 (July 30-Aug. 5, 1969), p. 4554.

Mohiddin, in his commentary on Ujamaa-ism, lists three criteria for it to be successful:

1) The state must control the levels of income and decrease the gap between incomes and privileges of the elite and the rest of the people;

2) New institutions are needed to promote and rejuvenate socialistic attitudes;

3) These institutions must be checked regularly to discern whether they are true to their purposes and then be adapted wherever needed.[15]

What are the main elements of this communalistic society? First of all, since socialism is an ideology, *imani* (a faith), a certain kind of attitude is required. It should be directed toward accumulated property rather than methods of production; a sense of obligation to one's fellowmen; and a sense of pride in an African identity. Without the correct attitude of mind, institutions can be subverted from their true purpose.

A social outlook requires communal undertakings. There must be no exploitation of one by another, and there must be a positive utilization of human resources cooperatively. There must also be freedom of conscience, democratic processes upholding the sovereignty of the people and the laws they make, production based on utility rather than purely on a profit motive, and leaders who serve along with and identify with the people.

Since its purpose is greater freedom and well-being for the people, economic development will be largely in the public sector. Cooperatives, self-help schemes, communal-land policies—along with the nationalization of banks, insurances, major industries, import and export firms—place the means of production and control into the hands of the workers and peasants. Projects operate mainly at the village level, thus creating a modern pluralism—decentralization and yet greater control at the center. Socialist villages depend on freedom, development, and discipline.

The democratic one-party system of government naturally developed and continues to develop in the framework of egalitarianism, freedom, and unity. The eccentric or critic is permitted.

---

15. Mohiddin, *op. cit.,* p. 139.

George Bennett, in "Kenya and Tanzania" (*African Affairs*, LXVI: n. 264 (1967), p. 334) claims Nyerere has been fighting from having *The Standard* nationalized, so that critics can be freer to criticize existing weaknesses in government leaders and their actions in letters to the editor. *The Standard* was nationalized in February, 1970, but given the challenge to expose any action of anyone that is not profitable to the country. Provision is made for free and open discussion before a consensus is reached; the problem is not whether the eccentric exists or does not exist, but how many. A great number would create an impossible situation. As President Nyerere says in *Freedom and Unity*, "One mosquito bite may keep the driver awake on a long and hard drive; a thousand might incapacitate him." Another natural expression of Ujamaa-ism is support for the United Nations organization and nonalignment with any particular power in the Cold War.

CRITICAL ANALYSES OF UJAMAA-ISM

A look at some critical analyses of Nyerere's Ujamaa-ism will sharpen our sensitivity to the implications of the application of these policies. The purpose of this section is to develop an awareness of not only the varying schools of thought held by scholars regarding Ujamaa-ism but also the probability for its future success.

The concept of the "psychocultural" theory, as defined by Maluki, states that "social values into which a young person is sequentially inducted during youth carry observable effects on his adulthood in conceptualization and adoption of similar reactions in structurally analogous political situations." He goes on to say that "it is now generally believed that political experiences are some of the earliest values formed by a child, first through his family and secondly through the community in which he grows up."[16] It would then logically follow, he asserts, that Julius Nyerere, born and raised in a traditional society, was socialized into political concepts by his family and then by the community. His community has also been confirmed as traditional in values and culture.

Like Nyerere, many of his political colleagues herded cattle in

---

16. Eliud Ikusa Maluki. "The Influence of Traditionalism upon Nyerere's 'Ujamaa-ism'" (Unpublished Ph.D. dissertation, University of Denver, 1965), pages iii, 19,20.

their childhood and are still close to the grass roots of traditional society. It is assumed, then, that they, and the 95 per cent rural population of Tanzania (as well as many of the urban dwellers who still hold onto traditional values), perceive political policies in much the same manner as Nyerere. The fact that many of the central political figures attended the same postprimary institutions adds to their similarities.

There are some, however, who favor policies based on a sharp break with the traditional past. This would be more disruptive to society than Ujamaa-ism, which makes the following distinction:

> A violent revolution makes the introduction of socialist *institutions* easier; it makes more difficult the development of the socialist attitudes which give life to these institutions. . . . Violence is a short cut only to the destruction of the institutions and power groups of the old society; they are not a short cut to the building of the new. . . . The new life has still to built by and with people who lived in the old society and who were shaped by it even if they reacted against it.[17]

On the point of disruptive change in society, leading sociologists and anthropologists do not even agree. Some advocate building on past traditions and others recommend a total change from a former way of life. There seems to be a greater tendency toward a gradual change than a total one.

Rweyemamu attributes the rise during this time of the subnational ideologies in Tanzania that conflicted with Ujamaa-ism to the slow clarification of Nyerere's ideology. He purports that in the absence of an ideology the people become confused and disenchanted.[18] Events in 1962 show that Nyerere saw a need for more immediate action. In response to the inconsistent party behavior and complaints about the slowness and moderation of the Africanization (the term changed to "localization" in 1964) program, he took some steps. During that time, he handed over the premiership to his later vice-president, stepping down to rejuvenate the party. He produced "Ujamaa: The Basis of African Socialism,"

---

17. Nyerere, *Freedom and Socialism*, p. 23.
18. Rweyemamu, *op. cit.*, p. 297.

"The Second Scramble," and "*TANU na Raia*" (TANU and the People) to further substantiate his goals.

One month after assuming the presidency in January 1963, he produced his "Democracy and the Party System" for the Annual Conference of TANU, and later, at the same meeting, it was decided in principle that Tanganyika should become a one-party state. His other papers, "Education for Self-Reliance" and "Socialism and Rural Development," which were contemporary with the *Arusha Declaration* (which, it is claimed, he wrote as a preliminary draft by hand at the TANU Annual Meeting in 1967 where it was adopted), were produced after the demonstrations of university students against the National Service Act of 1966 and the growing crisis of primary-school leavers who found neither further education nor jobs available to them at the completion of their primary-school course.

Rweyemamu, who wrote his doctoral dissertation before the *Arusha Declaration*, asserted that Ujamaa-ism was functioning as a "stop-gap" measure, giving rise to pressure groups, which—developing in the process of modernity—would cancel the need for Ujamaa-ism as such and call forth new ideologies and symbols. Later events show that new symbols have appeared on the national scene in the post-Arusha era, but there is also evidence of a greater commitment to Ujamaa-ism rather than a diminishing one.

The sociologist Meister accuses Nyerere of ignoring the fact that social change has already taken place; he postulates that the extended family pattern has already disintegrated in the urban areas and will continue to spread. Maluki would take issue with Meister, for he found that:

> . . . both Wallerstein and LeVine refute the assumption that modernization and urbanization logically lead to dissolution of traditional culture. . . . the allegiance to the traditional chieftancy declines while that of the traditional community, and the family with its extended systems, remains more or less unaltered.[19]

He goes on to say that LeVine gives two reasons for the possibility and, what is more, the reality of traditional values existing in urban settings: The cities themselves, first of all, are traditional in

---

19. Maluki, *op. cit.*, p.21.

values and composition; secondly, there is an intimate relationship between the villages and the cities. Meister's book, first published under the title *L' Afrique Peut-Elle Partir?* in 1966, and
Maluki's thesis, which was published in 1965, are contemporary.
LeVine's statements of 1963 are conclusions from his research in
East African cities. Meister does not include supporting evidence
with these statements of his. This researcher's first-hand observation since 1958 influence her more toward LeVine's and
Maluki's statements. One could hope that a comprehensive research
in this area would update their conclusions, supporting or refuting
them with current data.

There is common agreement over the application of Ujamaa-ism
at the general lower level of society to allow mass participation
and involvement. "It is at the general level that the strongest case
can be made for the importance of Ujamaa-ism in the evolution of
modern Tanganyika."[20] Burke sees new symbols and slogans as essentials to continued involvement; small societies tend to be in-
flexible and circumscribed.

General agreement on the higher- and middle-levels is harder
to obtain than on the lower levels, for it involves the politicians,
the government and party leaders, the educated and uneducated
themselves. Morse warns that strong measures are needed if the
development of class antagonisms is to be avoided. Meister sees
strong government, militant leadership, and coercion as the answer. Maxwell purports that a *laissez-faire* policy would create capitalism maldistribution. It has already been pointed out that Nyerere does not believe in coercion. Thus, the possibility for dis-
senters does exist, even though the majority of middle- and higher-
level leaders agree with Nyerere's policies.

Although they agree with the basic goals of the society, a few
middle-level leaders—not a clearly defined group—have different
ideas about its form at the top and middle levels of government.
The main point of contention is on the speed of modernization;
Nyerere advocating a gradualist policy, and they demanding more
vigor, dynamism, and drama in their scientific socialism. With the

---

20. Fred B. Burke. "Tanganyika: the Search for Ujamaa" in
African Socialism, edited by Wm. Friedland and Carl Rosberg. (Stanford:
Stanford University Press, 1964), p. 210.

great majority of the people supporting Nyerere, his policies are more likely to be adopted by the party in succeeding years than sharp, radical policy changes.

The technical aspect of implementing Ujamaa-ism has been analyzed by observers. They cite reasons why Nyerere has not married his ideas and symbols very successfully to programs of action: 1) the involvement of expatriates in arranging many of the programs, and 2) economic restraints, which undermine the applications of the principles of Ujamaa-ism. Both Arrighi [21] and Stephens [22] see the leadership as lacking in technical expertise for this revolution. One can assume that experience and inservice training, along with the induction of newly qualified leaders, may have the effect of gradually alleviating this situation. It is, however, impossible to predict whether or not the change will be rapid enough to meet present demands.

Critics express one other concern. They call for a paper on industrialization to coincide with the emphasis on rural development and agriculture. This criticism is built on the premise that agricultural development cannot be divorced from industrial development; the two must rise together in a developing nation in the modern world. If this criticism is valid, Nyerere's great emphasis on rural development and agricultural improvement for 95 per cent of his people must find room for more recognition of the industrial sector. An analysis of his goals for the nation will reveal whether or not he has indirectly added this dimension to his policies.

21. Giovanni Arrighi and John S. Saul, "Socialism and Economic Development in Tropical Africa," *The Journal of Modern African Studies.* VI: n.2 (1968), p. 167.

22. Hugh W. Stephens. *The Political Transformation of Tanzania*: 1920-1967. (New York: Praeger, 1968), p. 174.

CHAPTER FIVE

NYERERE'S GOALS FOR THE NATION

In the preceding chapter the underlying principles of Nyerere's beliefs and actions were discussed as a background to an identification and analysis of his goals for the nation. The purpose of this chapter, then, is to focus upon those goals that have implications for educational planning in Tanzania. This will be done by first examining his ultimate goals or general aims and then narrowing down to specific objectives with respect to social and economic targets, structure, method, and content—the segments that comprise the substance of the ultimate aims.

Nyerere's Ujamaa-ism is a statement of ideology in its orthodox meaning; it is in fact a broad statement of socio-political values or a system of beliefs. Beyond that it advocates a behavioral pattern responsible to and commensurate with such beliefs, functioning to integrate the social system and to legitimize the political authority. Ujamaa-ism is undoctrinaire, flexible, and realistic. It has elements of a theoretical ideology and many more of a nationalistic ideology in its pragmatism. Nyerere's ultimate objective and aims always project the best that man can become. The various goals for short- and long-range action are directives toward them.

That Nyerere is conscious of the importance of clearly stated purposes is substantiated by his writings. In 1964 he emphasized: "Only when we are clear about what we are trying to do can we begin to think about the way of doing it." In his education paper of 1967, he stressed: "Only when we are clear about the kind of society we are trying to build can we design our educational service to serve our goals." [1] He went on to say that Government has definitely decided to form a socialist society. Its responsibility rests on finding the means toward these Ujamaa objectives.

---

1. Nyerere, *Freedom and Unity*, p. 310.

99

An analysis of Nyerere's statements in the 1960's reveals a gradual evolution in his thinking as measured by clarity of statement. The consistency of thought shown in these statements leads one to think that he must have had a clear vision of the new society from the beginning of his public statements, at least on the general level if not in specifics. Additional details appeared whenever the climate was favorable, so one cannot do more than surmise how much sooner they may have been announced had the circumstances been conducive to action. Mention must also be made that his ideas were sometimes put forth and rejected; e.g., four years elapsed before his efforts to open TANU to other races finally convinced his colleagues. The greater possibility, on the other hand, is that the conditions themselves might have been factors pressuring him to reevaluations resulting in greater public clarification. In his preface to *Freedom and Socialism* he claims it is the people who have triggered his thinking; that the ideas expressed in his speeches and writings between 1965 and 1967 are "an attempt to formulate and to express in policy-making terms the basic ideals and desires of the masses of the people of Tanzania. It is they who have inspired the thought."

ULTIMATE GOALS

Three years before independence, Nyerere's ultimate goal was "the best that man can become.[2] After the fight for independence had been won, he focused on three great enemies—poverty, ignorance, and disease. Nyerere does not even appreciate the word "nonracial" as descriptive of Tanzania's society. He considers all citizens to be free and equal. He sees progress determined by "the attitude and participation of [the] people." The better-articulated goal then visualized free individuals in an expanded social unit. He wrote:

> We aim at building a non-racial democratic country, part of a united Africa, where every individual can stand in human dignity, free from ignorance, disease and the misery of poverty.[3]

While many targets of the Three-Year Plan of 1961-64 were not met because of various phenomena, including nature, Nyerere

2. *Ibid.,* p. 121.
3. Nyerere, in foreword to *The Tanganyika Way,* by Sophia Mustafa. (London: Oxford University Press, 1962), p. vii.

observed that not all projects were unsucessful. Wherever the plan had involved the people in nation building, there had been sensational success. "There has been," he said, " a quiet revolution and its heroes the people." Because of this observation of his, the plan that followed (1964-69) was a declaration of war with the people—everyone a soldier. Presenting a call for participation and involvement of all citizens in this new "war," he requested each one to do " his part" by fostering the Ujamaa attitude and being as good a worker, whether highly skilled or unskilled, as found anywhere in the world. This, he said, was true equality. In this investigator's opinion, the shift in Nyerere's thinking from a transformation approach—through programs requiring huge amounts of foreign aid—to an improvement approach—through voluntary involvement and participation of the people using their own resources—has been a crucial and significant decision. It is obvious that aids, with or without strings attached, connote paternalism and, no matter what the purpose for which it is given, seldom produce mature responses except in emergencies. Self-confidence is established, rather, through measures requiring social and work discipline that result in a feeling of accomplishment because of one's own effort.

By 1964 the ultimate goal was still "the betterment of our lives." [4] By this time he spoke of a revolution in order to induce fundamental changes in conditions, an economic revolution if any. The revolution he advocated was one that demanded first a recognition of facts, then scientific, objective thoughts, and lastly, subsequent action. The goal toward which he claimed the people and the Government of the United Republic were aiming at this time was much less ambiguous. The aspect of cooperation was added to the dimensions of equality, freedom, and unity;

> . . . to build a just society of free and equal citizens, who
> live in healthy conditions, who control their own destiny,
> and who cooperate together and with other people in the
> spirit of human brotherhood for mutual benefit. [5]

The revolution of which he spoke in 1964 seems biased toward

---

4. Nyerere, "How Tanzania's Plan Can Succeed" *East Africa Journal. I*: n.9 (Dec. 1964), p. 24.
5. Nyerere, *Freedom and Unity*, p. 311.

the economic aspect of Tanzania. This may be due to the emphasis of the Five-Year Plan for Economic and Social Development on immense projects requiring huge capital investments and to the great amount of energy exerted while setting the manpower program into operation. But before the year 1964 ended, Nyerere began to talk of conflicts and priorities. By 1965 the pendulum swung back toward center with the articulation of the social aspect of the revolution. Nyerere pointed out that Africa has two problems to tackle simultaneously: 1) to increase production and 2) to rebuild attitudes of equality. He warned that the economic and social revolution must be in accordance with the wishes of the people of Tanzania and "with their full and free cooperation." Due to the fact that Government has determined to build a socialist society on the principles of love, sharing, and work, discussion about whether or not a measure supports or nullifies these principles is permitted, but there may be no opposition in the form of advocacy of inequality.

Little has been added to the President's earlier general goals since 1966. The greatest change has been strategy and short-term objectives. Social rural development has become the core "for the socialist society we are trying to create." And by 1969 his schemes of villagization had changed from a highly mechanized "transformation approach" requiring huge financial investments to voluntary, cooperative endeavors of indigenous, self-reliant groups of farmers forming Ujamaa villages.

Summarizing this section, one can say with Arrighi that there seems to be "an evolution of President Nyerere's own thinking" noticeable throughout his statements.[6] The characteristics of his scholarship—an acceptance of reality, objective and scientific thought, and pragmatism—have determined changes in priorities and efforts, but make no significant change in the direction of his policies.

Making a choice between two good things when monetary balances are insufficient to promote both equally has not been an easy task. Choices were made most frequently between measures for rapid economic growth and those that retain the personal freedom and human dignity of all the people. Nyerere is concerned

---

6. Arrighi, *op. cit·*, p. 165.

with a development that encompasses society in its entirety; a comprehensive social development that touches all institutions in the society. This scope complicates governmental activities already confounded by few natural resources and wealth. But the ultimate goal, which Nyerere has consistently held forth as the purpose of all socialist activity, remains man and his well-being.

It is only fitting that an analysis of the ultimate goal or general aims for the nation be followed by an analysis of the various components through which efforts are directed toward the achievement of this ultimate goal. Most of the areas with which education is concerned—the development of the individual; home, family, and community life; economic demands; and civic and social duties—are implied in the quotation cited here from Nyerere's circular to the Government ministries in January, 1964:

> Each Tanganyikan citizen must accept the duties and receive all the rights, which our citizenship implies. All must be governed by the same laws, must receive the same respect from his fellows, and have the same opportunities to earn a living and to serve the nation of which he is a member.

For purposes of ease in organization, Nyerere's objectives are presented below in four different categories: self-realization; human relationships; economic efficiency; and civic responsibilities. There is some overlapping and interlocking in the subcategories, which cluster with several components of the main categories. Nonetheless, the objectives are presented in their separate categories inasmuch as it is possible.

OBJECTIVES OF SELF-REALIZATION

The goals pertaining to individual development are saturated with the principles of equality, freedom, and unity. Nyerere advocates that effort be made toward "a position where each person realizes that his rights in society—above the basic needs of every human being—must come second to the overriding need of human dignity for all," [7] and that, when an individual surrenders this kind of freedom, "his gain is that others do likewise." [8] In a sense, then,

---

7. Nyerere, *Freedom and Unity,* p. 17.
8. *Ibid.,* p. 8.

it is proper to say that objectives of self-realization can be described in terms of a collective development of individuals or of each man in his own personal way.

Nyerere believes that freedom is essential for all individuals because "only free people conscious of their worth and their quality can build a free society." This freedom permits each person to "develop the spark of divinity within himself at the same time he contributes and benefits from his membership in the community."[9] It includes freedom of speech, freedom of movement and association, freedom from ignorance and disease, freedom from fear of hunger, freedom from his fellow-man, and freedom of religion for everyone. There is freedom for all to live a decent life when men are "equal in dignity . . . have an equal right to respect, to the opportunity of acquiring a good education and the necessities of life; . . . and have an equal opportunity of serving their country to the limit of their ability."

Freedom is not something easy to obtain; it must be guarded, maintained, and expanded for the individual and the group. It is commensurate with a certain attitude of mind, that which respects and defends the individual. In speaking of democracy, Nyerere said that true democracy depends far more on that attitude of mind than on the form it takes. In the year following independence, Nyerere claimed the first task of the nation was one of reeducation in order to regain former attitudes of mind. These attitudes regarding individuals have been spelled out in recent years: confidence in himself; pride in his own race; and realization of his duty in working for the amelioration of his African world.

Speaking directly about education, Nyerere holds that education must encourage the socialist attitudes. (Most of the following paragraphs in this section are taken from Education for Self-Reliance, so the suplementary sources only will be given except for direct quotes.) Education has both economic and social functions in serving the intentions of Tanzania; its purpose is to prepare young people for their future membership in society and their active participation in its maintenance and development. An egalitarian society and egalitarian attitudes of mind are conducive to the educational purpose. Education was regarded in terms of ob-

---

9. *Ibid.*, pp. 121, 178.

taining skilled workers leading to high salaries in the modern sector, but Nyerere calls for a new kind of education, which is realistically designed to fulfill the common purposes of education in the particular society of Tanzania. Relevant knowledge, skills, and attitudes are more valuable to the socialist society than hoarded wealth. He told the university students at the time of their protest that spirit and determination are more important to the development of the country than money.

Specifically, the various objectives for free individuals in the Tanzanian society as given by Nyerere may be listed as follows (they are by no means weighted or listed by importance):

1) An inquiring mind.
2) Fluency in spoken Swahili.
3) Swahili literacy complemented with the habit of reading.
4) An ability to do arithmetic.
5) An ability to learn from others.
6) A healthy body.
7) Intellectual interests relevant to needs in society.
8) Esthetic interests that help to regain pride in one's culture.
9) The development of a sound, moral character.
10) An ability to provide for material well-being.

The inquiring mind is a *sine qua non* for an individual in a changing, developing society. Nyerere does not want robots who copy others and never questions the actions of the government and party. Individuals may criticize and oppose established practices; these ensure safeguards for the nation. Nyerere gives two reasons why an individual ought to be curious about ideas and, consequently, think: 1) He must judge social issues for himself, and 2) He must know how to interpret the decisions made through the democratic institutions of society and apply them appropriately to his own thinking and experience. He must be able to explain and demonstrate, not simply repeat things by rote. For example, a traditional farmer may not be just plain stupid; the inquiring individual may find he has reasons for continuing certain practices.

Nyerere prophesies a "big breakthrough in development when young people and adults have cultivated the habit of reading." In addition to the three R's, Nyerere lists a few other subjects to know. These include history, civics, and practical subjects leading to achievement of skills. Geography, health science, and English are considered important for one's enrichment in later life. Intellectual and esthetic interests will make a contribution to one's future life in society.

Malnutrition is not due to poverty, Nyerere purports, but to ignorance, indifference, and indolence. A hungry person cannot bring progress. He therefore advocates eating more meat, fish, beans, vegetables, and fruit, and the planting of fruit trees for shade in the new housing projects.

Nyerere considers it imperative that the student and his community be concerned with attitudes, character, and abilities beyond passing examinations. Education "must inculcate a sense of commitment to the total community." The values accepted must be appropriate to Tanzania's future. A member is valued for what he is, not for what he obtains. Dignity is not pomposity. Religious beliefs are private, he says, and not a concern of socialism, unless a certain practice inhibits the freedom of others.

Nyerere's goals for each individual, then, are that he be a healthy person contributing to his own well-being and society through his ability to communicate, to read, to inquire, and to provide for the necessities of life.

OBJECTIVES OF HUMAN RELATIONSHIPS

Man is a social being: "None of us liveth to himself and no man dieth to himself." It was mentioned earlier in the chapter entitled "The Philosophical Base of Nyerere's Ujamaa-ism" that Ujamaa-ism emphasized harmony of the individual and the group in African social life. In the preceding section, the goals for individuals within a group setting, i.e., in the family, neighborhood, nation, and world, as well as interrelationships between individuals and between groups were delineated.

In evaluating the situation around him in 1966, Nyerere concluded:

> We have a mixed heritage. We must make the choice whether Self or Service will be the dominant motive in Tanzania of 1990 and hereafter.[10]

Obviously, Ujamaa-ism is only compatible with the latter. Nyerere's objective is building a socialist society within the nation and look-

---

10. Nyerere, *Freedom and Socialism,* p. 228.

ing beyond its borders to greater African unity. The group is a community of hearts rather than an aggregate of individuals.

Characteristics (Goals) for Human Relationships

Nyerere's goals for human relationships can be described best by polarizing the positive and negative aspects in the application of the three main principles of Ujamaa-ism. His various writings have served as sources for this compilation. Many of these elements appear throughout his works.

1) Equality versus inequality:
   a) Positive: Same laws govern all.
                 Equal respect from fellow-men.
                 Mutual friendliness.
                 Equal opportunity to develop one's self.
                 Equal opportunity to serve the nation.
                 Common obligations and common rights.
                 Democratic decision making.

   b) Negative: No racism or elevation of a particular group over the good of the whole community.
                 No oppression or injustice.
                 No elites with luxuries before the standard of living is raised for the majority.
                 No class structure.
                 No demands for personal or group rights based on inequality or value of production.
                 No prestige structures while sacrificing freedom or priorities of human development.

2) Cooperation versus competition:
   a) Positive: Members of one society, dependent on each other, each contributing to the pool of the community.
                 The whole nation lives as one big family.
                 Self-help schemes for nation-building projects.
                 All members share fairly in the good and bad fortunes of the group.
                 The privileged responsible to serve.

Progress measured in human well-being.

Social security through group functions.

b) Negative: No exploitation of man by man or group.

Ends do not justify or gain precedence over the means.

No power-hungry master nor master and servants.

No wide gap between workers in the wage economy and peasants.

3) Unity versus discord.

Federations established on regional and continental basis.

The good of all takes priority over particular groups.

One of the major goals set by Nyerere at independence was that there must be an integrated system in the multiracial society. No one race can be educated separately. Since then he has given more thought to the role of the school in human relationships, and in his *Education for Self-Reliance* he has addressed himself more specifically to the problem. The school has two main functions in society.

1) To function as a unifying agent in society:

a) Positive: The school is a part of the community in which it is located.

The school makes use of wise, experienced citizens in the community.

Community activities by students during vacation time.

The school prepares youth to play a dynamic and constructive part in the development of society.

b) Negative: Does not increase the gap in society.

Does not create superiority/inferiority or failure feelings.

Does not induce growth of class structure.

Does not divorce students from the society it is preparing them for.

2) To foster socialistic attitudes, character, and other abilities:

Emphasize cooperative endeavor.

A spirit of service—a sense of commitment to total community.

Work and cooperation of students with family, communal farm, and community.

Education for the majority; only justification for educational privileges to the few is that they serve many.

Progress measured in terms of human well-being rather than in counting institutional buildings of grandeur.

In summary, Nyerere bases his aims of human relationships on the principles of Ujamaa-ism with education functioning as a unifying agent that fosters the attitudes relevant to a socialist society. Education prepares youth to live and serve in a community, the nation, and the world. The principles of love, respect, and unity undergird educational activities, making cooperation and harmony possible.

OBJECTIVES OF ECONOMIC EFFICIENCY

As stated in an earlier section, Nyerere's ultimate goal is always the betterment of society; the highest standard of living possible for Tanzania's stage of development must be enjoyed by everyone in the Republic. The socialist aim is a gradual rise in these standards of living among the masses. There are to be no master-servant injustices. No one is justified to live in luxury until the majority are experiencing a continuous progress in economical well-being. The idea of developing one district as a model for others to emulate clashes with the egalitarian principle of improving the whole area, however small. The whole purpose of the economic policy of government, from Nyerere's point of view, is to uplift the conditions under which the majority live. It is essential that government takes positive action in the field of agriculture and other aspects of the economy.

In Nyerere's ideal society, the goal is the development of man, not the acquisition of material wealth. He claims that Africans developed the idea that "the way to the comfort and prosperity which everyone wants is through selfishness and individual advancement" from their contact with the people from overseas. He suggests using the principles that Africans followed in their traditional system as a base; correct the shortcomings by adding elements that increase the output per person and make a man's efforts yield more satisfaction to himself; and adapt to its service the things that can be learned from technologically developed nations.

These double tasks of the nation—to increase production and to rebuild attitudes of equality or retain and expand personal freedom and human dignity—seem to have distinguished themselves in Nyerere's thinking around mid-decade. When he introduced the Five-Year Plan in 1964, he said its purpose was to increase the national wealth of Tanganyika as quickly as is consistent with the maintenance of national independence and the people's control over their own economy. At the end of 1964 he advocated investing in projects that are as profitable as possible. Group wealth and group power are considered virtues insofar as they serve man, the purpose of society. He was still concerned with economic growth in 1969 in his speech introducing the Second Five-Year Plan when he suggested that the rate they were then going to double the per capita income was too slow (it would require thirty years) and ought to be accelerated.

Nyerere advocates building village settlements in the rural areas following Ujamaa principles. "The villages must be made into places where people have a good life," he says, "and people find their material well-being and their satisfactions." [11] He aims at forming a nation in which "Ujamaa farms and communities dominate the rural economy and set the social pattern for the country as a whole." [12] In addition to internal cooperation, the community would then cooperate with other similar village settlements.

The Producers

Nyerere views man and their hard work as the chief natural resources in Tanzania. People are the developers as well as the purpose of development. Although Nyerere condemned human parasites in his Ujamaa statement in 1962, they did not disappear. In the Arusha Declaration and accompanying statements, they were given a greater exposure.

Following the establishment of the Manpower Planning Unit in 1963, the Five-Year Plan of 1964-69 was a declaration of war against poverty, ignorance, and disease. A target was set: to be fully self-sufficient in trained manpower requirements by 1980. The pur-

11. Nyerere, Education for Self-Reliance. (Dar es Salaam: Government Printer, 1967), p. 7.
12. Nyerere, Socialism and Rural Development. (Dar es Salaam: Government Printer, 1967), p. 15.

pose of government spending on education, as Nyerere saw it, was to "equip Tanganyikans with the skills and knowledge needed for the development of the country."

Nyerere placed adult education high on his priority list, reasoning that the effect of the change of attitudes among adults would produce an immediate impact, whereas it may take five, ten, or even twenty years to feel the impact from an expansion with an equal amount of money in primary education.

Choices must be made when it is impossible to experience two equally good needs. Not only did Nyerere set a goal for adult education, which indirectly limited funds for primary education, but he also gave secondary- and higher-education high positions on his list of priorities. He realized the clash of socialist principles with manpower-planning goals and placed universal primary education, a requirement in an egalitarian society, as a goal secondary to expansion in opportunities for postprimary education and training. The primary objective, the great need for skilled workers in every sector of the economy, was to be counterbalanced by a higher expectancy of output, especially in the agricultural or rural areas where 95 per cent of the people live. A crucial inadequacy, which he decried, was the lack of agricultural assistants who could communicate with the farmer. By 1969 Nyerere had yet another goal: greater efforts in cottage industries and craft workshops. He favors a mixed economy with emphasis on public ownership of the people's own institutions to get the most rapid and beneficial results.

Productive increase in the economy and expansion in education are interlocking. Nyerere views education as not merely a social service, but also as economic development. He envisions schools converted into economic as well as educational communities where pupils learn new skills for future life as a by-product of self-reliance. He says:

> We need the products of our schools to participate in, and guide, the enthusiasm and energy of the people, devoted to building our country and overcoming national poverty.[13]

A work-study program models his ideology quite well. Prosperity comes through better husbandry; he advocates educated

---

13.   Quoted in MacDonald, *op. cit., p.* 178.

people on farms with the educated doing manual work and not only office-type jobs. Also, by printing their schools' own textbooks in the country, Tanzania's economic growth is boosted, rather than another's.

To meet these aims in production requires a change of attitudes and habits. The individual as well as the nation must learn lessons of self-reliance. Education as a tool prepares people to change habits. Work discipline must become a natural characteristic of everyone. "A socialist society, therefore, will consist of workers— and only of workers . . . Each person has to produce more by harder, longer, and better work . . . working hard, intelligently, and together." Incredible income differentials and class structure must be reduced.

The Consumers

Nyerere calls for frugality as the watchword in consumption. Tanzanians must first accept the fact of poverty and then live correspondingly as poor men rather than on a pretense of affluence. Money should be spent on the essentials that make them "richer, healthier, and more educated in the future." They are asked to keep a balance, and to loan money to government for investments in education and health. By using their resources in the spirit of self-reliance, progress will then come slowly, but surely, and for the masses, Nyerere does not feel that a blueprint can be formed in the capital city that will be suitable for all the diversities found within the country; therefore, local initiative and self-reliance must go hand-in-hand for progress.

Nyerere does not expect youth to be consumers living off the older and weaker people, but to contribute to the productive force. Education does not serve as an excuse for withdrawal from the responsibility of production. Nyerere asks that those who complete the primary course be responsible workers and citizens, prepared for the work they will be called upon to do in a predominantly rural society. These citizens (primary-school leavers) should think for themselves and be valued for what they do, not what they obtain. Thus, schools must become communities practicing the precepts of self-reliance as a part of the larger community in which they are located and serve. For the few who are privileged to obtain education beyond the primary level, service to many awaits them.

OBJECTIVES OF CIVIC RESPONSIBILITY

Nyerere's objectives of civic and social duties encompass the individual, the group, and leaders in government. No one, irrespective of his work, is exempt from giving less than his best. Nyerere views the education of the leaders and the people as a *sine qua non* for development. Duties of citizens cover a variety of activities.

Social Justice

National ethics must be established and maintained in order to hand over with pride to the next generation. The Universal Declaration of Rights is to be used as the basis for internal and external policies. No discrimination shall be made on the grounds of race, tribe, color, sex, creed, or religion; nationalism and racism are incompatible. The only distinction that can be made is between citizens and noncitizens. This has been a highly emotionalized issue at times, especially since secondary education is free to citizens and allocations to noncitizens have become more stringent. Citizenship responsibilities and rights are based on loyalty to the country.

A "fair" share is always measured in relation to the whole society. The fact that diamonds produced by one man have greater monetary value than foodstuffs produced by another does not bestow greater importance on the former individual than on the latter. It is wrong to desire wealth and power in order to dominate someone else. Those who have been given special privileges or opportunities must use their eduction to help others gain the same opportunities they have had. "In order to do this, schools and universities must promote a national outlook among students," says *Freedom and Socialism.* In the Bursar System, a recipient is responsible to the group. Nyerere illustrates this by members of a starving village depriving themselves of their meager supplies in order to enable several representatives to reach a place of plenty. If those sent fail to return with aid for their friends, they have been very irresponsible and inhumane, and worse yet, traitors.

Critical Judgment

Nyerere warns that "one of the greatest dangers facing [Africans] is the temptation to stop thinking about an idea because the label "imperialist" or "communist" has been attached to it." He goes on to argue for the place of the eccentric who stops society from ceasing to think.

This admonishment is not aimed at the leaders only; the educational system must prepare young people to be able to "think for themselves, to make judgments on all issues affecting them," and to interpret the decisions made by their representatives and apply them to their local circumstances.

According to Nyerere, one of the hallmarks of a competent leader is his ability to think logically. The others that Nyerere lists are: a capacity to express himself clearly, and a mastery of his job that enables him to understand fully the implication of his decisions, as well as his character, intelligence, honesty, and willingness to learn.

Law Observance

Everyone is subject to laws; law is paramount in society. Three things are essential for peace in a society: 1) impartiality in respect of human rights; 2) equal treatment both in protection and restrictions; and 3) provision for change in laws by peaceful agreement of the citizens.

Political Citizenship (National)

Political participation is a right for all individuals. The people are expected to take the fullest part in the development of their country. "Our aim is to hand over responsibility to the people to make their own decisions," states *Freedom and Socialism*. In *Freedom and Unity*, Nyerere says that the Government cannot afford to carry "passengers" along in its service. In the society Nyerere projects, the people must have absolute freedom to choose their representatives who take part in discussions. On the local level, people must make decisions on those things that affect them directly; they control community decisions and are responsible for carrying them out. Village communities elect officers and committees; villagers adopt or amend their proposals.

TANU must be a broad channel through which communications pass both downward and upward. It is of vital importance that these lines of communication be kept open. Leaders must be aware of changing situations and keep in touch with the people. Thus, "public service must be efficient and embued with a sense of urgency of national need for revolutionary change."

World Citizenship

Nyerere is a strong supporter of "a United States of Africa" with African states cooperating and undertaking common activities wherever possible. In striving to promote African unity, Nyerere cautions that care must be taken to avoid African isolation. He feels that Ujamaa-ism can expand to embrace the whole of mankind. Tanzania can learn from other nations and can share its experiences with others. His own words are pertinent and very explanatory:

> Even the newest of nations has . . . duties towards all the nations upon earth and opportunities to influence by example of policies even of the most powerful.
> By thinking out our own problems on the basis of those principles which have universal validity, Tanzania will make its contribution to the development of mankind. That is our opportunity and our responsibility.
> We, the people of Tanganyika, would like to light a candle and put it on top of Mount Kilimanjaro which would shine beyond our borders giving hope where there was despair, love where there was hate and dignity where before there was only humiliation. . . . We cannot, unlike other countries, send rockets to the moon, but we can send rockets of love and hope to all our fellow-men wherever they may be.[14]

Nyerere lists four Government policy principles in regard to foreign affairs:

1) Recognition of the fundamental importance of the United Nations;

2) Basic and continued opposition to colonialism anywhere in Africa and elsewhere;

3) The attainment of African unity depends on the complete freedom of the continent [Tanzania is not considered wholly free because "Africa is not wholly free."]

4) Keeping out of the automatic conflicts in the world.[15]

---

14. *Freedom and Unity,* p. 142; *Freedom and Socialism,* p. 32; *Freedom and Unity,* p. 72.
15. *Ibid,* pp. 148-54.

Nyerere is a staunch supporter of an all-African government that would have "over-riding and exclusive power" in certain fundamental areas. This government is to be the one authority in Africa in relation to the outside world; i.e., Africa would be united in one voice in dealing with affairs external to the continent.

Nyerere's objectives of self-realization, of human relationships, of economic efficiency, and of civic responsibilities seem to be determined largely by the principles of equality, sharing, and an obligation to work. As stated earlier, Nyerere does not believe that ends justify the means. He has suggested some acceptable policies as directives toward securing these objectives. Those policies that have direct expression or implications for education will be considered under the categories of structure, method, and content.

EDUCATIONAL STRUCTURE
Administration

At independence one of the major goals set by Nyerere for administration was a rapid increase in the facilities required to train Africans for responsible positions in the territory. Later the term "Africanization" changed to "localization" to include all citizens. Nyerere's requirements for leaders are somewhat stringent. A leader is a servant wholly committed to his task. He is the representative of a group who expect him to occupy himself with their interests. The lines of communication permit messages to pass from these leaders to the majority and vice versa. These leaders are asked to be responsible—not to do all the thinking for others to follow blindly. They are to be living examples of their messages.

The only system admissible in Ujamaa-ism is an integrated one granting both racial and religious freedom. The system is designed to fit the community as a whole rather than a select few.

Institutions

It is obvious that an activity of any size requires an organization, and organizations usually work through institutions. Tanzania received and maintained a number of institutions from the former British administrators. Some of these were bound for change, and others had to be created to make feasible the new aspirations of Ujamaa-ism.

Not only should the institutions of government serve the people, but they must also be understood by the people. It is through them that suitable attitudes are built, ensuring freedom, equality, and unity through a social ethic. Cooperative societies and public enterprises build economic institutions. Institutions upholding the principles of Ujamaa-ism and actively vying against temptations to subversion have been on Nyerere's agenda for some years already.

As a main priority Nyerere argues for an adult education program that is actively directed toward the principles of freedom. The majority of adults, most illiterate, must understand and become involved in the nation's plans, according to Nyerere, if the country is to progress. Both social and economic reasons are given to justify the high position granted to adult education. He designated 1970 as "Adult Education Year," suggesting each citizen attempt to learn something new and teach a fellow-man something new. The task of socialist adult education is to strengthen people's self-confidence and pride and, consequently, lead to greater initiative and production.

Egalitarianism in a strict sense militates against the provision of education for some people at the exclusion of others. Thus, no one would have the privilege to go to secondary school until all had the privilege to complete primary education. However, manpower goals clash with this principle and Nyerere has been forced to help make choices that ultimately limited the expansion of primary education in preference to an increase in opportunities at postprimary levels. Universal primary education never ceased to be a goal of the President's, but choices had to be made and the target of 1989 for universal primary education was realistically set. With the number of pupils completing the primary-school course increasing and creating a problem for employment, the concept of the primary course as a complete education in itself, and not just preparatory for some training beyond, formed and took deep root in his statements; it was to affect the structure, method, and content of the educational activities in addition to shifting various objectives.

Entrance to secondary education—mostly boarding institutions—is very selective. The pressing issue, in Nyerere's mind, is how to utilize these institutional activities for integration with the communities of their location. These institutions are defended by him only because they are expected to produce skilled manpower to raise the conditions of many.

Nyerere values teacher training institutions very highly for their function in the country's development. He claims it is "the teachers now at work and now going through training college, who are shaping what Tanzania will become, much more than we who pass laws, make rules, and make speeches." [16]

In the realm of higher education, Nyerere gave a three-fold role to the university: to give ideas, manpower, and service for the furtherance of Ujamaa-ism. But that education must be relevant to the problems of the country, properly guiding the "servants in training." Nyerere had questioned the relevancy of the grand, modern buildings on the campus (grants were easily forthcoming from other nations and no money was spared in their erection), and concluded that the buildings become an issue if they are a factor in further dividing the student from neighbors in the surrounding community. He justifies professional training that requires many more years of education if this professional training is later translated into service.

As Nyerere sees it, all the foregoing institutions listed are to function as social and economic institutions, and none can be maintained on a purely academic basis. Students are to value working together with the nonstudents for the common good of all. Urban schools are not excluded. Although the institutional structure itself is conducive to superiority/elitist feelings, these should be counterbalanced by an emphasis on Ujamaa principles and behavior. Hopefully, universal education will alleviate some of these problems.

METHODS

There is no holy book, asserts Nyerere, nor any model for planners to follow when trying to blueprint a socialist society. Therefore, Tanzania should not copy others, but rather build its own patterns of societal and educational organizations, patterns that are relevant to its situation and needs.

In 1969 Nyerere asked teachers to create "new Tanzanians." Teachers, he feels, are the best instruments because they are ex-

---

16. *Freedom and Socialism*, p. 228.

perienced in explaining matters. He realizes that the method of persuasion may appear slower than force but in the long run, he argues, it is more effective. Even before he became President, Nyerere acknowledged intellectual freedom as an essential for progress to take place and that dogmatism functions as prison walls to confine it.

Nyerere gave four basic "duties" in his inaugural address of 1962 as steps toward the new society he perceived:

1) To recognize that the Tanganyika we have inherited is a different Tanganyika from the one that we are setting out to build and to bequeath our children;

2) To understand the problems facing us and to realize that there is no shortcut to their solution;

3) To avoid the temptation of blaming others for our difficulties;

4) For all to pool our resources and work together in trust and friendship in order to build a Tanganyika without the same problems we are experiencing.[17]

Education, to Nyerere, is not merely teaching little children in schools. It is a mass program aimed at benefiting all ages from the highest position to the lowest. For this task, he advocates the formation of Ujamaa villages. If people live together in communal settlements, the task of education would be facilitated. The way of life and agricultural developments would be built up together; as a natural result, the community might receive and benefit from social services.

Since 95 per cent of the population are rural dwellers, Nyerere views the attitude of the farmer as crucial. The ordinary farmer tends to be conservative. The earlier policies of education expected that a pupil would share the knowledge he gained at school with the adults of his family, but experience reveals that more often it was the pupil who was influenced by his elders rather than the elders changing their patterns of living. Nyerere cautions that force is not the way to change conservative farmers. He calls upon the student to know why the new method he learned was better and to remember the conditions under which it was successful. And, if the younger person must follow traditional practices on

---

17. *Freedom and Unity,* p. 181.

his father's farm, Nyerere suggests he cultivate a small plot of his own in the new way; and with several years of quiet perserverance, he may eventually prove his method to be better.

Another way of reaching the farmer is through the agricultural assistants who can communicate with him. Nyerere recognized the great lack of these workers and supported training the assistant in his own country, in his own language, and starting from his current knowledge, in order to enhance his efficiency. The agricultural assistant is considered just one of a team of people who work in the rural areas. All ministries should band together and supplement each other's efforts in a frontal attack in the rural areas. The Ministry of Education (when it was restructured in 1968) is the main ally of the Agricultural Department.

From the university level down to the primary level, these institutions are charged with the responsibility of fulfilling an integral part of community life. Nyerere lists three roles for the university: to produce technocrats, democrats and thinkers. One of the hardest things for a university student to accomplish is to identify with his fellows, including those who never went to school. University graduates are expected to transform the communities they live in from within. The staff and students must be objective and scientific in their search for truth, thinking and causing others to think in terms of humanity, collect and disseminate facts government needs to know, be "torchbearers" of society, "protectors of the flame" when leaders "endanger its brightness."

Much more is said regarding integration of schools with the community on the secondary and primary school levels in the White Paper, *Education for Self-Reliance*. In it, Nyerere recommends that these schools, in becoming social and economic institutions as well as academic centers, join the community folk with primary-school children in clearing acres for their school farm and that the knowledge and wisdom of the nonstudents be utilized to advantage. Secondary schools, mostly boarding, may well develop school farms and learn by doing so that their living standards improve when they do well and suffer when they do poorly. He wants to see pupils really involved in the developmental experiences from the planning stage up to and including allocations of the returns of productive projects. Conditions must be maintained that are parallel to those outside the school; Nyerere asks that no grants be given to the school that a farmer would not get. Flexibility on the local level is needed. Field work and class discussion should be coordinated so that pupils learn why, analyze failures, and consider possibilities for improvement.

Nyerere feels that citizens should change the expectations they demand of their schools. There are three areas of attitudinal changes that are basic to success in any socialist organizational change:

1) Emphasis on cooperative endeavor, not individual advancement;
2) Stress on concepts of equality and responsibility to give service that goes with any special ability (e.g., carpentry, animal husbandry, academic pursuits); and
3) Change in existing community attitudes.

Not only is the school to be integrated with the community, but its program is aimed at producing responsible workers and citizens at the completion of any particular course of studies. Since the majority cannot find opportunities in post-primary education or training, primary education should develop skills, attitudes, and abilities for successful rural socialist living. Nyerere suggests the entry age to primary school be raised above five and six years of age, so that primary-school leavers are not too young to contribute well to the community.

The content and method of teaching must be reconsidered if a socialist society is to be achieved. Teachers should uphold the ability to think and apply findings to the local situation. Pupil involvement and learning by doing is essential. Examinations, in Nyerere's opinion, ought to be downgraded in government and public esteem; ought not to adhere to international standards and practice over local situations; ought to be fitted to terminate education if one is needed. The usual examinations given to students, he reasons, do not assess the ability to think nor character and willingness to serve—all items of great importance in a developing socialist nation.

Another matter that Nyerere stresses from time to time is the wage differentials in Tanzania. For example, in 1959 he opposed the budget, giving the payment of extravagant salaries as one point of criticism. He argued that paying expatriates more than they would receive in England and more than Africans with the same qualifications was more than the territory's ability to pay. In 1963 he suggested that an increase in educational opportunities would decrease the scarcity value at the top. He realized that university graduates are guaranteed a good income with good living conditions when they attain their degree. The degree, however, does not guarantee a spirit of cooperation and services. Usually differences in wages "lead to social differentiation and attitudes supporting inequality." Social classes are incompatible with Ujamaa-ism. He later suggests a system of progressive taxation for a solution to this problem.

Work, he believes, is an obligation. If a man's production has more value than another's, it does not permit him, personally, to demand a greater share from society. Nyerere supports a work-study program. This increases the output of society by utilizing the youth in production, and hopefully, at the same time instills within youth the attitudes of Ujamaa.

By making education more relevant to the needs of that particular society, Nyerere does not feel that the academic standard will necessarily be reduced. Education should not be inferior if made relevant to life. He suggests that teachers try to coordinate their subjects and create problems relating to their textbooks.

Nyerere is not a defender of the status quo. In fact, he feels it is useless to concentrate on agriculture if traditional ways of agriculture and living are not changed. In order to improve rural life, the people must work hard and intelligently together. Young people have a double responsibility: They must learn the basic principles of modern knowledge in agriculture, and then adapt them to their own local situation and problems. Nyerere advocated the use of simple tools in order to release the time and energy of persons for other activities and development. By using oxcarts and simple plows, there should be more time for reading, experimenting, and leisure activities.

CONTENT

In 1954, seven years before independence and thirteen years before the *Arusha Declaration*, Nyerere asked the question: "What else can we do but to give them [primary-school students] a grounding in the three R's and hope they continue to benefit from it?" [18]   He went on to say: "I do not think we are too academic. We cannot expect to produce carpenters and masons from primary school-children." [19]   He argued that, although technical education was needed, it dare not be advanced at the expense of limiting the number of primary schools, which form a feeder for technical schools. Since then he has much more to say on this issue.

In 1961, when Tanzania decided to open a university, Nyerere spoke of the value of an African-oriented education versus overseas education. Although he favored training in East Africa, he did not exclude learning from other countries. "The future of Africa will be drawn from Europe as well as Africa, Islam as well as Christian, communalism as well as individualism." [20]

Throughout the years since independence, Nyerere has been partial to an African-oriented education given at a national university rather than overseas training. He feels that overseas training given to mature men is more profitable if they have had a good African education first. University education in a national institution should first be directed towards the villages. He supports the compilation of African history on the continent. African universities and institutions, he says, are best able to take a leading role in the interest of African history because the primary sources are local and because of the African's own desire to understand himself and his society. The result is a firm foundation on which to build. Understanding the attitudes of the past by the present and of the present by the past, according to Nyerere, helps to interpret history.

In order to help Tanzanians regain pride in their own cul-

18.   *Ibid*, p. 32.
19.   *Ibid.*
20.   *Ibid.*, p. 130.

ture, Nyerere created a Ministry of National Culture and Youth in 1962. In doing this, he cautioned, he was not rejecting other cultures. Realizing that "a country which lacks its own culture is no more than a collection of people without the spirit which makes them a nation," he desired to "seek out the best of the traditions and customs of all our tribes and make them a part of our national culture." From parents and grandparents, children can learn stories, poems, and their history, all a part of the Tanzanian heritage. They should also learn the trade skills of their people.

By 1966 Nyerere realized that, if the underlying principles of respect, freedom, and unity were to be taught, many changes were required in the material taught in the schools, in the press, and over the radio. Along with the *Arusha Declaration* came a greater focus on self-reliance and the needs of the majority. Self-reliance is not to be considered an additional subject to be taught or applicable at a particular time only, and neither is self-reliance considered just additional periods for labor. School farms are to relate work to comfort, he advocates, so that education prepares students for life.

As schools begin to hold a greater identification with the community and current national struggles, the curriculum will be determined by what a student needs to know, the skills he should acquire, and the values he should cherish. The content must be more Tanzanian, including the history of Africa, national songs and dances, the national language, and civics education. The notion that only knowledge obtained through book learning is respectable, has to be abandoned; many sources of knowledge can be tapped.

SUMMARY

Chapter IV dealt with the philosophical base and principles from which Nyerere has drawn his goals for the society. This chapter dealt with the ultimate goals; the objectives of self-realization, human relationships, economic efficiency, and civic responsibilities; and policies of structure, method, and content as directives toward the ultimate goal. It was pointed out in this chapter that Nyerere's statements take on greater details as the years progress, showing a gradual evolution of thought affecting policies and short-range programs. There has been no significant change in the direction of his goals, but his strategy has changed.

Goals are important to Nyerere; only after a people determine what kind of society they wish to build, can methods be considered. His goals cover all areas of life—individual aim, social relationships, economic betterment, and civic duties. Nyerere aims at a balance between social and economic objectives. This has not been easy to achieve, and, at times, there seems to have been conflicts between the two. Priorities have been set ("To plan is to choose," he repeats in the Second Five-Year Plan). His transformation approach to rural development has changed to one of the voluntary, indigenous formations of Ujamaa villages. Participation, involvement, and communication are the key elements in his policies. Nyerere's goals call for realistic, scientific thinking and pragmatism.

The African sees harmony between himself and the world about him. Individual rights are secondary to the need of human dignity for all. Free individuals create free societies. Nyerere does not feel that the Tanzanian people have approached the kind of freedom they should possess. Psychological attitudes of inferiority are hard to eradicate, but need to be attacked through self-confidence, self-reliance, identity, pride, and responsibility. These are approached through education addressing itself to all levels and age groups, including adults, in the community.

Critical thinking is given a prominent place in Nyerere's goals. He wants responsible men, not robots, in social, political, economic, and intellectual spheres of activity. Critical thinking must be accompanied by sound, moral character and relevant knowledge and skills for socialist living. These are relevant if they are addressed to the good of all.

In the "new society" there is no class structure. The welfare of man, not of individual greed and exploitation, is the only acceptable purpose of society. Processes that create an elite group must be downgraded or eliminated.

Economic goals are important—a hungry man cannot participate well in societal obligations. Since 95 per cent of the population are rural dwellers, the attitude of the farmer is crucial. Nyerere does not advocate maintenance of the status quo, but a revolution by evolution, slowly raising the standard of living of the masses. He thrashes against pomposity and frills, demands social and work discipline, and calls for community involvement and commitment. A work-study type of education is relevant to his ideas.

Nyerere sees education as a key factor in developing the nation, one among a variety of elements. No specific ministry can fulfill all the demands for education. All ministries must be allied in this great task. The Ministry of Agriculture and Ministry of National Culture and Youth are closely related departments of the Ministry of National Education.

Teachers are more influential in directing the way of life in the nation than lawmakers and politicians. It is the teachers to whom Nyerere turns to find local applications to his general goals. With their training and experience, they can explain governmental policy best, he argues.

One cannot stress too much that Nyerere's Ujamaa-ism is characterized by freedom of choice; it requires voluntary commitment and would lose its significance if it were to be made mandatory. His goals for the nation are influenced by his own commitment to socialism and self-reliance. As Nyerere's goals stem from a different philosophy than that held by the colonial administrators, it is only natural to assume that the educational policies that were developed before independence were influenced by the colonial leaders (and the earlier chapters of this study support this). If postindependence policies were influenced by Nyerere's philosophy and goals, changes in the trends of educational policy in the 1960's should be significant.

CHAPTER SIX

NATIONAL EDUCATIONAL POLICIES IN FORMATION, 1961-66

BACKGROUND TO THE PERIOD

As independence approached, Nyerere raised two main issues: 1) integration of four separate racial systems of education and 2) Africanization of the civil service as soon as feasible. After several years of patient perseverance, he was able, with the consent of his political colleagues, to change the term "Africanization" to "localization" in order to include all citizens of Tanzania.

Changes were taking place in the wider society; nationalism affected social, economic, and political spheres. Skorov evaluated the situation well when he wrote that the manpower requirements at independence demanded an expansion in the educational system, a remodeling of structure, an improvement in the quality of education, and a reduction of wastage.[1]

Reforms of various degrees were initiated during the 1960's. Some resulted in meeting targets on or before schedule, but they have also met unanticipated consequences as well. Since 1967 the reforms have taken on something more like revolution. For this reason, the policies of 1961 to 1966 will be studied as a unit and the policies of 1967 to 1971 inclusive will be dealt with later.

The trend in educational reform since independence has gravitated toward integration, unification, and greater control from the center. Africanization exacted a shift in emphasis from primary to secondary and other postprimary education. Quality controls were exercised in this great expansion period. Although 14 to 17 per cent of the Government's budget was used annually for education, funds were inadequate and various

---

1. George Skorov. "Integration of Education and Economic Planning in Tanzania," *Africa Research Monograph* No. 9 (Paris: UNESCO/IIEP, 1966), p. 40.

methods were utilized in order to accomplish as much as possible with available money.

The Development Plan for Tanganyika, 1961-64 was largely a product of expatriate influence. In 1963 an Education Planning Unit was created. With the additional advantage of this unit, the Five-Year Plan (1964) became the first coordinated and comprehensive plan, not only a collection of plans from each ministry, but an integrated plan in which the people were involved and felt responsible for its implementation. A second difference between these two plans is that the Five-Year Plan did not depend on foreign aid as absolutely as the Three-Year Plan, but neither did it reject aid that was available and forthcoming. The Five-Year Plan, one might conclude, was the first significant reference to a measure for self-reliance. After the plan was introduced by Nyerere, it was regarded as the first stage of a general attempt to reduce inequalities and expand opportunities for the population as a whole.

Nature itself had not been very kind during the Three-Year Plan. The worst drought of years came in 1961-62, killing crops and cattle and putting half a million people on famine rolls. Funds that had been allocated to development were used for this purpose. The export business also diminished; coffee prices were cut by one-third and the sisal market was low. Gold began to decrease in quantity in several mines.

So, when the Three-Year Plan was over, Tanzanians conceded failure. But the President had noticed a quiet revolution going on. In the self-help areas, the plan had succeeded. This observation gave incentive to the educational planners for the Five-Year Plan, which became, not a plan of ministries but of the whole nation—a "People's Plan," as it was called.

EDUCATIONAL POLICIES, 1961-66

As mentioned before, integration, unification, and decentralization with greater control at the center were the most significant elements of the policies of education during this period. Many of these changes had been instituted by the colonial administrators and were instigated by African demands and the imminence of independence. They are covered in greater depth in this section than in Chapter III since they took effect in postindependent Tanzania.

Chapter III mentioned the Committee on the Integration of Education in Tanganyika organized in 1958, which published its report in 1960. The committee could have recommended wholesale nationalization or confiscation of schools in Tanzania with impending independence, but chose instead moderation and suggested far-reaching alterations in the governance of Tanganyikan education. The Government's official reaction to the twenty-six recommendations of the committee, submitted in March, 1960, was contained in the Government Paper No. 1 of 1960, debated and approved by the Legislative Council in 1960.[2]

The most significant change abolished the various statutory advisory and authoritative bodies, i.e., European and Indian Education Authorities, Advisory Committee for all other Non-Native Education, and Advisory Committee on African Education, and in their place a single advisory council on education functioned under the jurisdiction of the Minister of Education (Recommendation No. 22). Nongovernmental schools were not restricted; they could continue to operate and receive grants-in-aid as long as they were approved and they abided by the principles of the integrated system of education (No. 1). In actuality, schools were categorized as 1) Government and Government aided and 2) private or nonaided.

In order for a school to be Government aided, it had to comply with the following principles: Admission to any school was open to any child whose knowledge of the language was sufficient (No. 2), but priority was to be given to the children for whom the school was built; admission to secondary schools was based on a common, competitive examination (No. 4); selection to higher secondary courses was done on the results of the Cambridge Overseas School Certificate exam results and general school record (No. 6); and teacher-training centers were commanded to admit students of any race (No. 7).

---

2. *The Basis for an Integrated System of Education.* (Dar es Salaam: Government Printer, 1960).

The length of the primary course was ultimately to be eight years (No. 3). All existing and future schools were to develop on the 8-4-2 pattern (No. 10). If a student merited admission, a lack of finances should not deny him entrance (Nos. 17-20). Integration was to be completed with a uniform system of nomenclature used for all schools (No. 23) and a common syllabus for the basic subjects (No. 8). Various minor items were included for measures of integration, which will not be mentioned here other than its recommendation that a Unified Teaching Service be established as soon as possible for all local teachers (No. 5).

Another far-reaching decision recommended the creation of Boards of Governors and school committees appointed for postprimary institutions (No. 14). Members of Government and the VAs concerned were to be represented on the boards. This measure did not delegate authority for policy making, but it did assign authority to a body for implementing Governmental policies and tapped sources of funds, personnel, and expertise to supplement Governmental resources.

In the *Education Ordinance of 1961* the new Government made provisions for integration, uniformity, and decentralization. The *Education Ordinance of 1961* repealed former Tanganyika laws, *The Education (African) Ordinance (Cap. 71), The Non-Native Education Ordinance (Cap. 264)*, and the *Non-Native Tax Ordinance (Cap. 265)*; and legally established an integrated system of education in Tanzania. This ordinance made no reference to race. It was not bogged down with structural questions, but dealt essentially with the power and limitations of various bodies to control education in the country.

The Minister of Education (or his chief professional officer, the Chief Education Officer) received an almost endless list of powers. Though the structure of Government and mission school categories remained unchanged, the changes in the maintenance and administration of the VA schools effected as great a far-reaching impact on the future of education in Tanzania as had the more visible abolition of former racially separate systems. In respect to VA schools as well as Government schools, the Minister of Education took complete and effective control over:

1) staffing—e.g., certification, promotions, pay;
2) admissions of pupils;
3) syllabuses and secular instruction;
4) common standards of discipline and internal organizations;
5) the opening of a school and closure, if necessary.

VAs owned and managed the schools and helped in moral instruction and in the shouldering of administrative burdens.

Powers bestowed on the Local Education Authorities (hereafter LEAs) in Section 8 were more far-reaching than those formerly granted to the NAECs. These committees were composed of TANU members of LAs (not less than one-half) and representatives of societies and bodies concerned with management of schools in that area. They submitted development plans, estimates, and revenues for approval, received and disbursed grants-in-aid as approved, and received school fees from Local Authority schools. LEAs could voice local views, but had to abide by Central Government policies. If they acted contrary to Central Government's wishes, others could receive their delegated authority. The body concerned—either LA or VA—financed the unapproved school, not the Central Government.

Another new group that received a statutory delegation of power with the *Education Ordinance of 1961* was the Board of Governors for postprimary institutions; the move was considered a distinctive policy of the new Government as few such boards had been organized before. The Government added this provision for greater efficiency in management and, by including a local citizen on the board, provided greater integration in the local community. Mission schools lost their privacy as its management, Government officials, and other representatives mutually agreed upon met together and shared a voice.

In analyzing the educational reforms at this time, Dodd concludes that the delegation of powers to LEAs and Boards of Governors was done in an effort to tap sources of funds, personnel, and expertise that would supplement the Central Government and also keep it sensitive to local needs. He aptly says that what appeared to be decentralization was delegation of authority and, at the same time, greater concentration of control at the center.

This *Education Ordinance of 1961* remained in effect throughout the 1960's, was amended and appended with regulations of 1965, and finally was repealed by the *Education Act of 1969*. Thus, the structure for educational governance of Tanzania's schools projected integration, uniformity, and decentralization with greater control at the center. These reforms reflected both what was happening in society at large and reinforced those steps toward national unity. Working through the application of these powers was bound to bring changes, but the extent to which they adhered to the colonial influences or the aspirations implied in Nyerere's Ujamaa statement of 1962 depended upon the interpretation of the principles by the persons directly involved.

Integration was not a spectacular, single process. The policy started from the top where it existed and gradually worked down. The common use of English in the higher levels of education was a deciding factor in this policy. Doubtless to say, there were many briars along the path of integration. But in general, the process was quite smooth. There was no exodus of school administrators. Years later one could still find schools with a predominance of one racial or religious group of students. As Hinkle says: *"The critical and essential change required was to ensure that the power to govern the pace and extent of eliminating inequities in educational opportunity was in the hands of a single, politically accountable individual, e.g., the Minister of Education."* [3] [Emphasis his.] With the powers clearly defined, the process of implementations could proceed.

Dodd categorized the attack on integration of education as a four-pronged assault: 1) by legislation, 2) by the use of exams, 3) by syllabus revision, and 4) by the manipulation of

---

3. Hinkle, *op. cit.*, p. 50.

language policy.[4]   The various elements of this attack will be discussed under structure, method, and content where relevant. The Asians were hardest hit by the integration policy. They needed to compete for vacancies henceforth, and only 10 per cent could expect to be granted places.   Up to 1961 the Asians' schooling had been purely academic.   Now they would have to seek more diversified educational opportunities.   The language policy demanded one of the greatest reforms, but also resulted in greater integration with the African society.

With the responsibility of the educational system of Tanzania defined and relegated to the Minister of Education, education framers began to search for measures to bring uniformity into the single system.   The formation of a Unified Teaching Service was one of the first significant measures adopted.   Following closely on the heels of the colonial administration that repeatedly considered introducing a Unified Service after the Binns Mission in the early 1950's and just as often rejected it for financial reasons, the new Government pursued the issue.   It passed in Legislative Council "An Act to provide for Common Terms and Conditions of Employment amongst Teachers by the Establishment of a Unified Teachers Service and for Matters Incidental Thereto and Connected Therewith" (No. 6, 1962).   The law went into effect January 1, 1963, and for months offices were busily engaged with the registration of UTS applicants.   Its membership was open to all Tanzania teachers and to some noncitizens teaching there.   Teachers were still employed by the various school managers (LA, VA, Board of Governors, Central Government or individual managers), but they could now enjoy the same salary, same conditions of service, the same pension rights, and fringe benefits.   With the UTS Board established, the individual employer could not alone control the opportunities of the teacher. The Regional Educational Officer in the ex-officio chairman of the regional board composed of teachers' and employers' representatives, so grievances are heard by a whole representative body.

---

4.   Wm. Dodd, "Centralization of Education in Mainland Tanzania" *Comparative Education Review*. XII: n.3 (Oct. 1968), pp. 268-80.

Just as the establishment of UTS was a measure for unification and integration, the next significant measure—the reform in the inspectorate—not only aimed at unification of the system, but also gave Central Government greater control over implementation of its educational policies. After the Inspectorate Reform in 1963, the responsibility for inspection lay with the Central Government and not the owners of the schools. The earlier system had previously had Government supervisors who inspected LA Primary Schools and overlapped with the mission supervisors in the inspection of VA schools. Following the recommendation of the UNESCO Education Planning Mission of 1962, VA supervisors were abolished, Regional Education Officers and District Education Officers shed inspection duties, and a new cadre of Government Primary-School Inspectors (hereafter PSIs) were created to visit all schools.

PSIs carried supervision responsibility for all schools and were civil servants acting as "mobile teachers' colleges" on professional advisory service. They were no longer adjuncts of educational administration, nor inquisitors. As such, they were not feared and endured by the teachers. As an additional change, these inspectors assessed "learning by the pupil" rather than "teaching by the teacher" beginning with the pupil and ending with the teacher— just the opposite from what they had been accustomed to doing.

In this system the Central Inspectorate of the Ministry of Education coordinated the inservice training as well as the preparation of the PSIs. The responsibility for raising the quality of primary education was bound in such duties of the PSI as 1) refresher courses of various lengths of time for inservice teachers; 2) establishment of model schools as centers of quality from which to influence the surrounding schools; 3) exhibits of visual aids and other educational materials; and 4) dissemination of information and circulation of advice on teaching methods.

In addition to the circular of PSI duties of 1963, the Government issued a second circular, this one detailing the functions of the DEO who complemented the PSI in the sphere of educational administration on the district level. That same year (1963) a number of new syllabuses were issued. The content of them was revised for greater relevancy to national aspirations and required the expertise of the new inspectorate in implementation.

As the single educational system took on greater uniformity and expanded by leaps, the Tanzanian government became more aware that "the development of education must be viewed in the larger context of economic and social development, and that the planning of education should, therefore, be seen as an integral part of overall development planning."[5]   Thus the Educational Planning Unit was set up in 1963 with the Assistant Chief Education Officer in charge.   According to this plan, he has three professional officers: An assistant is mainly concerned with organizational and financial matters; an education officer supervises the collection and processing of statistics; and another officer supervises the school-building program. The appointment of a qualified architect to the staff in 1965 also proved invaluable. Their task is one "for educators concerned with an appreciation of priorities rather than specialists who understand the economy's manpower situation but not the possibilities of educational development." A plan, when issued, was not considered absolute, but is followed by a period of reflection and reconsideration, then changes are made whenever needed.

The Educational Planning did not initiate manpower goals in the system; it increased them, since they were already present before independence. The mission of UNESCO and the Tananarive and Addis Ababa conferences on African education were influential.   Many opportunities for Africanization in the civil service surfaced at independence. Only 17 per cent of Government middle- and high-level jobs were occupied by Tanzanians. Among 560 locals in the 4,000 civil-service senior posts requiring postsecondary education, only 380 of these were Africans. Only 245 Africans held S/S certificates in 1959.   Only 15 of the 116 graduate teachers in African S/Ss in 1959 were African and only 29 Tanzanian Africans were in higher teacher-training programs and preparing for careers. There were no African judges, or magistrates, nor any African permanent secretaries or principal assistant secretaries in 1960. The focus in expansion of education moved from the P/S level to secondary and higher education and other training courses. In 1963 there was still difficulty in getting a great enough intake into Grade A training. Tables VI and VII

5.   Skorov, *op. cit., p.* 11.

show the actual increases in enrollment and percentages on various levels during the period between 1961 and 1966.

TABLE VI
PERCENTAGE ENROLLMENT INCREASE
ON SELECTED LEVELS [7]
1961-66

Primary schools:	1961	1966	increases
Std. I	121,386	154,512	27.3%
Std. IV	19,391	60,721	215.8%
Completing P/S	11,740	18,946—Std. VIII	490.9%
		46,816—Std. VII	
		65,762—Total of Std. VII, VIII	
Secondary schools:			
Form 1	4,196	6,377	50.9%
Form 4	1,603	4,723	188.8%
Form 6	176	761	332.4%

TABLE VII
EDUCATIONAL OPPORTUNITIES
1961-66

Std./form	Pupils	Std./form	Pupils	%-age on
1961 to 1962				
IV	95,391	V	26,803	28
VIII	11,732	1	4,810	41
4	1,603	5	286	18
6	176	U.E.A.	95	54
1965 to 1966				
IV	126,536	V	60,721	48
VIII	46,647	1	6,377	14
4	4,505	5	826	18
6	603	U.E.A.	410	68

6. Extracted from *Annual Report*, Ministry of Education, Tanzania.
7. R. C. Honeybone and J. K. Beattie. "Mainland Tanzania," in *Examination: The World Yearbook of Education*, 1969. Lauwerys and Scanlon (eds.) (New York: Harcourt, Brace & World, Inc., 1969), p. 133.

The Five-Year Plan (1964) listed three major long-term objectives for 1980: 1) to raise the per capita income from Shs. 386 per annum to Shs. 900; 2) to be fully self- sufficient in trained manpower requirements; and 3) to raise the expectation of life from thirty-four and forty years to fifty years. These objectives greatly influenced educational planning. For instance, note the targets that they set for expansion in secondary education for the five years:

Form 1   5,250 (1964)   to 6,755 (1970)   Increase of 28%
Form 4   4,165   to 5,915   Increase of 41%
Form 5   680   to 1,220   Increase of 79%
Form 6   520   to 1,080   Increase of 107%

Note also the focus on manpower goals as stated in excerpts from a speech delivered by the Minister of Education at a conference at University College at Dar in March, 1967 (less than six months after the university students' demonstration against the National Service Act):

> It is the policy . . . to invest in education almost exclusively in relation to its contribution towards providing the skills needed for Tanzania's programme of economic and social development. Education for education's sake, whatever the value agreed for it, must wait upon the "take-off" . . . whatever may be said of the cultural and social aspects of education, it would hardly perform its functions if it did not serve economic development efforts to the fullest possible extent.[8]

He listed five major contributions that are expected of the university "in furtherance of the policy of self-reliance and socialism." The list, all manpower goals, follows:

1) Provide higher education for an adequate number of people to fill the high-level manpower requirements of our country;

2) Prepare its graduates for entry to specific professional careers;

---

8. "The Conference on the Role of the University College, Dar es Salaam, in a Socialist Society." Mimeographed.

3) Provide the institutional arrangements that are necessary to keep the precious high level of manpower force up to date and thus prevent obsolescence;

4) Assist in the development of the content of educational courses so that people who are highly educated are also well-suited to undertake the tasks that are most important in development;

5) Carry out research activities related to high-level manpower.[9]

He did not include the cultural responsibilities of higher education that UNESCO's conference at Tananarive had listed.

In this researcher's opinion, the foregoing statements of the Minister of Education reflect well the trend in educational policies by the mid-sixties. Even the Five-Year Plan includes the following statement to that effect:

This educational policy admittedly differs in the short run from humanitarian ideals which attach great importance to moulding human minds and strive to have the greatest number possible benefit from education as a source of moral enrichment and aesthetic satisfaction. Indeed, it should be stressed that the results of this idealistic position are most frequently ephemeral and even become harmful to society as a whole when not accompanied by a simultaneous improvement of material living standards . . . the Government has henceforth decided to pursue a policy of educational development in line with economic requirements.

Policies of structure, method, and content adjusted to this trend were widely accepted and implemented quite well. The earlier charts reveal the expansion achieved until 1966. These figures of expansion in formal schooling juxtaposed with Hunter's figures of the estimated educational attainment of the rural labor force expose a great need for improvement in the economy at that time. Hunter's figures follow:

---

9. Resnick, *op. cit.*, p. 43.

1,966,000 who have no education
1,000,000 in Standard IV
545,000 from V to VII/VIII
152,000 above Std. VIII

———————

3,663,000 — total rural labor force [10]

TABLE VIII

EDUCATIONAL PROGRESS OF AGE GROUP
(APPROXIMATELY 8 YRS.) AVAILABLE TO ENTER STD. I
IN 1961/62 (TANG.) [11]

Age group	In thousands	%-age
Did not enter school (1962)	117	46.8
Up to four years of education	81	32.4
Up to seven years of education	45	18.0
Entering secondary (1969)	7	2.8
	250	100.0

As mentioned before, Nyerere's speeches in 1964 seemed biased in favor of economic values, partly because the great expenditure of effort went into the establishment of the Education Planning Unit in 1963 and its impact on the Five-Year Plan (1964). But then his attention to social goals by 1965 soon brought a balance between economic and social goals. It seems quite obvious that the educators were not influenced by his switch to obtain an equilibrium, and they maintained a focus on manpower targets up to and beyond the adoption of the *Arusha Declaration* with its commitment to socialism and self-reliance. The P/S- leaver problem and university students' demonstration had not yet revolutionized the thinking of the Minister of Education, as seen by his speech referred to earlier.

Mwingira, Chief Educational Planner of Tanzania, addressed the conference on "The Challenge of Development" held in Nairobi in September, 1966, on the topic, "Priorities in Educational

———

10. Guy Hunter. *Education for a Developing Region: A Study of East Africa.* (London: Allen and Unwin, 1963), p. 14.
11. *Ibid.,* p. 15.

Development." [12] His paper also supported manpower goals, but recognized as well the problems of P/S-leavers instigated by these policies. The representatives of seventeen African nations and observers from four European countries seemed to be more aware of the clash between manpower and social goals than he was, as seen by their discussions on the conference papers. They listed the following series of choices, involving a number of factors, and recommended that governments give high investment priority to research into the implications of those choices for further development in each country:

1) Willingness of the present generation to sacrifice itself for the benefit of future generations;

2) Establishment of an order of priority between advanced technological development at heavy cost in human and in economic terms, and a slower development more harmoniously adapted to the existing society;

3) Establishment of an order of priorities between development of already favored areas and nationwide development based on regional planning;

4) Choice between speeding up development by offering an economic stimulus to efficiency, and acknowledging egalitarian aspirations of the people might result in slower development;

5) Choice between modernizing traditional outlook and introducing new ones;

6) Choice between using literature and true arts for political purposes, and allowing the widest possible freedom for artistic creation, in keeping with African tradition. [13]

EDUCATIONAL STRUCTURE, 1961-66
Administration

A description of powers granted to the Minister of Education in the *Education Ordinance* of 1961 and to the LEAs and Boards of Governors has appeared in the last section on policies of 1961-66. After powers had been delegated to LEAs for primary education

---

12. A. C. Mwingira, "Tanganyika's Educational Development" in *The Challenge of Development*. (Nairobi: East African Publishing House, 1968), pp. 130-40.

13. *Ibid.*, p. 147.

and Boards of Governors in respect to postprimary institutions, it logically followed to define the powers of Education Secretaries. On a local level, an Education Secretary represented his agency in communication with the government officials. An Education Secretary General headed the secretariat of each major group in confering with Government on the national level. There were five Education Secretary Generals: of the Tanganyika Episcopal Church (Roman Catholic); of the Christian Council of Tanzania; of the Tanganyika African Parents Association; of the East African Muslim Welfare Society; of H.H. the Aga Khan's Education Department. Their main responsibilities were to ensure that Governmental policies were implemented in their schools, to receive subventions and grants-in-aid, and to produce reports on their use.

Mention has also been made of the change in functions of the District Education Officers. They took on administrative duties only, connecting LEAs with the Central Government while PSIs became agents of teacher education. Education administrators increased in number at the center as well as in the districts. There were 8 Regional Education Officers in 1961 and 17 in 1966. DEOs rose correspondingly in number during the same.

The Five-Year Plan (1964) was a comprehensive plan that united all departments. All became responsible for the educational task. The Ministry of Local Government and Housing checked the stewardship of funds. The Ministry of Community Development and National Culture was in charge of nonformal education. The Chief Education Officer approved a syllabus on courses for each school; this ministry delegated the LEAs to check that local goals corresponded to national goals. The Ministry of Education held responsibility for vocational and technical adult education. Other Governmental departments had inservice training programs for staff. For these, the Ministry of Education produced an adequate flow of trainees in quantity and quality. The University of East Africa implemented plans for higher education.

Institutions

With Africanization as a major goal in middle- and high-level jobs, the Government restricted the expansion of primary education severely in both its Three-Year and Five-Year plans in order to concentrate its efforts and finances on secondary, teacher training, and higher education. The officials quieted the demands of

African parents and justified their decision by citing wastage figures in the primary-education institutions. Thus, one of the aims of the policy makers in the early years of independence was to find the best ways to reduce wastage by utilizing the existing structures, both in primary and secondary education.

Primary education was largely the responsibility of the LEAs. But, since at least half of the teachers' wages was paid by the Central Government, it was impossible to open many new schools without some assurance that the community could indefinitely finance the cost of operation before the Central Government's approval. More than half the population was under sixteen years of age. The inability to provide many P/Ss for each succeeding age meant that the task of adult education would be great for many years to come. Again, there is the fact that over half the people are concentrated on one-sixth of the land and only four per cent live in towns. This makes it difficult to evenly distribute education throughout Tanzania. Popular pressure demanded development of education at the primary level as well as at other levels. The focus of expansion on secondary and higher education and a lack of attention to primary and postprimary training involved a political risk. Yet the Government's policy to restrict the expansion of primary education was partly due to the problem of P/S leavers. A Std. IV leaver could revert to illiteracy if he did not exert any effort for using his skills, perhaps a useless investment. Employment for Std. VIII leavers, and for Std. VII after 1964, was becoming scarcer by the year; only ten per cent could expect to be employed, and each year the new leavers competed with the leavers of all former years.

During the Three-Year Plan, the Government adopted the 8-4-2 cycle and extended Std. V and VI in selected P/Ss as a step toward a full primary course. In 1964 there were 1,115 classes (44,000 pupils) of Std. V level and only 548 classes (18,000 pupils) in VIII. Std. I-IV schools were then called Lower Primary Schools, I-VI were Extended Schools, and V-III were Upper Primary Schools. Std. VII was added to the extended P/Ss when VIII was eliminated in the M/Ss of the region. An ordinance of 1961 forbade the opening of more boarding facilities on this level. Primary education absorbed about half of the budget, but the expenditure mounted to £8 at the primary level, £85 at the secondary, and £1,145 at the university level. So, one of the first objectives in the Ministry of Education's plan was "to make every effort to ensure that the standards of quality in primary education are maintained at a level adequate to lay the foundations of permanent literacy for pupils who proceed no further." [14] Grade A teachers were to replace Grade Cs in whole-day sessions for Std. III and IV.

Secondary education was the bottleneck in Tanganyika's quest for Africanization; there were insufficient secondary graduates to enter training courses. Of the few qualified African graduates, only about a score opted to remain in the teaching profession and the rest were lured by power, prestige, and the benefits of other positions. There were fifteen in 1961/62. At one point in 1964, there were only nine Tanzanian African graduates serving in the secondary schools. Thus, the very institutions that required African influence were left to expatriates to keep them from collapsing during this expansion. Note the large number of teachers required from abroad:

TABLE IX

TEACHERS IN SECONDARY SCHOOLS [15]

	Tanzanian Citizens	Others	Total
Holders of degree equivalent to Univ. of East Africa with professional training (3 did not)	13	323	336
Holders of university degree:			
a) with a professional qualification	10	109	119
b) without professional qualification	10	120	130
Holders of diplomas (equal to Makerere)	39	42	81
Grade A teachers (or equivalent)	108	9	117
Teachers of Domestic Science or handicrafts otherwise not specified	14	—	14
Other teachers	32	29	61
Laboratory assistants	61	—	61
Totals	287	632	919

14. Page 37 of the Plan and Mwingira, *The Challenge of Development*, p. 133.

15. A. C. Mwingira and Simon Pratt. "The Process of Educational Planning in Tanzania," *Africa Research Monograph* No. 10. (Paris: UNESCO/IIEP, 1967), p. 77.

One of the first experiments in educational integration of multiracial dimensions began in 1960 at St. Michael's and St. George's School, originally opened for the benefit of European children of junior- and senior-high level. Twenty-one Africans and twenty Asians were admitted after interviews and testing. This group met high standards, both academically and in sports. They followed the customs and standards of the European setting.

After independence this school met with immediate problems. Many expatriates left the country and, with European enrollment dropping from about five hundred to one hundred eighty, fees dropped considerably. The Property Fund was not available either. The Government took over, but could not maintain the cost. Thus, in 1963 it was closed, not as a failure in integration of the student body, but for purely financial reasons. In 1964 the school reopened under the name, Mkawa High School, and has been invaluable in its capacity for science and art streams. It has served well as a catalyst of human understanding among the agriculturally oriented Africans, the commercially oriented Asians, and the Europeans.

The majority of Tanzania's S/Ss, which were twenty-eight in number in 1960 (fifteen were full S/S) and ninety-seven in number in 1966, had VA operations. They did not present any great threat to the Government, which gained greater control through the provisions of the Education Ordinance, 1961 (discussed earlier); the volunteers rather served as an additional source for the receipt of funds, personnel, and expertise so much in demand at this time. This situation was not without its peculiar problems. The 150 teachers supplied through Teachers for East Africa (TEA) in 1961, as well as Peace Corps teachers who began to arrive in 1963 to teach in upper primary grades, were only on a two-year assignment. With a twofold adjustment—to the African way of life and to the British-influenced system of education—they probably learned more than what they could contribute of a very permanent nature to the youth of the nation. At least, the expatriate staff generally served only two-year terms, and most of the time the turnover was around fifty per cent.

Due to their selective nature, secondary-education institutions were boarding schools. Even urban S/Ss were forced to provide accommodations for rural students in 1964 as most urban P/Ss had achieved full primary course by then. Evan's characterization of the S/S in 1962 might well have been repeated during the next few years:

> The secondary school is an exotic institution which bears little relationship to the community desires or wishes except . . . economic preferment and a white-collar job.[16]

This was a political decision based on conflicting views—social equality and economic efficiency.

In compliance with the recommendations of the Tobias and Thomas manpower surveys, secondary expansion, as well as all other postprimary-level education, has been determined mainly by manpower requirements. The survey on trade-school training, as mentioned in Chapter III, revealed that industrial employers did not look to these graduates for their labor supply. Therefore, technical and vocational education, one of the weakest links in the educational system in the past, needed to undergo change. The emphasis shifted from traditional to modern crafts and technical education. Evening classes opened for commercial and technical training. Ifunda and Moshi Trade Schools were converted into secondary schools with a technical bias in 1964 and 1966 respectively. The intention of the new curriculum was to encourage students to pursue upon completion professional studies, e.g., architecture, surveying, civil engineering, mechanics, and electrical engineering. Dar es Salaam Technical College was the only institution providing postsecondary technical education in Tanganyika in 1964. Training in agricultural college was shortened from three to two years. Agricultural courses were introduced into five S/Ss. Bwiru Girls Secondary School became a territorial school for girls with a commercial bias. Although Tobias and Thomas had recommended that industries provide training on the job and formal technical training became supplementary, the Ministry of Education still favored providing formal technical training and argued that employers were either unable or unwilling to provide it. The ministry expected to eliminate defects by revising the syllabus, improving pupil selection, and training in crafts that were in short supply rather than in excess.

---

16. P.C.C. Evans, "American Teachers for East Africa," *Comparative Education Review.* VI: n.1 (June, 1962), p. 76.

Again, as in secondary and teacher training, the lack of Tanzanian teachers with high qualifications was a grave problem. The following chart reveals the problem:

TABLE X

TEACHERS IN TECHNICAL EDUCATION [17]

Teachers	Tanzanian citizens	Others	Total
Education Officer			
(i.e., grad. equivalent)	4	75	79
Grade A teachers	6	—	6
Technical assistants	20	—	20
Junior technical assistants	47	—	47
	—	—	—
Totals	77	75	152

This need for African staff with high qualifications continued up to the end of the sixties. This was partly due to the unwillingness or inability of School-Certificate holders to undergo technical training.

The arguments given by the critics in regard to Kenyan secondary education are the same ones leveled at Tanzania's secondary-education institutions: too superficial; available to too few; too bookish and impractical; productive of too many clerks and too few farmers, artisans, technicians, and reliable administrators; and conducive to the drift to the towns, the decay of agriculture, the breakup of the family, and the loosening of moral standards. Thus, by training a few to such quality of learning (1.7 per cent of secondary-school age in 1964), the upper layer of society was moving away from the lower layer. Meister put it this way:

> Secondary and higher education have very little effect on social change . . . The kind of education given does not answer the needs of underdevelopment, and takes place in the highbrow and falsely humanist framework of Western university traditionalism.[18]

Meister asserts that secondary and higher education cannot be

17. Mwingira and Pratt, op. cit., p. 78.
18. Meister, op. cit., p. 70.

used as tools for preparing committed leaders, but that adherence to only manpower requirements is inadequate and some consequences will appear out of necessity. And this is, of course, just what happened in Tanzania. The crises of 1966 did not come directly from the secondary-education level, but undoubtedly many secondary students shared similar feelings and, since secondary education was linked to all other levels either above or below, it made an impact during that time.

The great expansion in secondary education in the Three-Year Plan provided for teacher-training candidates who were needed in Upper Primary Schools and Extended Schools, made it possible to plan postsecondary technical courses, and supplied a number of ex-secondary students to vocational training by other agencies. In 1964 the output of secondary schools met Government demand and the private sector began Africanization.

The expansion of secondary education provided more candidates for Grade A training (note the change in teacher categories in Table XI), but also lowered the prestige of teacher training since secondary and higher-education institutions had first chance in selections. Grade C TTCs received those who could not merit secondary education, and some Grade As had not even passed one subject on their Cambridge Overseas School Certificate Examination. The "no-fail" policy of a two-year training did not encourage high standards. Most educational planners consider teacher training to be one of the nerve centers in the educational system. Economists feel also that more can be done to raise the standards of education through teacher training than through other activities. Tanzanian educational planners supported this concept and expended much effort and attention to improving the quality of teacher training. Instead of fees, allowances were paid monthly to students in the colleges as incentives for joining teacher training.

Because of the Africanization process, TTCs were taxed to the limit to produce as many highly qualified teachers as possible for all types of educational programs. The following table reveals the shortage of qualified and experienced Tanzanian citizens in this type of education:

TABLE XI

STAFFING IN TEACHERS' COLLEGES, 1964 [19]

Category of teacher	Tanzanian citizens	Others	Total
Trained graduates	6	42	48
Other graduates	2	54	56
Makerere diploma and equivalent	19	—	19
Grade A	22	9	31
Grade B	31	—	31
Grade C	15	—	15
Other	3	—	3
Total	98	105	203

By 1966 five categories of teachers were in training: The former Grade I category was changed to Grade A; Grade Bs finished Std. X and had two years of training; Grade Cs were the former Grade IIs; ex-Form 6s trained for two years as Education Officers III, beginning in 1965; and University College offered education as one of the three subjects with the Arts and Science bursaries for a BA or BSc beginning in 1964/65.

Despite the great expansion in education and the rush for Africanization, Tanzania kept its policy of not using untrained Swahili teachers in P/Ss, a practice that some of the neighboring countries still maintained. Problems did arise from the fact that some teachers had only slightly better qualifications than their students, and measures were taken to improve the situation. Because of the focus off expansion on primary education, one of the best ways to affect primary education and all subsequent levels was to improve the quality of teacher training. In the Five-Year Plan (1964), the 320 places for Grade A expanded to one thousand five hundred while the 680 Grade C places were slowly phased out. Grade C training was considered inadequate. Therefore an intensive program of upgrading took place. As a result of the elimination of the Territorial X Certificate Examination, Grade B, by 1963 became a promotion grade only.

---

19. *Ibid.*, p. 79.

Upgrading was done by merit, as a result of performance. The key to upgrading was English. A "B" merit required an ex-Form 2 level and Grade A required a pass on the English Qualifying Exam. One hundred thirty teachers annually on full salary were seconded to an upgrading course, but this method was considered too expensive and dropped at the end of two years. Instead, a two-year correspondence course was developed with two six-week vacation courses at selected colleges. By 1966 there were 870 teachers upgrading. Until enough Grade A and B teachers were available, the surplus of Grade Cs was used in Standards V, VI, and VII where As and Bs should have been.

Teacher-training centers were also consolidated and decreased in number by half, 22 to 11, with 240 to 280 pupils each. This action took place to achieve economy of scale and to make full use of specialized staff and equipment.

Another significant feature in teacher training was the formation of the Institute of Education in 1965. Castle very eloquently defines its function:

> ... it is a coordinating and advisory institution ... co-operating with all agencies engaged in the education of teachers. It has no control over its constituent colleges, except in establishing standards through its qualifying exams; interference with the government of schools or colleges, or with their internal autonomy, is not involved.[20]

As Skorov asserts, "The link between education and employment is at its closest at the university level. Higher education is, therefore, the educational sector most affected by manpower requirements." [21] He goes on to explain three different lines of action that can be taken:

1) Projecting entries into specific courses of study in accordance with requirements;
2) Making the flow of students follow the planned pattern of studies; and
3) Ensuring that graduates take jobs for which they have not been trained.[22]

---

20. E. B. Castle, *Growing Up in East Africa.* (London: Oxford University Press, 1966), pp. 182, 83.
21. Skorov, *op. cit.*, p. 48.
22. *Ibid.*

Before independence Tanzania offered no university-level education. University College opened in Dar with a Faculty of Law in 1961, the University of East Africa formed in 1963, a Faculty of Arts and Social Sciences opened in 1964, and a Faculty of Science began in 1965. By 1966/67 there were 552 Tanzanians in the student body of 812, 45 5enrolled in the other East African sister colleges, and 818 Tanzanians in postsecondary institutions abroad.

Prior to 1964, experience revealed that students failed to choose courses leading to occupations where there was a critical shortage in manpower. In response to this, the ministry adopted several policy instruments, which will be discussed in the next section entitled "Methods, 1961-66": vocational counseling, tied bursaries, and control of overseas scholarships.

Although it cost £250 per pupil annually to be educated on the university level abroad and £850 per pupil per annum to be educated in the University of East Africa, the development of university education in East Africa demanded that the Ministry of Education be willing to pay the difference. Also, university development had priority over all other educational development. In alignment with Tanzania's goals to maintain as high a standard of education as possible, higher-education admission requirements were not lowered in general to meet manpower requirements sooner.

It was not until after independence that adult education gained great impetus. Adult education, used in the sense in which Prosser defines it in relation to developing countries, is:

> that force which in its ideal application can bring about a maximum of readjustment of attitudes within a society to any new and changed situation in the shortest possible time. . . .

and which also "imparts new skills and techniques required and made necessary by the change." [23]

The Social and Community Development Department took the responsibility for adult education with others joining forces for literacy campaigns. Kivukoni College, under the aegis of

---

23. Roy Prosser, "Social Change and Audlt Education," *East Africa Journal.* XV: n.4 (1963), p. 176.

TANU and its trade-union affiliate, was established in 1961 with the hope of equipping each student with a new approach to learning, to enhance his capacity to apply himself to study, and to provide him with a set of valuable keys to man's store of knowledge. A graduate does not receive a diploma, only a certificate of completion of the course at the college. An important place was given to social studies, attention given to practical skills, and the inculcation of a team spirit. According to Burke, Kivukoni has been making an "extraordinary contribution to the political life of the nation." He credits the alumni for being among the few who understand Ujamaa as a national theory and as a guide to action.

The Institute of Public Administration and the Institute of Adult Education in Dar es Salaam and University College respectively reached an enrollment of one thousand by 1966 and offered courses in many subject areas. Skorov felt that these courses would be more helpful to manpower needs if they were attached more closely to formal education. Inservice training, operated by various departments and industries, were directly linked to manpower planning.

With literacy and adult education recognized as an economic function by the Five-Year Plan (1964), the Ministry of Community Development and National Culture provided more than further training in citizenship at the national level at the Institute of Adult Education. There was available, too, the Community Development Training Centre at Tengeru; the Swahili-speaking stream at Kivukoni College; basic literacy at the village level; and basic development and citizenship training at district training and community centers.

By the end of 1962, there were three hundred thousand enrolled in literacy classes. An estimated six hundred thousand were to enroll in courses in 1965. King has categorized them, but did not include evening classes arranged by the Ministry of Education:

TABLE XII

ENROLLMENT IN NONFORMAL EDUCATION [42]

569,642 in literacy classes
16,539 in community development follow-up classes

24. Jane King. "Planning Non-Formal Education in Tanzania, 1966" *Africa Research Monograph No. 16* (Paris: UNESCO/IIEP, 1967), p. 12.

    5,000 district and farmers' training center enrollment
      189 in training-in-industry (TWI) classes
    2,010 in civil-service inservice training courses
    5,100 in correspondence and evening courses
       60 in residential adult courses (Kivukoni)

  598,540 grand total

King reported one hundred thousand in women's groups, some of which would be offering literacy courses also. Eleven thousand persons were involved in teaching these courses: eight thousand teachers for literacy, 833 community development officers, 1,864 agriculture-extension officers, and three hundred in other forms of nonformal education.

METHODS, 1961-66

Having accepted educational policies for integration, unification, decentralization with a strong central authority, and the manpower approach to educational planning, the new Government sought ways to meet the educational demands of the new nation. Their policies reflected measures for equality, but whenever economy measures for producing more manpower were envisioned, the choice was generally given to the latter.

The objective of the salary revision accomplished in 1965 was the equalization of money incomes between wage and salary earners. The salary structure recommended by the ADU report of 1961 was not put into effect until after the implementation of United Teaching Service. A graduate's salary in education now compared with a graduate's income in other professions. Wages in the higher-level-income brackets were at that time frozen in comparison to the greater wage hike for the lower-income workers. This policy had the indirect effect of requiring professionals to pay for their training. The Tanzanian Government paid expatriate teachers on the same scale it did a Tanzanian of equivalent qualification. The difference due to cost of living, an overseas addition, was added by the sponsoring government to match the expatriate's salary with market rates in the country of his origin.

The status given to Swahili by the new government built greater uniformity into the educational system. The use of languages other than Swahili and English was forbidden in schools after 1964. Swahili was made a compulsory course in all S/Ss, as well as a subject in the School Certificate exam.

The Government was forced to decide whether or not to allow the richer and most progressive areas to take the economic responsibility for educational expansion or to opt for a slower process, which, through aiding the poorer areas, would bring educational opportunities and privileges to all. They tended to favor the former. LEAs were made responsible for primary education. Grants were given on the condition that the local government would contribute either cash, labor, or materials. Through self-help schemes, energetic regions pushed ahead.

As a counterbalance, Central Government put on the brakes by withholding approvals for new buildings when they questioned the area's ability to pay additional teachers' wages. Self-help was not without problems: It was rather easy to coordinate community effort to build a new classroom, but it was usually a different proposition to supply houses for teachers and schools with latrines. Building standards were sometimes poor and deterioration was rapid. In some cases, better economy measures in self-help projects would have had greater lasting results.

The new government was well aware of the necessity to enact economy measures. It sought ways to utilize the existing structures as well as to expand at a moderate cost. Educational investments were initiated to produce manpower. A seven-year primary course, shortened from eight years, required thoughtful reorganization to accomplish it without a loss in educational content. Standards III and IV read all day instead of half-days. For a few years the products of the P/Ss possibly were of a lower academic competency, but in several years' time the increasing number of leavers made selection much more competitive, thus ensuring a higher quality of the ones chosen. After this time period, no more boarding schools were built on the primary level. Forty per cent of the Upper Primary Schools, the former M/Ss, were boarding institutions in 1965.

The savings made possible in the use of the secondary-education school plant was a hotter and more protracted issue between the Ministry of Development Planning and Ministry of Education. The Ministry of Education would hear nothing of "double streaming" the schools and offered arguments that the development planners could hardly substantiate. The ministries finally decided that they would allow the plant to grow in size in the first Five-Year Plan (1964) and then double shift after 1969.

One policy that eliminated wastage in the schools was the removal of fees as a cause for not attending school. Primary children in day schools could be remitted up to 20 per cent, and students in boarding in upper primary schools were given as high as 33 per cent of the fees required. S/S fees were abolished in 1964. This raised the question of payment by the noncitizen. The whole matter followed closely with the President's circular of January 3, 1964 (*Tanganyika Standard*, January 8, 1964), in which he stated that discrimination shall be no more by race or class, but by citizen and noncitizen. The Ministry of Education adopted a policy that provided for the selection of noncitizens for attendance in a secondary institution in proportion to the "children of citizens of the same age-group, i.e., not less than 2%" and preferences were to be given to certain parents. Children of noncitizen parents who were wage earners and liable to transfer were given preference. If admitted, they paid fees. According to Cameron's estimation, "Few other countries with the same or similar problem have tackled it so understandingly and to date [1967] so successfully." [25] Primary education was not offered free as secondary education because fees lessened the great number of primary-school leavers, who would have ordinarily finished under a free system but who would not have been qualified for the higher-level manpower demands.

The most significant method adopted to reduce wastage in schools was the energy expended in teacher training to improve classroom teaching. Wastage was due to inadequate teaching, it was suggested. With the expansion of secondary education, a corresponding advance could be made with more advanced teacher education. English was used as a medium of instruction in TTCs. Upgrading courses and inservice refresher courses along with the newly trained PSIs, provided new exposures for the cadre on the job. Model schools in each PSI's district, abolition of half-day sessions for Stds. III and IV, and syllabus revision attacked the situation from many angles.

---

25. John Cameron. "The Integration of Education . . .", p. 52.

Critics argued against and for the exam program and the exit points. Those who supported the exams claimed that they kept a high standard of learning. Opposers contended that they produced "rote" learning, and that selection on the basis of a special exam was more like a lottery than actual evaluation and choosing. This argument caused Government to consider better selection techniques and also suggested that general school records be submitted for each child before he sat for the exam. To ensure a greater number of science-oriented Form 4 graduates for entrance to the Higher School Certificate course, Government introduced the Mock Cambridge Examination technique. Pre-selection was done on the basis of this mid-year exam, and science-qualifying students could resit the English exam in Form 5.

Educational policies of method during 1961 to 1966 were highly spiced with manpower goals: The Territorial X Examination was abolished in order to give all secondary students the privilege of finishing the School Certificate course; University College provided opportunities for further education in several fields; Grade A TTCs expanded, and two other higher categories of teachers were established. Arrangements with America for Teachers of English Abroad and Peace Corps teachers lessened the short supply of teachers. Firms were required to supply technical inservice training while the Ministry of Education provided formal training on a secondary level. Form 6 graduates were required to teach six months in adult education before entering university. In 1964 the publication of *Careers for Nation Building: a Career Guide Book for Secondary Students* was designed to overcome the serious lack of occupational labor-market information in Tanzania. The adoption of an 8-4-2 cycle with P/S expanded to Std. VI was the first stage to a full course. Finally, the Government, in a controversial measure, offered bursaries for courses that would produce skills needed for manpower development.

Since past experience revealed that students failed to choose courses leading to occupations where there was a critical shortage of manpower, the Tanganyikan Government decided to follow a different approach to ensure the flow of students into planned courses of study to meet manpower requirements, and to guarantee that those students would fill the positions for which they trained. Tied bursaries, operating as of 1964/65 entry, were offered according to manpower needs. Even before university level, four-sevenths of all Form 5 places were given to science students and three-sevenths to arts. After steering students into required courses, the Government offered bursaries as scholarships for further education. Forty per cent had been offered in education in order to train every possible undergraduate for teaching. Science bursaries were given higher priority, so that "the number of arts students admitted into the university straight from school will be determined not by the number who qualify, but by the number of bursaries left after the science bursaries have been awarded and these again will be allocated to specific courses, such as Law, Education, Accountancy, Commerce, etc." No student was forced to take a bursary, but could accept or reject the offer, or pay tuition. He usually accepted it and was bound to work any place the Government placed him for the first five years at the completion of his training. The Government gave overseas scholarships only in the areas of study not offered in East Africa.

This system of bursaries came under attack. Critics felt free choice was virtually impossible in this system, and that students were forced into areas of study for which they had little interest. Their opponents focused on the huge number of primary and secondary leavers and even farmers who had no opportunity for further training and were forced into employment that they certainly did not choose, and argued that slight attention had been given to this greater number of people with a similar problem. The opponents also demonstrated the efficiency of the system in meeting manpower targets and warned of the dangers of an oversupply of arts graduates whom the economy could not absorb.

As a means for providing contact for the university graduates, Form 6 leavers, and postsecondary training graduates with the average citizen, the National Service Act of 1966 required that all graduates of postsecondary courses serve the Government for two years under a specified program and that approximately 60 per cent of their salary be paid to the Government. The bill was debated for only two days in the National Assembly and approved with a single dissenting vote on October 4, 1966.

The passing of the National Service Act literally blew the top off the education system. Students cried loud and angrily against the bill during the debate. On October 22, less than three weeks after the bill's approval, 393 students (310 from the university and the remainder from S/Ss) gathered outside the State House and submitted a statement to the President. They said that they opposed the law for its compulsory features and were unwilling to serve under its present proposals. One placard, "We were better off under colonialism," cut deep to the core among TANU leaders. Nyerere listened to the students, angrily condemned their attitudes, fingerprinted them, and expelled them from the university outright. They were given armed escorts to their homes. But to have 310 students rusticated from a student body of 552 in a developing nation where manpower planners counted positions for everyone was tragic. An editorial in TANU's official paper expressed well the nation's shock and disappointment:

> The memorandum of the students must give the govern-
> ment the occasion t oreview extensively the educational sys-
> tem in the country. When students who have so openly
> benefitted from the reclamation of our political birthright
> of independence so earnestly tell the world that they would
> rather be under colonialism there must be something wrong
> with their educational institutions and methods . . . they
> were not, in a word, being educated.[26]

Hinkle, who carefully analyzed this incident, believes the crisis was an isolated incident; that a whole group of youth was not out of agreement with the governing body. He believes that these students felt threatened by the act and responded singularly, and the President's response was unique to the occasion. The students and the university, as well as the President, made a number of concessions in later responses as they reviewed educational policies and purposes and realized the ramifications of their initial responses to each other.

CONTENT, 1961-66

What steps were taken by curriculum planners to induce true integration among the races, religions, and geographical areas; to unify the educational system and nation; and to develop a nation with cohesive, upcoming, qualifying Africans and a growing economy?

---

26. *Then Nationalist* (Oct. 24, 1966), p. 4.

Most of the syllabuses for this period were the same ones used in the fifties. In 1960 a *Primary School Handbook* was issued. This proved to be very helpful—a good guide to the techniques of teaching, administration, and discipline. In fact, in this investigator's opinion, the P/S handbook was more relevant professionally to the P/S teacher than the sister volume—the *Middle School Handbook.* These two handbooks with current syllabuses became the "bible" of supervisors and teachers.

By 1963 a number of syllabuses were prepared for various subjects. Nature study, health, physical education, arts and crafts, and music were given more specific attention with separate handbooks or syllabuses for each. The P/S syllabus stressed school gardens or demonstration plots and beautification of the school compound (planting of shade or fruit trees) rather than the full-scale periods of Kilimo (Agriculture) as previously taught. Gardening, for example, was to be done as a part of a science lesson.

With the great emphasis on manpower planning and expansion of opportunities for entrance to secondary education and higher learning, it is not surprising that rote memorization was considered the best guarantee of a good performance on the entrance examinations to the next level. In fact, S/S students reacted negatively toward a teacher who was including "frills"—not examinable material (in their estimation)—in his teaching. Handicraft, agriculture, and domestic-science lessons rated lower in prestige, so that if there was any difficulty in obtaining supplies for these periods, or if the exam date was approaching, a teacher of these subjects might either have used the period for 1) giving them a study period, 2) supplementing other lessons, or 3) arranging with another teacher to take the period.

Thus the type of syllabus and teacher attitudes influenced students away from farming as a career. The curriculum was less important in actuality than matriculating and finishing school. Attempts to change the curriculum did not always succeed. Africans clamored for a literary education, and the vocational and aesthetic skills that they needed were neglected. Hector suggests that the root of the problem may not have been in the curriculum, but in changing social patterns of culture, and that the revision of the syllabuses may not have solved the problem. The courses lacked relevancy or efficiency, for why did one see broken windows, desks, and benches in a boys' school where a specially trained shop teacher had shop classes? Why did the school lack fresh fruits and vegetables if they had large agricultural blocks of time in the Middle School timetable? Why did the domestic-science teacher introduce less African and more European foods and ways of cooking? And why did the Std. VIII girl fail to clean the dormitory properly on a Serengeti class safari?

Examinations, and subjects examinable, then, dictated the curriculum. Peace Corps teachers complained about the academic type of learning and the lack of activity method (as was upheld in the M/S syllabus) and appeal to judgment, observation, and reasoning. With Stds. V and VI added to the day I-IV P/S, it was hard for them to compete with the established M/Ss. Even when Grade A teachers became available as Full P/Ss developed (to Std. VII), the academic standard of the P/S leaver was lower because many of these classes had not been full-day sessions on the Stds. III and IV level and were therefore forced to cover more in their middle grades than they could accomplish. As the seven-year course went into effect, the eight-year course was kept by allocating Stds. III and IV material to Std. III whole-day sessions and by covering in Std. IV the Std. V material, etc.

Not only in P/S but also in M/S, craft training and agriculture gave way to academic subjects. But by the mid-sixties, the trend away from craft training to technical education in a general S/S curriculum was noticeable as Bwiru Girls' Secondary School became a territorial commercial girls' S/S, and Ifunda and Moshi converted into technical S/Ss. Manpower goals were gaining precedence over moral and aesthetic values and the satisfaction and pursuit of pure learning. Klinglehofer's research on the occupational preferences of S/S students clearly revealed that manpower needs and the desires of individual students badly mismatched.

Lest the impression remain that the Ministry of Education had no policies of value that were adopted regarding the content of the curriculum at this time, some policies should be cited that more closely interpreted the President's goals for integration of Tanzanian citizens, localizing the civil service, building a national ethic, and raising the nation's economy. A common syllabus was adopted, religious instruction was encouraged, but not made mandatory, the medium of instruction was reduced to Swahili and

English only, and a common examination and selection system began to function. Secondary- and higher-educational institutions and postsecondary professional courses were training graduates for manpower needs. French was introduced into S/Ss, not as a required subject, but to enable Africans to communicate with their brothers in Francophone Africa or to enter diplomatic service. As the P/S-leaver problem increased, educators in the Ministry of Education and in the Institute of Education began to work on schemes for the reintroduction of agriculture into the P/S curriculum.

Postprimary education had been oriented toward a foreign culture, but now more attention was drawn toward current affairs and the history and geography of tropical Africa. The Cambridge Overseas School Certificate exam was printed in an East African edition. Arts and science streams of Forms 5 and 6 were added to comply with manpower requirements. Education courses were given as an option for courses leading to the B.A. and B.Sc. degrees. The Institute of Education began to take on responsibility for coordinating inservice teacher training, advising the syllabus revision, and researching into national problems.

Since its inception, the University College has experimented with new approaches to educational problems and adapted to the needs of the country in its teaching and research, as specified by the Ministry of Education and the Ministry of Development Planning. University College was not a part of the national system of education, but could not exist without the lower echelons of learning nor escape the ramifications of it. That something was out of tune in the university's function in nation building was unquestionably clear in the university-student demonstration against the National Service Act of 1966 (already referred to in Methods, 1961-66). The university responded to the crisis by searching for much greater relevancy in meeting the educational needs.

SUMMARY

The educational policy makers seem to have been quite successful in a number of the points listed for revision by Skorov (cited on the first page of this chapter); expansion in the educational system; remodeling of structure; improvement in the quality of education; and reduction of wastage. (Note the absence of measures to strengthen cooperation and an attitude of service.)

1) Expansion of the education system:
   a) Primary schools began extending to Std. VI and a few to full primary status (Std. VII).
   b) Secondary Std. X exam abolished and most students on to Form 4; more on to Form 6 also.
   c) University education offered.
   d) Technical education offered on secondary-education level.
   e) Expansion in adult education.
   f) Education Planning Unit set up and manpower goals entrenched the expansion.

2) Remodeling of the structure of education:
   a) Integrated single system with measures for unification.
   b) Inspectorate reform—PSIs, the "mobile teachers' college."
   c) Decentralization by delegation of authority.
      i) LEAs responsible for primary education.
      ii) Boards of Governors in charge of postprimary education.
      iii) Education Secretaries' duties defined as VAs were drawn further into the public system.

3) Improvement in the *quality* of education:
   a) Upgrading and inservice courses with PSI help.
   b) Teacher training of better grade (five categories) with lower grade slowly decreased.
   c) Syllabuses and handbooks of better quality.

4) Reduction of wastage:
   a) Exit points reduced by abolition of exam and more places provided for further training.
   b) Fees abolished in secondary education, allowances for teacher trainees, remissions for some in primary education.
   c) Tied bursaries to ensure five years of service wherever Government wished to place a graduate.
   d) Salary revision placed graduates in teaching field on same scale as in other fields.

The very structure of education with its competitiveness intensified by the allurement of power, prestige, and benefits of position opening to Africans after independence attributed significantly to the narrow goal of educating for the examination. Fox believes the school, as well as other institutions, stifled creativity in the students and developed regurgitators rather than critical thinkers:

> Much of the inborn creativity and imagination of the children "seems to be trained right out of them," as an astute American colleague put it, unconsciously or consciously, by every major institution which touches their lives—the home, the tribe, the school, the church, and industrialization with its growing impact.[27]

It was rather paradoxical that the students, who were being trained under the influence of manpower planners, should have such a "purely" academic education and spurn vocational opportunities in the curriculum and in the workaday world. Vocational and technical training were neglected in the desire for high passes on highly academic examinations that would guarantee a good position with economic and social benefits.

P/S leavers carried a feeling of failure when they were not fortunate enough to be selected for further schooling or training. For them, opportunities for further training or employment decreased. With Std. VIII being eliminated in Tanzania over a period of three years, one-third of the territory's Stds. VII and VIII pupils were leaving P/S together. Only thirteen out of one hundred could be selected for further education, and only 10 per cent of the rest could hope for employment. Formal education, then, was actually relevant to a few, while many were frustrated for not having been chosen to realize their aspirations.

Secondary-education graduates faced restrictions in some areas of their highest aspirations, but still found the manpower market sufficient to grant them some salaried positions. They, and the university students even more so, were on the whole purposely isolating themselves from the average citizen. Their participation and involvement in self-help schemes was at a minimum. It was on

---

27. Lorene K. Fox. "Learning Ventures in East Africa," *Childhood Education*. XLI (March, 1965), p. 344.

this point the Government decided to pass the National Service Act of 1966, hoping that exposure to and communication with the common man would deepen commitments of service to the nation.

Had the educational policies been less biased or slanted to segments of Nyerere's goals and been more in touch with the changes and needs of the young nation, the problems that drew to a head in 1966 might have been avoided. The march of the university students to the State House in a revolt against the National Service Act and the increasing problem of P/S leavers (the educational crises of 1966) called for responses from the Government policy makers. To continue with the same plans would only deepen the wounds, and to revolutionize a large system would present immense ramifications. By 1967, however, changes had been made, and a new era began in educational planning.

CHAPTER SEVEN

THE POST-ARUSHA PERIOD, AFTER 1966

BACKGROUND TO THE PERIOD

Many social, political, and economic changes have taken place since the beginning of Tanzania's drive toward independence and its struggle for nationhood. These alterations have had a profound effect on the educational pattern of Tanzania. The manpower approach to educational planning and its close ties with, and demands on, the educational system were analyzed in the last chapter as well as some of the consequences of the relationship. The unattainable aspirations of many parents for their children, and of the children themselves, the limited expansion of the educational system in comparison to the population growth of 2.7 per cent per annum, and the lack of qualified Africans in the higher-and middle-level manpower categories all together provided a situation for change. The demands, then, on the few who were responsible for developing plans for the nation were burdensome. After independence they were gradually able to give more careful thought to a national philosophy or ethic.

Nyerere expressed himself on various issues relative to the educational system before the crises of 1966 (e.g., pomposity, parasitism, inequities, responsible leadership, and critical thinking). Some of his concepts were widely accepted and included in the educational planning and system; some were fit into a plan without application; and some were undoubtedly not fully comprehended and either implemented in policies, which in turn resulted in a reversal of the desired effects, or were ignored or rejected. It was not altogether surprising then that elements of Ujamaa-ism that up to this time were expressed as an attitude of mind found little application in the educational planning and system, and that manpower requirements embodied in concrete, visible terms gained precedence over the social aspects.

Nyerere was able, therefore, to use the crises in education of 1966 as a catalyst or springboard to action. His analysis of the educational system and plea for "a more thorough examination of

165

the education we are providing" were sequential to the *Arusha Declaration*, the official commitment of TANU to a socialist state. With lucidity he laid bare the features of the system that were antagonistic to the socialist commitment the nation had just made. His immediate suggestions for change focused on the curriculum, organization of the schools, and the entry age. Using these general guidelines, the educational planners were then responsible to interpret Ujamaa-ism and to determine appropriate policies for implementing socialistic principles and self-reliance.

The lack of new and appropriate materials, trained personnel, adequate finances, sufficient time, and appropriate scheduling were a constant liability. But despite shortcomings, the Government gave educational planning and policy making a top priority. That it was necessary to revolutionize or transform rather than modify the education system was clear. And that there was no blueprint in any other nation to imitate was also evident, for no other nation had a similar situation. What has been done then, one might say, was and continues to be an experiment.

EDUCATIONAL POLICIES, 1967–

The period beginning in 1967, sometimes called the post-Arusha era, includes the last half of the Five-Year Plan (1964) and the formation of the Second Five-Year Plan, which began operation on July 1, 1969. The Five-Year Plan (1969) stated that the basic educational policies of the Five-Year Plan (1964) would continue at the end of the decade:

1) to achieve essentially full self-sufficiency at all skills in the economy;
2) to achieve basic primary education for all (set as a goal for 1989 in the second plan);
3) to provide postprimary education as needed by manpower requirements and fill these places by offering busaries.

Government, it may be said, had chosen to pursue an educational policy strikingly inegalitarian, for the phrase "high-level manpower" itself suggests a strata of workers and is difficult to infuse with egalitarianism. The Five-Year Plan (1969) repeats over and over, "To plan is to choose." But Terrence O. Ranger in his article, "Students and the Nation" in the May, 1967, issue of the *East Africa Journal*, seems to feel that many people would agree that the Government had no other choice than the one it took. Therefore, the elite system that appeared was not the intention of Government but rather a consequence. While the Five-Year Plan (1964) focused on strengthening leadership in the ministry, the 1969 Plan was seeking the advancement of revolutionary education to the masses.

Immediately after the announcement of the *Arusha Declaration* and the issuance of *Education for Self-Reliance*, a permanent committee formed within the ministry to study the two documents and to prepare proposals for their implementation. A conference, called by this committee in April, 1967, was attended by senior members of the educational establishment in the Ministry of Education, Regional Education Officers, heads of S/Ss and TTCs, and Education Secretaries—all members who would be actively involved in carrying out the proposals agreed upon at the conference. Some of their recommendations for implementing *Education for Self-Reliance* reaffirmed existing practices. Others supported reforms, such as readjusting the school year to the locality, encouraging teachers and tutors (even expatriates before they left their homeland) to study the contents of the *Arusha Declaration* and *Education for Self-Reliance* and to devise steps to implement their principles, and promoting school-community integration in cultural activities either on or off the premises.[1] Various proposals for the different levels of education were presented at this conference to unify the general applications agreed upon.

The sociological milieu does not immediately transform the very day an official commitment to a new ideology is pronounced. Neither are attitudes of long standing replaced by others more suitable to the new indoctrination and social experience. The educational planners in whatever degree they themselves understood the spirit of Ujamaa-ism were forced to reckon with teachers, administrators, and community people who had very successfully learned, and held quite dear, the manpower emphasis and narrowed educational aims of the period between 1961 and 1966. The task they faced was formidable, but urgent. What was formerly a state of mind under the title "Ujamaa" now initiated action corresponding to socialistic attitudes.

---

1. See Hinkle, *op. cit.* pp. 221-25.

Many of the post-Arusha educational policies took on the flavor of earlier colonial policies: relevancy or adaptation to the community; mass education for community living; keeping social and vocational goals in balance and emphasized on par with or over academic achievement; the increasing use of Swahili as a language medium; teacher-education emphasis; checking the danger of overdevelopment; expansion emphasis on primary education; and viewing education as one aspect only in the development of the community. The structure, organization, and curriculum were altered to correspond with their comprehension of Ujamaaism and self-reliance. These steps came slowly, each one by experimentation, aimed toward the goal of creating a socialist society permeated with socialist attitudes.

One of the most significant policy changes restructured the purposes of formal schooling on the primary and secondary levels. In order to produce pupils who would return to and enrich rural life rather than become social misfits, these institutions were expected to serve as a catalyst for community and national development in their locales and to promulgate the spirit and theme of Ujamaa. This policy required changes in structure, in staff, in curriculum, and in school-community relationships. The main objective of primary education became rural development. Secondary education was expected to produce more and better graduates with skills prepared to meet manpower needs and, in addition, expected to increase prospects for employment through a more diversified curriculum.

These objectives have immense implications for the role of the TTC of the present time. As much as possible, the Government aims at reducing the gap between school and community so that what is learned in school can more readily be practiced at home.

EDUCATIONAL STRUCTURE, 1967—

Administration

The administrative structure made significant alterations in order to present a cohesive, unified front in the educational revolution. The Ministry of Education has been both reorganized and renamed and, in general, charged with an enlarged scope of jurisdiction. The Ministry of National Education, as it is known since February, 1969, is headed by a director whose responsibilities correspond to those of the former Chief Education Officer. A reshuffling of staff within the ministry put younger men into positions of greater responsibility. This action also manned the professional and operational positions with citizens.

The 1968 Act Supplement No. 62 gave the Director power to set up Boards of Governors for private schools. This delegation of power enabled him to gain control over these nonaided institutions. The Director was given the responsibility of approving fees set by private schools in the *Education Act of 1969.*

The greatest changes came at the end of 1969 in the *Education Act,* which repealed the *Education Ordinance, 1961.* This act placed all Government and public schools under the management and administration of the Director of National Education except in the case of P/Ss, which were handed over to the Local Education Authorities. This act required all Voluntary Agencies to hand over their assisted schools to the Government and all teachers to be employees of the Government and members of UTS (unless exempted). The offices of Education Secretaries were abolished, and the Education Secretary General in the new provision would be the coordinator for the educational activities of private schools.

The reorganization in the Ministry of National Education abolished the former British-oriented inspectorate system and replaced it with a system of directorates for all professional departments, each headed by an Assistant Director. Secondary and technical education were joined and have been separated again after a year, the inspectorate division is now known as "Curriculum Development and Examinations," and the addition of Higher Education and Adult Education has currently fallen under the jurisdiction of the Director. The responsibility for adult education has been brought into this department, and responsibility for craft training has gone to the Ministry of Commerce, Labor, and Works. By the end of 1969 the course and direction of this new organizational structure seemed to make little difference in its operation. Officials indicated that it allows for more flexibility, and that the staff and professional personnel were concerned with supervision rather than periodic inspections as heretofore.[2] One advantage was evident; the Director could coordinate more easily the political education in all educational institutions.

Institutions

The period of the plan (1964) was primarily a time of institution building. With the plan of that period uncompleted, the plan (1969) continued this element in some areas.[3] Manpower planners readily opted to continue the structure of selection and expectation. If the education system was examination-oriented and competitive, adult-education agencies would feel the brunt tomorrow, and have to do remedial socialistic education. Adopting a policy for eliminating boarding schools on the primary level and elsewhere wherever feasible, they had more money available to open more schools in the local constituency and reduce the sharp competition created between 1964 and 1967. Day schools were also necessary if the institutions were to become communities interacting in the areas where they were located.

Although expansion in primary education in the plan (1964) was relatively small in comparison to secondary education,[4] and the focus of expansion was put on secondary and higher education, popular demand for primary education accompanied by self-help schemes was the main force behind the actual quantitative growth. The plan (1969) proposed to effect progressive increases on the Stds. I and Std. V levels, thus shifting the emphasis to rural primary education. P/Ss are scheduled to increase sufficiently by 1974 to abolish the Std. IV exam at that time. The target for universal primary education has been set at 1989. School premises are viewed as community education centers, and primary education is considered only one function of the educational process.

---

2. American Embassy, "Some Comments on the Achievements of Tanzania's Program of 'Education for Self-Reliance' " Memo A-248 of Nov. 7, 1969.

3. A 51.6% plan performance had been reported for 64-9, Vol. H, p. 2 of the Plan (1969).

4. A. 27.4% increase in total primary enrollment and 50% increase in secondary enrollment. Abstracted from Vol. I, p. 23 of the Plan (1969) and *Tanzania Education Journal*, V: n.13 (June 1969), p. 2.

The combination of secondary and technical education directorates in the ministerial organization was an example of the trend in secondary education for vocational biases. Secondary Schools, with their influence on higher education (the basis for further training at university and intermediate level colleges and TTCs) and on primary education (through TTCs, teachers, and extension workers) hold a key role in the educational system of the country. Since 84 per cent of the S/S teachers at this strategic level were expatriates, a vulnerable situation, the planners of the Three-Year and Five-Year (1964) plans emphasized post-primary expansion. As a result, manpower self-sufficiency in staffing of secondary education has run ahead of the 1980 target. By 1973 it is expected that all but a few teachers will be citizens and that 100 per cent citizen cadre will be reached by 1977 if not before.

A policy that received much attention later than the staffing issue was the shift from purely academic to vocational biases. Enrollments and outputs of S/Ss were planned to meet the needs of the labor market for immediate employment, and through pre-professional courses and university training for later employment. The plan (1969) calls for thirty new streams, all in the science subjects, i.e., agriculture, commerce, manual crafts, and domestic science.

A radical change in the secondary institutions has been their involvement in adult-education literacy and self-help schemes in community-development projects and the introduction of poultry, gardening, beekeeping, and other work-study activities. Tabora Girls S/S was awarded the Mohammed Raza Pahlavi Prize of $35,000—in Paris for its outstanding literacy work in the community.

The unsatisfied demand for technical workers has been an obstruction to Tanzania's development in self-reliance. Vocational education, in addition to the conversion of trade schools to a secondary-education level, has been expanded through Dar es Salaam Technical College, which will continue to enlarge its technical facilities, and, as planned, will be joined by a sister institution during the period between 1969 and 1974. The commercial courses offered at the college will be moved to a specialized institution at Tabora in the same period. The College of Business Education will be enlarged and, if possible extend training to the Swahili-speaking businessmen. UNESCO's willingness to make a Technical Advisor Component available at the Government's request by the end of 1969 was highly appreciated.

The main expansion in teacher training at the end of the decade supplied the teachers required in the primary-education expansion. The premise on which they are working is that teachers at grass roots must be of the people and hold the same attitudes they wish to persuade. The policy to reduce the number of Grade A trainees and to increase Grade C (the inverse of 1961-66 policy) and to introduce Grade D (later called Grade C special) training is an economy measure; a lack of buildings and the inability to train and then to pay Grade A wages influenced this decision. At the end of 1967 a 100 per cent citizen teacher cadre was effected in primary education. The expectation for secondary and teacher training staffs is set for 1976. Technical-education cadre can not localize as soon.

The integration of National Service with the training program was a response to the criticism that national education came too late in the student training to be effective.[5] Not only does political education become a component of teacher training, but since 1968 socialistic understanding and practice are examined along with practical and theoretical pedagogy. The candidate's commitment to socialism had also been assessed upon entry to the TTC, or College of National Education as now called.

The approach to community service as a role of the teacher followed the British mandate policy, which, after successful implementation for several years, had been replaced with an emphasis on pedagogical quality. This time, however, the spirit and theme of Ujamaa was the dynamic force guiding the action. Places for two hundred in two training colleges are reserved for the retraining of inservice teachers in the new methods and materials pertinent to nation-building attitudes. Upgrading courses by correspondence and vacation classes at TTCs continue.

Higher education has, and is continuing to, expand rapidly with a Faculty of Medicine established in 1968, a Faculty of Agriculture in 1969, and plans for Faculties of Commerce and

---

5. Terrence O. Ranger. "Students and the Nation," *East Africa Journal.* IV: n.2 (May, 1967), p. 5.

Engineering in 1972/73. President Nyerere appointed a committee in July, 1969, to do a ninety-day evaluation of the total
program of the university in respect to its performance and relevancy to Tanzania's developmental needs.[6] It was a timely act
just when the huge institution was about to break up with the
University of East Africa and become the nationalized University
of Dar es Salaam. This step was assumed crucial for better integration with national programs and the educational system of the
country. Reorganization within the ministry placed higher education under the Director of Education in the 1969 act. The university itself has been experimenting and devising schemes for
more active involvement of the students in the nation's problems
while they are still students.

Adult education was transferred to the Ministry of National
Education so that teachers could be better integrated with the
people. Although literacy was an important goal in adult education, it was not the only one; the main emphasis was on rural development. "Literacy will be included in response to popular
demand, as people become aware of its functional importance." [7]
A work-oriented project was organized by the UNESCO for 1967-
69 in selected areas, and is still in full effect in 1971.

An earlier British policy that placed an additional teacher in
primary education for involvement in adult education has come
back in a revised form; with the school functioning as a community
education center in the new policy, the general responsibility for
adult education rests with the teacher. He surveys community
needs and arranges for suitable personnel and classes. Every department is expected to cooperate in this endeavor. The Institute
of Adult Education is responsible for urban needs, for training an
adult-education staff, for research, and for developing a National
Correspondence College for isolated, literate persons. Kivukoni,
the nation's socialist college, has explicitly indoctrinated its student body in that doctrine since the adoption of the Arusha Declaration. Mzumbe and Rungemba, other leadership-training

6. General Notice No. 1657 in the Gazette of the United Republic
of Tanzania. V: n.32 (July 25, 1969), p. 519.
7. Vol. I, p. 157 of the Plan (1969).

courses, fall under the same department as Kivukoni, the Ministry of Regional Administration, and Rural Development.

Special education has recently been included in the annual reports. The Government's policy regarding abnormal children encourages them to attend open schools with other children. Special schools are provided for the blind, deaf, and mute.

The addition of a national culture and antiquities division to the Ministry of National Education reveals the value placed on the cultural aspects of education. This division is concerned with cultural centers, national stadium facilities, and museums.

METHODS, 1967—

The revolutionary policies had first been stated in general terms, so the problem of implementing them involved a search for methods relevant to each locality and level of instruction. Powers and functions of components were defined by law, but the operation was tempered by the humanity and understanding of those who direct it. Those involved in implementing the policies are not those who made the decisions. The elitist mentality of successful students has been another inhibiting factor.

Post-Arusha policies are aimed at national integration and self-reliance. Further integration has been attained in the system by reorganizing the structure, placing the Voluntary Agencies' assisted institutions with the Government schools and giving the Director certain powers over the private schools. This action removed those wrinkles that remained in the UTS. This measure also ensured the implementation of the nation's socialistic commitment in all its schools. In line with nationalization of firms, Tanzania Elimu Supplies, Ltd., was authorized as the sole suppliers of textbooks and equipment to schools. Central Government also took over the responsibility to pay P/S teachers' wages, which amount to 80 per cent of the cost of primary education.

Swahili, the official language of Tanzania, was made the medium of instruction in all P/Ss, effective January 1, 1968. This policy has now been extended to primary-education TTCs and possibly to S/Ss during the succeeding development plan. English, though not eliminated as a class subject, is considered a less positive instrument in rural development than Swahili.

Political indoctrination of the cadre of teachers and administrators of various levels has required much effort. DEOs, of both Administration and Inspectorate branches, attended courses in 1967. All inspectors, at one time or another, also attended a three-week agricultural seminar in order to enable them to give better advice on agricultural projects. Teachers were called to seminars on socialism and self-reliance. Some attended upgrading courses and inservice short courses designed to acquaint them with the current reforms in organization and curriculum. Headmasters and principals share ideas at conferences each year. TANU Youth League set up branches in most schools. University College recommended a Common Course compulsory for all Tanzanian students; the contents would "be determined by the necessity of making the students dedicated to the national goals." [8]

University College has a greater role in national integration than it played in the first years of its existence.[9] Rather than play a passive role, it is taking the position of a third party with government and TANU as the other members. It has social, cultural, economic, and political duties to fulfill. In addition to its function as a center par excellence and its political education course, the college is developing a policy for staff and students that encourages work and service to the community and social integration within the community. The Institute of Education aids by providing special courses for teacher education and researching the needs of Tanzania. The East Africa Examination Council was established to gradually take over the responsibility for the East African version of the Cambridge Overseas Examinations. Beginning in 1968, the certificate awarded was known as the East African Certificate of Education.[10] By June, 1971, the Ministry of Education withdrew from the East African Examination Council in order to provide their own examinations more suited to their educational philosophy.

---

8. "Report and Recommendations of the Academic Board Committee to Consider Suggestions for Change" that have come out of the *Conference on the Role of the University College, Dar es Salaam, in a Socialist Tanzania*, 11 *March*, 1967. Mimeographed.

9. See Resnick, *op. cit.*, which discusses the role of the university from various viewpoints.

10. Earlier the University of East Africa granted degrees for the University of London, Honeybone and Beattie, *op. cit.*, p. 137.

Manpower goals and emphasis have not disappeared in this new era. Educational plans continue to train as many as necessary in the appropriate fields. This policy indirectly gave precedence to the revival of rural development, since few could expect to find a place in the wage economy. Primary schools are geared to rural life, and agriculture has been introduced into the secondary schools. The secondary-school graduate should feel as much a part of the community on the day he returns as on the day he left.

Therefore, schools are to make a way for the student into rather than out of the community. This policy touches the crux of the revolution in education. The Government has stated it clearly:

> The agricultural effort of the school shall be directly linked to that of the community. . . . Agriculture should form part of the life of pupils in and out of school.[11]

The Ministry went further in stressing the need for a "committee of teachers and pupils to plan a program of scientific, productive farming of a reasonable acreage."[12] It also suggested the establishment of a school committee of parents, teachers, and officials of the LEAs at every school for more effective integration within the community. As much as possible, the Government sends teachers back to their home communities. The policy of selecting students and sending them to distant boarding schools has also been revised. Familiarity is the underlying asset.

In order to reach its target for skilled manpower, tied bursaries continue, combinations of arts and science offerings in schools with the High-School Certificate courses are controlled by the Ministry, and a vocational-guidance counseling service has been put into operation. Bursaries are given for study overseas only for courses not offered in East Africa. The reorganization of Forms 5 and 6 is an attempt to diversify the national curriculum and at the same time utilize the resources to their advantage. The vocational-guidance counseling service was pilot tested in 1967 and ready for full-scale operation in 1968. In this service, students are

11. Herrick, op. cit. 161, quoting from the Minister of Education.
12. International Yearbook of Education. "United Republic of Tanzania: Educational Developments in 1967/68" from Mr. Eliufoo's Budget Speech, June 1968. XXX (1968), p. 533.

aided by local advisers who give counsel about the location and availability of courses and opportunities in chosen vocations, and who make preparatory contacts with firms before a student's referral.

Because of its competitive, inegalitarian nature, the issue of examinations and selection has fallen under the hardest attack and scrutiny. With Forms E.F. 65 revised to provide data on a student's school academic achievement, personal health, recommendations of staff regarding his character and potentials, and a Cambridge Mock Examination, pre-selections remove the death threat from evaluation of performance solely on one battery of test answers. These tests exist as the main instrument by which mobility from one level to another is accomplished.

What has been done to ensure quality in the schools other than revamping teacher education and exams? The Government acted quickly on a policy of Africanizing the heads of S/Ss and TTCs after its new commitment to socialism, which, they said, could best be implemented with Africans themselves in positions of authority. In some cases the successor was less academically qualified than his predecessor, but the Government was willing to accept a temporary weakness in favor of an increased understanding and commitment to the national goals. But even though the Government preferred a speedy Africanization, it was not ready to implement the policy at an obvious loss to academic standards. It recognized the need for expertise in certain areas, such as child growth and development, curriculum development, teaching methodology, and specialized technical areas. Expatriates were recruited from a variety of countries with various ideologies to enrich Tanzanian education. In these situations the Government insisted that counterpart training be built in so that qualified citizens can train for eventual control of the position. It is too early to evaluate the holding power of bursaries on teachers, which should improve the quality of secondary education if the high staff turnover in postprimary institutions is reduced.

The plan (1969) speaks of providing vehicles for itinerant educators but does not enlarge upon that function. Certainly this measure must aim for quality in primary education. A delay in practice teaching until Grade C trainees have had two years of concentrated preparation and their National Service experience could increase the efficiency of the student teacher, since it involves more intensive and well-supervised planning. Practice teachers should have no financial problems since they receive 80 per cent of the Grade C entry salary during the year of supervised teaching.

As an expression of self-reliance, Tanzania expects to finance 60 per cent of the expenditures of the current plan and more than 30 per cent of the parastatal investments. IDA is helping to initiate vocational biases into S/Ss, but much of the educational expenditures are and will be shouldered by the communities and the Tanzanian Government. Fees are still levied in primary education as a means of increasing the revenue as well as mollifying parents whose children are not privileged to attend. This has been an issue of contention. Some DEOs report a wastage in Stds. VI and VII, which may be due to a lack in the quality of education; some parents and/or pupils withdraw when they feel the investment is greater than the foreseen results of completing the P/S course.

Schools are encouraged to emphasize the vocational bias of the community in which they are located, e.g., fishing, herding, farming, or commerce. Primary schools join cooperative endeavors or initiate their own projects of self-reliance in agriculture. Boarding schools now aim at self-contained units. Education policies of national integration and self-reliance have not forgotten the teacher. He participates with the school and maintains his own plot of land in a way that reflects his teaching. He also has community service responsibilities, which integrate this key person with the members of all ages in the community, including P/S leavers.

CONTENT, 1967—

In order to implement the principles of Ujamaa and self-reliance, new policies for curriculum content and materials had to be defined. The curriculum had been revised slightly in the 1963 syllabuses, but the classroom content was actually more highly academic than before. The 1966 crises in education forced the planners to recognize that the curriculum in the P/Ss was adequate for only 13 per cent of the students—those who would enter post primary schools. They also realized that the curriculum in educational institutions of all levels could not be relied upon to instill the attitudes that the young nation desired in the products of their education system. They decided it would be wiser to adjust education to the African culture and economic setting and to gear the education offered in formal institutions to the needs, both current and future, of the majority of the pupils. It was time to remove the irrelevancies, which were rooted in the inherited colonial system. Attention was given to both content and to instilling attitudes for socialistic, self-reliant living. The Minister of Education believed that:

> Ultimate success will come when our own teachers, dedicated to socialist principles, are provided with teaching materials that reflect socialist values, to teach pupils who are practising self-reliance in their own communities.[13]

The basic academic program of the P/S and S/S remained essentially the same, adding a few practical courses as they developed. The responsibility for curriculum development was decentralized in 1968, assigning a subject to a relevant department in a TTC for primary education. For secondary education, the country was divided into ten regions with an appointed teacher-coordinator for each subject. The coordinators are representatives to a national panel. Modern curriculum methods of other countries have been analyzed and adapted to Tanzania's situation, e.g., the new math courses and the Nuffield approach to chemistry. The fundamental innovation has been in activity methods and practical studies. The principal aim for primary education is rural development. The intent for introducing biases in secondary education is:

> . . . not to provide vocational or craft courses but rather to give students a general education in which the background to principles and practices in the "bias" area forms a part.[14]

The physical experience in the fields for all levels is a significant part of the work-study, self-reliant type of education.

Since 96 per cent of the population are rural dwellers, agriculture has filled the Government's goals as it related to educa-

---

13. *Africa Research Bulletin.* IV n. 6 (July 15, 1967), p. 812.
14. Simon Pratt, "Report on the Supply of Secondary Level Teachers in English Speaking Africa" *Country Study No. 8: Tanzania.* Overseas Liaison Committee of the American Council of Education. (East Lansing: Michigan State University, 1969), p. ix.

tion, political goals, and ideology. The P/S curriculum, built around agriculture, displays some of the same characteristics of the M/S syllabus of the fifties. When one-third of Tanzania's Std. VII's joined the Std. VIII primary-school leavers in the selection race in 1965 as the first stage for abolishing Std. VIII, in February, 1966, the plight of the majority of leavers became the subject of many letters to the editor of Dar es Salaam's daily newspaper, The Standard, and in Parliamentary debates at that time. The Minister's response in June, 1966, used the manpower approach to appeal for a return of agriculture in the primary course.[15] Because education should fit pupils for future occupations, and because most students returned to the land, schools should prepare pupils through agriculture. Government then requested the Peace Corps to supply vocational- and agricultural-education teachers for upper-primary education. These teachers had barely understood their assignment (educational officials were very slow in finalizing an agriculture program for them) until the university demonstration took place. Less than half a year later the Arusha Declaration and Education for Self-Reliance documents followed, which exacted a revolutionary response quite foreign to the reform barely begun in this one particular area.

The new syllabuses of 1969 and textbooks introduced since 1967 incorporate socialist principles. They find various applications in the school curriculum—both in the academic courses and in the extracurricular activities—that link classwork to manual labor. A period of National Service is now scheduled early in pre-professional training for future teachers. Self-reliance is scheduled for five hours a week on all timetables and is included in the evaluation of a student's progress. It is not a course that can be introduced and ended at will. The course is marginal; students must see the superiority of a socialist world view as applied to the academic experience. These periods are used for keeping school gardens, poultry raising, maintenance of school buildings, and assistance in community-development projects. Students are cautioned to:

---

15. United Republic of Tanzania, Ministry of Education. "Schools and Agriculture: It is the Responsibility of all Schools to Prepare Pupils for Agriculture," EDTT/SI/10/36 of June 4, 1966.

Seek and follow the advice of experts for better results.
Use the harvest for enriching the school's diet before selling
the crops.
Avoid exploitation.
Build a spirit of cooperation at work and share in the
planning.[16]

Radio Tanzania supplements the self-reliance periods with two
weekly programs to schools in self-reliance activities. They also
broadcast weekly for their TANU Youth League branches in the
schools.

Civics courses, compulsory for all levels since 1968, provide a
means for making students realize their social obligations. These
courses are taught by Tanzanian teachers only. Social studies aim:

> . . . not only to make pupils think, but to motivate them
> politically, so they are proud of the past, understand the
> achievements of the present and have the skills and knowl-
> edge to improve their future.[17]

African and Tanzanian history are replacing the imbalance of
the British Commonwealth and European social studies taught
heretofore. This policy builds a solid base of Africanism first and
then conditions the people to reach out to understand other cultures and to feel a part of the world and of Tanzania. The lack of
teaching materials in Swahili impedes the introduction of Swahili
as a medium of instruction in higher education. However, the
ministry has been trying to produce new textbooks as cheaply as
possible and to schedule their introduction according to available
funds.

The Institute of Education, in liaison with the Department of
Education, is busily engaged in practical research and has coordinated many subject panels and workshops. A few of the results of
their efforts had reached the schools by 1968 and 1969, and many
materials were in the developmental or pilot-testing stages. The
Institute of Education has also been researching selection procedures for primary up to secondary education and various social
and education psychology problems.

---

16. "Elimu ya Kujitegemea katika Vyuo kwa mwaka 1968"
Tanzania Education Journal, op. cit, p. 14.
17. *International Yearbook of Education,* 1968, p. 530.

The necessity to concentrate on teaching a body of technical knowledge has perhaps caused the weaker emphasis on the arts and on character training. While primary education is focusing more on the arts, secondary and higher education are still bound strongly with science-based subjects. Mr. Mgonja, the new Director of National Education, declared that Government is "streamlining and reviving the national culture of Tanzania." [18] There is much, however, to revive in traditional arts that is compatible with Ujamaa and self-reliance. For instance, folk tales tell of the person who seeks advancement and personal gain and is punished by natural or supernatural events.

Physical-education courses and forthcoming music syllabuses are reviving national songs and dances. Condon has analyzed Swahili poetry and has found several common themes: political (at national level), moral or philosophical commentaries, and observations about daily living.[19]

Last, but not least, were the curriculum innovations on the university level. The committee appointed by President Nyerere to evaluate the performance of the University College submitted its report to the President before the end of 1969, but the nature of the report was not publicized. Rumor had it that considerable changes would be recommended regarding curriculum reform as well as staffing. However, the staff of the university had already been experimenting with micro-teaching that "applies the principles of student self-involvement, student self-evaluation, group (rather than individualistic) procedures of learning, and tutor-student equality." [20] They had also worked on more political-education relevancy and cultural promotions.

SUMMARY

Educational planners at first responded to the crises of 1966 with infrequent and general directives to their cadre of teachers, but by the end of the decade specific features of the anticipated

18. *The Nationalist,* June 6, 1969.

19. John C. Condon, "Nation-Building and Image Building in the Tanzanian Press," *Journal of Modern African Studies.* V: n.3 (November, 1967), p. 530.

20. See Louis L. Klitzke, "Micro-Teaching at the University College, Dar es Salaam, *"Tanzania Education Journal,* IV: n.12 (May 1968), pp. 19-20.

changes had begun to take shape. African culture and selected colonial educational policies have been revived and adjusted to the current African socio-economic setting.

Because the purpose of the primary and secondary institutions was changing to fit the role of a community education center, a whole new set of organization and curriculum was required. The Education Act of 1969 placed adult education directly under the Director of National Education's control and disbanded the VA's managerial control over assisted schools, thus granting power to the Director to coordinate political education in all institutions. African administrative and supervisory cadre have been called up to replace the vulnerable position of expatriate control. The national culture and antiquities division as well as library services in the Ministry of National Education have been expanding its social responsibilities.

A new concept of the function of formal institutions aims at greater integration in the community of educated and uneducated in cooperative endeavors of a social, economic, and academic nature. This involvement of the school in community life, therefore, assists in developing an attitudinal change toward education and the educated. This concept of integration has influenced the revival of African history and culture, the extended use of Swahili as a medium of instruction, and a curriculum geared to rural development on the primary level and to a vocational bias on the secondary-education level. Basic academic education has changed little, but has been infused with socialistic thinking and enriched with practical experience and self-reliant activities.

Although the Education Department receives around 17 per cent of the Government's budget annually, choices must be made regarding its most profitable use. Universal primary education, a target for 1989, is not yet a reality. Selection procedures at the end of Stds. IV and VII and Forms 4 and 6 remain. The country's economic needs determine postprimary educational expansion. The inegalitarian structure of education with its corresponding selectivity is not an intention of the planners, but a result of the system. It is impossible to eradicate this inequity at present, so efforts have been directed toward tempering the process with pre-selection measures and changing the elitist mentality of those who pass through this system.

In focusing on an education that is more relevant to the national goals, Tanzania has not blinded itself to other ideologies and educational practices. It has examined various modern methods and adapted them to Tanzania. The nation has, however, in becoming more national, cut itself off from its neighbors and other educational systems. Foreign experts will be useful in certain areas for awhile and will be accepted, if the national goals are not jeopardized by their presence.

POLICIES FOR SELF-REALIZATION, 1961-66

1) Although the P/S syllabus of 1963 stated a twofold purpose for primary education—terminal education and a foundation for further education—the latter aim took precedence over the former one. The majority viewed education as a means to a white-collar job, an escape out of the rural community.

2) Integration policies provided for open admission on merit and slightly reduced imparities due to race, religion, sex, and geographical differences as it moved very slowly from the top down in a medium of English. Even then, few could reach positions of leadership.

3) Universal primary education as a target for 1980 operated at lip-service level as expansion in primary education barely kept up with the rate of growth in school-age population.

4) Exams became ends in themselves, and rote learning contributed little to the future of students after the cut-off point.

5) Teacher training was made more appealing by paying monthly allowances to trainees.

6) Adult education, under another ministry, offered courses for adults in urban areas, but no major breakthrough occurred in adult education in the rural areas.

After 1966

1) Primary education expanded to touch the majority; universal primary education was set realistically at 1989.

2) Primary education was planned for life in a rural economy; it was adapted to the needs of the school leavers.

3) The use of Swahili increased in schools.

4) A cultural revival took place, emphasizing traditional arts and crafts.

5) Basic education changed slightly, but was infused with socialist thinking and self-reliant activities.

6) Theoretical and practical experiences were linked together for more effective problem solving.

7) Religious instruction was encouraged, but not made mandatory.

8) Selection to further education was made on merit, school record, and character recommendations.

9) Secondary- and technical-education divisions joined, and a vocational bias was introduced in each secondary school.

10) Courses with a science base emphasized higher education over arts subjects; entrances and courses were controlled to match manpower demands.

11) Organization of adult education was placed in the hands of the headteacher in the community.

12) Adult education aimed for rural development; work-study projects and literacy were provided on public demand.

13) Private schools, although limited in autonomy, were permitted.

The policies of the post-Arusha era emphasized self-realization more than the earlier policies did, especially in primary and adult education where they touched the majority. Special further education was geared to meet the demands of the nation of people.

POLICIES FOR HUMAN RELATIONSHIPS
1961-66

1) Schools were considered agents or models for social change; what was learned at school was supposed to be shared at home, and in that way raise the standard of rural community life.

2) The school, with its use of English and "foreign" curriculum features, was an alien in the community; as they proceeded farther up the educational ladder, students were proportionately divorced from their peers and their families.

3) The system of selection was competitive and stirred up feelings of failure and of personal aggrandisement.

4) Buildings of prestige drained finances that might have been used for social and cultural goals rather than to further separate an elite in a special class.

5) The policy of integration disbanded discrimination and upheld competition by merit.

6) University colleges in the three countries formed the University of East Africa and cooperated in an integrated program.

7) Self-help projects built classrooms, and in some instances, school committees organized the construction of teachers' houses.

8) Uniformity of conditions of service for teachers of VAs and Government was established through Unified Teaching Service.

After 1966

1) Education reorganized on all levels for school-community involvement.

2) All institutions of the community mobilized in a frontal, or broad-base, approach in order to make some gain toward Ujamaa.

3) The Ministry of National Education took responsibility for all educational institutions, including adult education and higher education.

4) The practical content in education increased with communal school gardens, etc.

5) TANU Youth League branches were organized in schools.

6) National Service and tied bursaries required service under a contract.

7) Equality of opportunity became the goal for primary education, but educational privileges beyond primary education were restricted to the needs of skilled manpower.

8) Cooperative endeavors were essential in the competitive system.

9) A break with the University of East Africa was effected to nationalize university education; cooperation in educational research continues.

10) French was taught in S/Ss to facilitate communication with Francophone Africa.

POLICIES FOR ECONOMIC EFFICIENCY
1961-66

1) Basic education was for further training; the targets of the plan (1964) were to raise the per-capita income and to train manpower.

2) The transformation approach with its dependency on foreign aid provided large, prestigious structures, but self-reliance changed the policy to one of frugality and self-help schemes.

3) Selectivity in recruitment for higher levels of education, control of those courses and faculties entered, and tied bursaries for control of employment were introduced.

4) Fees were removed to end educational wastage.

5) Decentralization or delegations of power to local authorities touched a greater amount of resources.

6) New policies called for centralization of the educational system with extensive powers in the hands of the Minister of Education and unification of the curriculum, teachers' conditions of service, supervision, etc.

7) A few teachers' colleges were consolidated for greater efficiency to utilize resources.

8) The Education Planning Unit was established with an emphasis on development of skilled manpower.

9) A salary revision introduced equality with other branches of civil service and high rates of increase at the bottom of the scale.

10) Plans are not made absolute and can change according to need.

After 1966

1) School emphasized making rural life worth living.
    a) Primary education took a rural-development emphasis.
    b) Secondary education was geared to the vocational needs of the community.
    c) Higher education emphasized technical education to meet the practical needs of society; it shifted away from traditional arts subjects.
    d) Upgrading and inservice courses for teachers were established.
    e) Various departments interrelated in political education, especially agriculture extensions and community development, with education.

2) Frugality in program.
    a) Multiple use of buildings.

    b) Staff consolidated for specialized training.

    c) Schools helped provide for operation through income of self-reliant activities.

3) Manpower demands.

    a) Expansion was limited in postprimary schools.

    b) Subjects in Forms 5 and 6 reorganized to meet needs.

    c) Bursaries were offered in areas of greatest need and for certain faculties.

    d) Students were bonded with a five-year contract of service.

    e) Vocational counseling and overseas scholarships were directed toward concrete needs.

4) African-oriented syllabuses and textbooks were produced by national institutions.

5) Nationalization of schools abolished dual management (Government and voluntary agencies); nationalization of university attended directly to nation's needs and problems.

POLICIES FOR CIVIC RESPONSIBILITY
1961-66

1) Integration of four separate racial systems.

2) Distinction between citizen and noncitizen duties and privileges.

3) Civic or citizenship courses on selected levels.

4) Leadership courses under a ministry other than Education.

5) Self-help projects for nation building.

6) Higher education on a regional basis.

After 1966

1) Participation in school-community activities in nation-building schemes.

2) Service to others in self-reliant activities and in National Service.

3) Political education through the Ministry of Education to all educational institutions including adult education and institutes.

4) All organizations joined in a broad-base approach for a frontal attack at community level.

5) TANU provided motivation for rural development.

CHAPTER EIGHT

EMERGENT EDUCATIONAL POLICY PATTERNS IN INDEPENDENT TANZANIA

The purpose of this chaper is to identify the emerging patterns or trends of postindependence educational policies in Tanzania. The data of Chapters VI and VII have been analyzed for expansion patterns, structural trends, patterns in organization and methods, and trends in curriculum.

EXPANSION PATTERNS

The main thrust of expansion during the sixties occurred in postprimary institutions. Secondary education had its lower-school growth acceleration during the Three-Year Plan and higher-school development during the Five-Year Plan (1964). Teacher Training was upgraded over the years and new categories for secondary-education teachers and college tutors appeared. Grade A entrants greatly increased while Grade Cs began a phasing-out process. Technical and commercial training rose to secondary-education level in a few specialized institutions. University College was established and expanded swifty.

Then the main emphasis shifted from training for leadership and skilled manpower to education for the majority in the post-Arusha era. Up to this time P/S expansion was the responsibility of the LEAs, and self-help and local initiative provided the planning for most of the new schools. A new policy moved the emphasis to primary education where Grades I and V are opening at an accelerated pace. Boarding schools on the primary level are rapidly disappearing as day primary schools are beginning to offer a complete P/S course, a step toward universal primary education. Teacher training is expanding to meet the demands for teachers of primary and vocational education. A new Grade D (Grade C special) training course has been created, Grade C has been revived, and a temporary restraint has been placed on Grade A entrants.

A new faculty is formed each year in University College since the nationalization process called for a breakup with the University of East Africa.

Secondary and postprimary schools are now entering a period of restriction in expansion. Education on this level is geared toward practical vocational needs in the country. The issue of overdevelopment has again concerned planners.

Adult education was given much emphasis in the sixties. The latest plan stresses rural-development activities and suggests that literacy not be the initial activity but should be introduced when it is demanded. By 1971 fingerprinting in lieu of a signature has been eradicated in several areas.

The expansion patterns developing in Tanzania coincide with the main emphasis of the development plans—first, preparation of a leadership, and later, education for the masses.

PATTERNS DEVELOPING IN THE EDUCATIONAL STRUCTURE

Integration

a) *Cooperation with other Governmental agencies and departments.*

The plan (1964) was the first comprehensive development plan in which the programs of each ministry joined to form a unit. The creation of the Ministry of Development Planning and cooperation with National Service and TANU Youth League has increased interministerial communications.

b) *One national, centralized system of education.*

At independence there were four racial-education systems. The four separate councils and systems were replaced by one new advisory council and one system in the *Education Ordinance of* 1961. There was also a dual system of management—government with central and local authorities and voluntary agencies with assisted and unassisted schools. Dual management was not abolished until the Education Act of 1969, although the Minister of Education had been granted such extensive powers in 1961 that the assisted VA schools were categorized as "public" with Government schools rather than "private" with unassisted schools. To receive assistance, VAs accepted open enrollment, followed a common syllabus, common selective procedures after a common exam, and the same disciplinary measures with LA schools, and shared authority for governance of postprimary institutions with Government representatives on the Boards of Governors.

Steps toward a national education system progressed in the sixties. VA supervisors were withdrawn in the reorganization of the inspectorate in 1963 and Central Government took complete responsibility for the supervision of schools. UTS unified the conditions of service for teachers in the various agencies. All teachers of assisted schools were placed directly in the civil service when the Education Act of 1969 required managers of VA schools to hand over all assisted schools to the Director of National Education. When adult education and higher education were placed directly under the jurisdiction of the Director in the same act of 1969, the scope of the national system of education increased, for the Director now had control of political education in educational institutions of all levels and even of informal education. The nationalization of the university came in 1970. The name of the ministry itself has changed to befit a national system of education.

Private schools have not been abolished, but they lost some autonomy in the Education Act Supplement No. 62 of 1968 when the Minister of Education was granted power to establish Boards of Governors in these schools also. They remained with certain restrictions at the end of the sixties and had a coordinator—an Education Secretary General—at the national level functioning between them and the ministry.

c) *School-community integration.*

The emphasis on basic education on further education or training set the school apart from its environment. Schools on all levels, especially boarding institutions, tended to become islands. Nyerere commented in *Education for Self-Reliance,* "The school . . . is not part of the society. It is a place children go to and which they and their parents hope will make it unnecessary for them to become farmers and continue living in the villages." P/S leavers and postprimary graduates looked for employment in urban areas. The illiterate farmers remained with their growing children in the community. Had the leavers filled a particular niche in the community, there would not have been any such school-leaver problem. Higher levels, by virtue of the boarding situation and European-biased curriculum, accentuated the gap between students and their home villages. Separated from their communities a large part of their lives, students never really shared the poverty of the community and village.

The post-Arusha concept of school-community integration and involvement is revolutionary. First of all, the school functions as a community education center with primary and secondary education as only one aspect of its educational activities. The head-teacher is responsible for ascertaining the needs of the community people, identifying suitable instructors, and arranging for classes.

Secondly, primary education is geared to vocational needs of the community. The curriculum includes self-reliance activities on communal farm projects. The increased usage of Swahili as a teaching medium in P/Ss and in primary education TTCs reduced the use of English, a non-African language, in the African milieu. Secondary education has not yet reached this point of change, but educational planners expect to make the transition in the next plan, i.e., later in the seventies.

Thirdly, education and political organizations have joined. National Service and TANU Youth League branches have reached into the schools. These both provide opportunities for contact between school and nonschool personnel.

Decentralization versus Centralization

Great powers were vested in the Minister of Education by the Education Ordinance of 1961. In turn, certain of his powers were delegated to other authorities, i.e., LEAs and Boards of Governors. According to Dodd, the delegation of power was accomplished in such a way that, even though LEAs and Boards of Governors were responsible for specific levels of the system, the central control was strengthened.[1] These bodies of authority mustered together resources for expansion and implemented Central Government's policies. They were not granted policy-making rights. Central Government maintained a policy of granting priority to those districts that joined in self-help projects.

The hierarchy of structure and operation has been defined throughout the sixties: the powers of the Minister of Education, of the LEAs and Board of Governors in 1961; of the DEOs and

1. Dodd, "Centralization of Education . . ."

PSIs in 1963; of the Education Secretary Generals and Education Secretaries in 1965; and the rights of public and private schools. The inegalitarian structure that formed was not the intent of the planners, but the result of the system.

Africanization

Since there were few trained Africans to man the innumerable positions opened to them at independence, they had the opportunity of choosing to remain in teaching or to join government or industry. As a result, there was a brain drain from teaching; African staff in secondary education and teachers' colleges were few. Teachers for East Africa and Peace Corps programs supplied teachers during this critical period.

With many more positions in government filled by Africans by the mid-sixties, African staff in educational institutions increased more rapidly. Self-sufficiency in manpower by 1980 was set as a target in the plan (1964). Then, the *Arusha Declaration* appeared and self-reliance included in the educators' interpretation Africanization of the staff and heads of schools as soon as possible. Africans were appointed as heads of boys' S/Ss and TTCs early in 1967. The lack of qualified African female staff impeded a similar action in girls' S/S. By 1969 there was almost a 50:50 or 1:1 ratio of secondary expatriate and citizen staff. The increase of citizen teachers is approximately two hundred per year. There is still a lack of vocational-education citizen staff. Technical and higher education had a higher percentage of expatriates. The operational positions of the ministry were manned almost exclusively by citizens at the end of the decade.

PATTERNS IN METHOD AND ORGANIZATION

Language Policy

Swahili, English, and Asian vernaculars were the main language media used in schools at independence. By 1965 they were reduced to English and Swahili only, and Swahili was made compulsory as a subject in S/S for the School Certificate exam. By 1968 Swahili was extended in the P/S (except in a few selected English medium schools for expatriate children) as the medium of instruction to the end of the primary course. As a counterbalancing measure, educators proposed to introduce English as a subject in Std. I instead of Std. III and to provide an intensive English course to students recruited to S/S. English, the medium for instruction in primary-education TTCs, has been replaced by Swahili. Swahili is also used in S/Ss for religious instruction and other subjects not included in "pure" academe. Lack of literature published in Swahili is a hindrance toward a complete transition at this level. In summary, the language pattern has been toward greater Swahili usage in communication, but English remains the second language.

Economy Measures
a) *Self-help projects.*

Primary education was placed in the hands of the LAs in 1961. Nation-building schemes, such as dispensaries, roads, schools, and other assets, were not an integral part of the Three-Year Plan. These projects were a result of "unplanned enthusiasm" and formed the basis for the inclusion of nation-building schemes in the first Five-Year Plan.

b) *Buildings.*

Local councils drew up approved patterns for proposed school buildings and teachers' houses, which would be followed by self-help schemes for primary education. Secondary-education buildings needed the Central Government's approval at different stages during the building process before the next part of the grant-in-aid was delivered. These boarding schools, as well as teachers' houses on the lower levels, maintained a standard above that enjoyed by the majority of Tanzanians.

The greatest gap between student life and the average citizen occurred at University College, an institution well endowed with gifts from many nations and agencies. No economy measures of frugality were involved in its planning. When the issue of this extravagance was raised, various means for better utilization of the property were proposed.

The educational planners have become increasingly concerned about using resources to fullest capacity. Double-streaming schools, increasing the ratio of pupils per teacher in higher education, and extracting multiple use from existing buildings are some of the measures developing under the self-reliant approach to education. In fact, some of the latest UNESCO advisory missions suggest that the planners may be overdoing this point, as for instance, in the use of Technical College facilities for the proposed Faculty of Engineering.

c)   *An Education Planning Unit was established.*

The need for an education planning unit was presented in the World Bank report. Thomas and Tobias conducted manpower surveys, and the establishment of the unit followed in wake of the planning of the Five-Year Plan (1964).

The Planning Unit considers investment in education that serves the economy. Postprimary educational opportunities were determined by the manpower requirements, both in the accelerated expansion in further education throughout the sixties and the slowing down of this expansion in further education in the post-Arusha era. The efficiency of its program was substantiated by the degree of self-sufficiency reached in many occupations by 1970. In fact, its economic goals have overridden the social and cultural aspects of education; e.g., the certificates became more important than what was learned.

A commendable feature of the Planning Unit has been its ability to reevaluate policies and to change its programs during a plan period.

d)   *Manpower restrictions and programs.*

Acceptance into higher-education programs in the late sixties has been limited in order to avoid overdevelopment in areas where the economy could not absorb graduates. This was done in various ways: Expansion itself was controlled by the planners; Forms 5 and 6 offerings were reorganized in order to control the higher School Certificate course offerings; vocational counseling steered students into careers or preparation for careers where the need was greatest; bursaries were offered with priority given to the most urgent need; and scholarships for overseas were granted only for courses that are not offered in East Africa.

In addition to controlling the training for certain positions, the bursaries offered are tied with a contract for five years of service to the Government. Equally important is the National Service requirement of two years of service.

The decision to shorten the P/S course from eight to seven years required fewer teachers in full primary schools and makes universal primary education possible at an earlier date. The demand for teachers in the primary expansion at the end of the sixties has been met by training teachers with less prerequisites than Grade A trainees. National Service provides Grade A teachers for two years of service in P/Ss at a great reduction of cost. Providing seven years of education for one child is considered a better investment than dividing the same amount of money between two children and then abandoning them to illiteracy.

e) *Salary scales.*

The recommendations of the ADU Commission were incorporated into the 1965 salary revisions. Salaries of teachers were equalized with salaries of similarly qualified Africans in other services. The rate of increase in wage in the higher levels is frozen in comparison to the upward swing in lower-category manpower job salaries.

Quality of Education

Quality in education during 1961 to 1966 was approached through improvement of pre-service and inservice training of teachers. Teacher-training courses themselves were upgraded and syllabuses were improved.

The quality of post-Arusha education focused more on the relevancy of education and on a practical, problem approach. Political education was used as a motivating force. Schools are considered economic as well as educational institutions. Secondary education and technical divisions were fused in the reorganization of the ministry. Teachers are given refresher and upgrading courses and preservice training has been revised to follow the new emphasis.

Additional preselection features of recruitment to the next higher level of education affects the quality of students. Instead of a selection on one battery of tests taken in one day (or several), the school record of the student has become increasingly important. In the case of the secondary-education student, a Mock Cambridge exam is taken in mid-Form 4 and its results are used as a basis for pre-selection. Primary Form E. F. 65 has been revised to include data on the student's health, the staff's recommendations of the student's character and potentials for further training, as well as detailed academic records for several past years.

PATTERNS IN CURRICULUM CONTENT

Academic versus Practical Learning

A set of new syllabuses for primary education were issued in 1963, and those of 1969 showed very little change in basic education. The purposes and biases of education change the relevancy of the education offered during the years. The 1963 syllabuses were academic centered. For example, agriculture up to that time had been practiced in school *shambas,* or small fields. The 1963 syllabus reduced the amount of ground to garden size and considered the subject an outgrowth of the academic courses, which referred to agricultural science.

The 1969 syllabuses subscribed to the same basic education, but the difference involved infusion of socialism and self-reliance into the total curriculum. Socialism, rather than agriculture as in the colonial policies, is the key factor of the curriculum. Self-reliance activities are not limited to certain blocks of time.

Since primary education aims at rural development, agricultural education has also been entered into the timetable through various subjects and activities. Local biases and adaptations are made on the primary- and secondary-education levels in agriculture and vocational education. In secondary education, the introduction of a vocational bias has been slower, but good progress into the planning stage was made in 1970. Adaptation to the community bias has changed the school calendar in some localities.

Practical learning in the post-Arusha era appears revolutionary compared to the highly academic learning of the mid-sixties. Rote learning for exams had become so common that students were criticized by expatriate teachers for their difficulty in problem solving. Generally, exams were still deciding factors in recruitment, but now questions on political and vocational education were included on the various levels, and as scheduled, all exams—even School Certificate—will be set in Tanzania by the end of 1971.

Practical learning links theoretical learning with reality. It provides motivation through its economic and educational rewards. Physical and mental exercise are required of students as well as teachers. This kind of learning carries the classroom into the community at times.

Africanization of the Curriculum

The 1963 syllabuses began the process of decreasing the over-balance of European history and geography and increasing that of the African and local units. By the end of 1966 the Institute of Education at University College was involved in cultural research, and the syllabuses of 1969 were decidedly more Africanized in their viewpoints as well as in subject matter.

Since 1967 certain subjects are reserved for African teachers, such as political education and history.

New Subjects in the Curriculum

Political education has been offered on more levels and given greater time in the weekly schedule. French language is not compulsory, but expanded in the sixties in many S/Ss. Swahili as a subject was made compulsory on the secondary level in 1965. While not a new subject religious instruction is encouraged, but not mandatory.

SUMMARY

In an analysis of trends and patterns emerging in the post-independence educational policies, it became quite evident that the purpose of formal education changed during the decade. Whereas education in the pre-Arusha years focused on future educational opportunities and rewards, the post-Arusha years emphasized terminal education at each level and education for the masses. Even though the major focus of most educational expansion during the sixties was on the training of leadership, primary education managed to keep a growth rate approximately equal to the school-age group increase through the initiative of parents and local leaders in self-help schemes.

The sixties were years of great institutional expansion. The increases in enrollment are indeed striking for such a poor, developing nation. Basic education was still geared to future prospects in training and occupations. Those who were a part of the few selected to achieve their aspirations have filled esteemed positions in the civil service and in industry. At the end of a decade of independence, targets of self-sufficiency in skilled manpower were on the verge of being realized as a result of this former educational purpose.

But there were other consequences of a narrow, academic curriculum manipulated for a high number of "passes" on entrance examinations. The end became greater than the means, and relevancy was that which developed skill in taking exams. Rote learning and fluency in English became advantageous skills.

The post-Arusha policies changed this direction and built around a purpose of education for the majority. This change required policies of a revolutionary flavor, wherein the 1961-66 policies were carry-overs of the colonial days with certain added reforms. Even post-Arusha policies repeat the jargon of the colonial eduacators from pre-World War II days—"adaptation" and education for the community. Now terminal education at each level does not change basic education, but demands school-community integration and learning experiences with practical, everyday problems. "Foreign" features in the curriculum are giving way to local and African awareness, tradition, political education, and local vocational biases; and the whole curriculum is infused with socialism and self-reliance. Cooperation with other departments and agencies has increased in order to implement this policy. Adult education has become a part of the Ministry of National Education and thus tied to formal schooling.

In the post-Arusha policies the school is not conceived as an "island" where pupils and teachers live on a different scale from that of the masses. Integration through Ujamaa activities in the neighborhood and ties with TANU Youth League and National Service provide practical political-educational experiences.

The system of education has slowly taken on a national character, one area in which the evolution of educational policies has not been skewed by a revolution. First, the separate systems were unified into one. Certain rights and privileges of the VAs were curtailed in the powers granted to the minister, the new PSIs and the Boards of Governors; and dual management was finally discontinued by the Education Act of 1969. This system had developed greater control at the center even though the delegation of power has spread. Private schools still have a place.

Nationalization and adaptation brought Africanization into personnel and curriculum. Swahili, the national language, has been replacing English as a medium of instruction.

One of the greatest controlling and limiting factors of postindependence education in Tanzania has been the scarcity of funds. The plan (1964) set a target for universal primary education for 1980. Even though the educational planners have supported the policy for universal primary education, they were unable to shift the emphasis of educational expansion to the primary level until the end of the decade. Despite their support for this principle, other policies gained priority and only about 50 per cent of the school-age population has entered P/S each year. Money was invested in higher education instead of postprimary education at a much greater cost per person. But frugality was not an outstanding feature of higher education, especially of Dar es Salaam University.

The introduction of self-reliance in the plan (1964) affected educational policies several years later in consolidation for better use of resources, tied bursaries, National Service, salary revisions, and reducing the eight-year primary course to seven without a loss in curriculum content. Multiple use of structures has been a more recent policy. The Education Planning Unit implemented a fusion of secondary- and technical-education divisions in the ministry and introduced a vocational bias in selected S/Ss. At the end of the decade the issue of overdevelopment became a real concern.

Between 1961 and 1966 policies of expansion, organization, and curriculum focused on developing a few for leadership roles. The many who were not so privileged had difficulty finding employment, and a school-leaver problem developed. A commendable feature of the system was the ability to change policies and programs in the middle of a five-year plan. The policies of the post-Arusha era contain socialism as the key and are geared to education for the majority. The structure of the system has changed slightly and economic stringency, although practiced, has not permitted all the changes that might otherwise have taken place.

CHAPTER NINE

A LOOK AHEAD

A GENERAL STATEMENT

The objectives, structure, method, and content of the period between 1961 and 1966 were built on the Government's decision to "pursue a policy of educational development in line with economic requirements." The Government, therefore, emphasized institutional building. Basic education at the primary level was geared to further education.

After 1966 the policy for educational development still involved economic development, but the emphasis shifted to the educational needs for rural masses.

CONCLUSIONS

1) There is less congruence between the goals of the President and the educational policies in the pre-Arusha days than in the post-Arusha days.

2) The newer policies of post-Arusha days emphasized social and cultural goals; whereas Nyerere's policies balanced social and vocational goals. The pre-Arusha policies, in general, emphasized vocational goals; while policies of social and cultural aspects were deliberately given second place. Nyerere's goals show more concern for individual rights and group relations than had the previous educational policies.

3) In general, educational policies regarding economic efficiency have emphasized self-sufficiency for leadership and highly skilled manpower, pursuing one of Nyerere's aims for economic efficiency, but they failed to do much for the middle-level categories, for the education of the rural adult population, and for primary-school children in preparation for raising the standard of living.

4) There is a trend in educational policies similar to Nyerere's transformation approach with large investments, and the framework for his later Ujamaa village approach.

201

5) As the seventies began the educational planners were formally committed to the principles of socialism as stated by Nyerere, and the policies of the time were significantly in agreement with the aggregate of his goals. The policies, however, that support competition, such as selectivity, strict control of higher-education entrees and courses, and insufficient opportunity for primary education, mitigate against Nyerere's goal of building attitudes of equality.

IMPLICATIONS AND RECOMMENDATIONS

Several inferences can be made about the new patterns in educational policies that had been forming in the post-Arusha era.

1) Tanzania is committed to a revolution in education that will touch the majority of people. Its leadership has articulated national goals and has been shaping up the nation's resources for maximum use toward achieving these goals;

2) The education planners are formally committed to the principles of socialism as stated by President Nyerere, and a few specifics of the changes anticipated have begun to take form;

3) Their commitment includes a thorough revision of education at all levels;

4) The formal education of children is only one function of the educational institutions in the community. An integrated front of all members of the community (with all departments offering their expertise) is considered essential for practicing socialist principles and self-reliance;

5) African culture is important, but needs adaptation to the present milieu; and

6) The high cost of postprimary education (e.g., £1,000 per annum per pupil in the University of Dar es Salaam equals the per capita income of fifty ordinary Tanzanians) is permissible if translated into skilled manpower for nation-building service.

This chapter considers the question: Are the nation's policies suited to the achievement of its goals? There is no blueprint that its citizens can follow, for no nation has a similar situation. Therefore, all experimentation is trial and error.

There were many variables in the educational patterns of the late sixties that can confound the purposes of the educational planners at this trial-and-error stage:

1) Remote control at the center versus local face-to-face relations in the formation of attitudes and values during social change;
2) Motivation and mobilization of the majority in a manner appropriate versus inappropriate to their commitment;
3) The social environment of schools complementing versus alienating the aims of the schools and vice versa;
4) Traditional culture streamlined to a modern milieu versus conservatism;
5) Frugality promoting efficiency and manpower goals versus social goals and egalitarian demands;
6) Teachers instructing in the way they were taught versus an untried method;
7) Teachers', students', and parents' countersocialization from the formerly accepted goals; and
8) The replacement of the gap between uneducated and educated by a gap between education of the majority and of the few.

There are also external factors that need to be considered:
1) The success of the Ujamaa villages both socially and economically;
2) The ability of TANU to motivate mobilization;
3) The place of the other agencies—churches, cooperatives, etc.

The recommendations that follow center on two main themes or tasks of education: rebuilding attitudes of equality and increasing production.

1) It is recommended that initiative and experimentation take place at the local level:

The key to revolution, in this investigator's opinion, is social change arising through a change of aspirations and attitudes on the local level; paper work in Central Government offices is useless unless its effect reaches the local level.

Why stress the local level? First of all, face-to-face intensive relations with others are essential for changes of deeply rooted attitudes, for attitudes are changed through experience and through adoption or imitation. Secondly, from the historical perspective of experience, paper work was remote and did not effect the changes desired. Thirdly, an analysis of culture reveals that cultural clusters in oral literature and social organization that are not similar indicate a need for local or regional planning for varying emphasis. Fourthly, the more integrated the values and institutions are in a society, "the more successfully [the society] can respond to social change by resisting, facilitating, incorporating, or adjusting."[1] Where could the greatest integration take place but in a closely knit group of people? Fifthly, according to Mazrui's stages in African cultural emphasis—an attempt to prove that Africa could master Western culture, an attempt to repudiate Western culture and unearth Africa's traditional heritage, and a capacity to take pride in some aspects of African culture without need to renounce Western culture at the same time—[2] Tanzania appears to be entering the third stage.

The second stage, one of nationalism, was observable by its concentration of power in the Central Government and development of National Education. Mamuya feels that the Government had no alternative but to identify more closely with their forefathers and less with Western culture at the time of independence.[3] In most scholars' opinion, the third stage—the synthesis of the two cultures—is the healthiest stage. And Government has chosen a pattern of rural development at this time. It is logical that education follow with progressive methods of learning geared to rural development.

Sixthly, a theory of state determines the system of education. Tanzania's Government has chosen a democratic, egalitarian way of life. This choice requires less central control and autocracy. Seventhly, most educators feel that it is necessary to understand one's own community first and then, through that understanding, the broader world. And last, a lesson from Nyerere's transformation approach and birth of the improvement approach to rural-community development through indigenous, voluntary Ujamaa

1. A proposition of Bernard Berelson and Gary A. Steiner. *Human Behavior: An Inventory of Scientific Fndings.* (New York: Harcourt, Brace & World, 1964), p. 615.

2. Ali A. Mazrui, *The Anglo-African Commonwealth: Political Friction and Cultural Fusion* (London: Pergamon Press, 1967), pp. 107-08.

3. Matthew Salim Mamuya, "Religion and Society in Tanganpika: An Encounter of Western Civilization with Traditional Culture" (MA thesis, University of Pennsylvania, 1965), p. 81.

experiments is an example of the need to concentrate on initiative and experimentation at the grass-root level.

2) It is recommended that groups in the community join together through participation in common experiences:

Social scientists believe the greater the common experience, the greater the social cohesion of a group. Common experiences cannot be found in formal education because the literacy rate is too low. Again, the school has been an alien institution in the community, which has trained students out of the community. Those who remained there have relapsed to traditional methods instead of influencing the adult members of their families with the knowledge they acquired in school.

The school, therefore, appears to be a poor agency for community development unless there is a team spirit developed among the school, the party, the church, and the cooperatives. A political apparatus must provide the strongest motivation for this cooperative endeavor and serve as a catalyst to join the school and community on new principles, not on former ones covered over with a new facade. And education must be viewed as an exchange of ideas among members of society.

Recognition of the power structure in the community is an important factor for initiating common experience. Not all the uneducated are unwise; only half of the school-age group have entered Std. I. They have not been abandoned because of their lack of intelligence, but because of inadequate educational facilities. The brain drain has removed educated leaders to the urban areas. Certainly some of the wise, illiterate farmers who remain have natural leadership abilities. Hapgood feels that community innovators hold more power on the land than politicians.[4] By using the power structures of the community and joining various groups in common experiences, the participation of each one is crucial and stabilizes social change.

If Kaayk's conclusion is true—that it is not so much primary-school leavers who are unwilling to return to the land as the community who mistrusts them[5]—then peer-group interaction of both

---

4. David Hapgood, "The Politics of Agriculture," *Africa Report*, XII: n. 8 (November, 1968), p. 11.

5. Jan Kaayk was a member of the Dutch research team in Sukumaland in the mid-1960's. His book is not yet published.

educated and uneducated on common projects during formal schooling years is crucial and might be the remedy to promote greater cohesiveness and to avoid "misfits" in society. If formal schooling truly becomes just one of the many facets for education in the community and agriculture is held in esteem by all ages and groups of people, common experiences can occur.

The common experience, then, takes place on the land and the organizers are the leaders of the various agencies plus the community's local structural leaders. The attitudes of the community are important to consider, and the economic progress is a must to provide incentives for improving the standard of rural life.

3) It is recommended that the Central Government continue to maintain a national system of education, but limit its power to selected areas of control:

Cultural clusters of similarity in oral literature and social organization indicate some bases for educational planning on a national level, emphasizing a common cultural heritage. Political stability and national unity are encouraged through an emphasis of a common heritage. Decision makers should be free to display what is to be taught and which attitudes should be implanted.

What are the main areas in which, in this investigator's opinion, the Central Government ought to function?

a) Engage in educational research throughout the Republic, then disseminate the findings to the public;

b) Provide for expert assistance or counseling to the innumerable local communities, provide general directions regarding content and methods, an indicative rather than prescriptive approach;

c) Provide for citizenship training throughout the nation;

d) Continue to make provision for and coordinate private schools;

e) Provide some means for recruitment to postprimary education on some general terms; and

f) Coordinate the educational institutions that are not on the local level.

4) It is recommended that primary education continue to receive main emphasis, and rural adult education and primary-school leavers gain consideration in work-study projects:

In these efforts, education planners should join the force of other departments and agencies. For instance, education planners could accompany their efforts with rural-education programs on Tanganyika Broadcasting Corporation (TBC) programs as well as receive and announce progress reports from the communities.

This recommendation is related to the first one and is very important for bridging the generation gap. Dumont feels that adult education should follow only after children have been educated, for children, he says, are a better long-term investment.[6] Castle, on the other hand, would support the above recommendation; he says women and girls need to be educated in order to raise all parts of the social economy together.[7] Unless women are involved in the new national culture, their children will not be weaned away from tribal or sectional interests.

Doob's study on communication among various African groups shows no great difference between illiterate and educated groups in respect to *knowledge* of the world outside, but he suggests that "the psychological effects of literacy are significant because being literate seems to affect *attitudes* of motivation toward participating in modern ways and to increase awareness of life outside the immediate environment.[8] Thus, as Edward Shils argues in "Political Development in the New States" in the April, 1960, issue of *Comparative Studies in Society and History*, it is not so much what is taught as the fact that an experience gives one an intensified feeling of his own value. Lest the impression be left that no thought need be given to WHAT is taught, a warning ought to be thrown out that misinformation and ignorance can weaken progress and can turn large groups of peasants into counterrevolutionaries, according to A. Langa in "Socialism and Rural Revolution" in the November, 1968, *Africa Report*.

Adult education, then, may be an indirect technique for the countersocialization or the creation of new attitudes. If this were verified, it would be just as significant to expose adults, and nonschool youth, to the same experiences of development as youth

---

6. Rene Dumont, *False Start in Africa*, translated by Phillis Nauts Ott (New York: Praeger, 1969), p. 209.

7. Castle, *op. cit.*, p. 140.

8. Leonard Doob, *Communication in Africa* (New Haven: Yale University Press, 1961), p. 257.

in formal educational institutions. (It would probably be less expensive also.) Much more research needs to take place in reference to the communications of attitudes, values, and the formation of behavior. Roach declares that there is also a dearth of research on the development of child behavior as well as the attitudes of those exposed and those not exposed to education.[9]

5) It is recommended that more research and experimentation on granting rewards for contribution rather than for degrees take place:

a) Material rewards of further education should be reduced; the fortunate have the most interesting and responsible jobs and ought not to be rewarded with incomes enormously higher than people who have primary education or less. Housing and transportation privileges should not be so much greater. The student of higher education has already had his self-awareness increased through selectivity and does not need luxurious rewards to increase his self-aggrandisement.

b) The self-taught man is one who knows self-reliance from experience. Provision should be made for him to prove his ability and join the ranks at the level on which he can make the greatest contribution. The policy of self-reliance is not only having what you use, but also using what you have.

c) As a corollary to this recommendation, programs could be implemented for imparting high-level prerequisites outside the formal educational system. These could be offered at much less cost than formal education programs, since the prerequisites for a certain job do not carry the gamut of curricular content given in the higher-education curriculum. Inservice training and adult-education courses can supplement for the individual what he desires after he is already employed.

d) At the same time, education planners should not lower the academic standard for entering the University of Dar es Salaam, for the school-leaver problem would only rise to a later age group.

6) It is recommended that concept learning receive greater effort:

---

9. Penelope Roach, *Political Socialization in the New Nations of Africa* (New York: Teachers College Press, 1967), pp. 22-23.

Education psychologists on the American scene have shifted in the past two decades from an emphasis on social adjustment and personal development to an emphasis on intellectual development and achievement. If American children can profit by concept learning, so can Tanzanians, and doubly so since they have had a much greater emphasis on repetition of facts and memorization than Americans have had. They are also growing up in a land where emergent values are different from traditional values, and they need to resolve the conflict of the two in the most effective way for their own development as well as for their society.

Concept learning offers the best method for understanding and evaluating the changes taking place in the society and nation. The introduction of the school farm and other practical experiences in S/S met with unfavorable reactions by the students who felt threatened that this action was undermining their security. Even upgrading the esteem for agriculture and manual labor did not guarantee that the attitudes of students have changed. The concept method of instruction is therefore recommended as superior to the more factual approach that has taken precedence in the past. Concepts and principle methodology require a general education and integration of much knowledge for productive thinking. It also requires a study of the environment and the application of sciences to everyday technology.

7) It is recommended that traditional values are respected and preserved as much as possible, but traditional methods are streamlined to the modern technological age:

Most sociologists and anthropologists agree that traditional values cannot be completely ignored or despised; that schooling should not be divorced from the African background. Two scholars propose that "the more a social change threatens or appears to threaten the traditional values of the society, the greater the resistance to the change and the disorganization." [10] The risk of uprooting a child from his environment is minimized by respecting traditional values.

Cultural values contribute to the humanistic and artistic part of education, which helps to bring out the full potential of an individual. The consequences of the absence of security derived

---

10. Berelson and Steiner, *op. cit.,* p. 614.

from the cultural heritage will be ambivalence, uncertainty, and bewilderment in the face of the moral problems.

Much of the Africanization of the curriculum and revival of African culture has been done in conjunction with African neighbors, but the commitment to socialism and self-reliance has narrowed the international cooperation in favor of greater nationalization. And yet, the isolation is not so great as one might assume, because most of the Bantu philosophy is egalitarian and compatible with Ujamaa-ism. Bantus cover much African territory.

Time will reveal how successfully traditional culture can be adapted to modern situations. One observer contends that many of the very institutions that gave expression to customary virtues "are condemned and are being rapidly demolished because they are inconsistent with national unity and the development of a modern state." [11] Societies in which traditional principles worked are usually categorized as circumscribed, static, and conservative.

8) It is recommended that, in adapting (ruralizing) the curriculum, a general education with Ujamaa-ism at its center receive special attention:

Since most of the people (over 90 per cent) will need to depend on the land for their livelihood in future years, education will need to emphasize skills that are usable in rural occupations. British colonial policies emphasized agriculture, but did not change the Africans' aspirations toward urban salaried jobs. In fact, a negative attitude developed toward agriculture in general in the colonialist era.

To raise the dignity of agriculture, viewed as the lowest form of labor in the colonial days, to an honorable position, is a delicate task. Students rate modern farming high on the occupational lists, but see that it does not pay, according to J. D. Heijnen's "Results of a Job Preference Test Administered to Pupils in Std. VIII, Mwanza, Tanzania," in Education, Employment, and Rural Development, edited by James R. Sheffield (Nairobi: East African Publishing House, 1967). Secondary-school students rated "Training more young people to be good farmers" as second in problems

11. Burke, op. cit., p. 207.

facing the country in Koff and Von der Muhll's study.[12] Joel D. Barkan, in his 1968 ASA paper, "Elite Perceptions and Political Involvement in University Students in Ghana, Tanzania, and Uganda," concluded that students are more concerned with acquisition of security than power. In order to convince students individually and collectively that farming is satisfying, they must see success.

The issue of agricultural education in primary and secondary schools has been controversial. The general consensus of scholars is that "the teaching of vocational agriculture in primary schools is of little or no value in producing future farmers or agricultural technicians." [13] With the exception of Meister and Dumont, sociologists and economists agree that schools have more important work to do than be bogged down with special vocational training. They must prescribe a course that builds the essential skills of literacy and, as Guy Hunter says:

> . . . an emphasis on the practical, illustrations from the real conditions of the rural economy, and a power to awaken the imagination of pupils as to the possibilities of a fruitful, modern life in a rural economy which has been transformed by the application of scientific methods.[14]

Adviser Anderson prescribes a general education, heavy in sciences, that permits shifts easily between curriculums. He suggests that an individual postpone occupational choice as long as society can allow him to remain out of employment.[15]

The school-leaver problem is probably more of an agricultural-economics problem than one of formal education. As such, it is probably more important to control what is done outside the

---

12. David Koff and George Von der Muhll, "Political Socialization in Kenya and Tanzania," *Journal of Modern African Studies,* V (May, 1967), pp. 13-51.

13. AEG Marham, FAO education adviser, based his conclusion on an "impressive volume of experience" in his 1965 lecture cited by Skorov, *op. cit.,* p. 61.

14. In "Manpower Employment and Education in the Rural Economy of Tanzania," *Africa Research Monograph No.* 9 (Paris: UNESCO/IIEP, 1966), p. 38.

15. C. A. Anderson, "The Social Context of Educational Planning," *Fundamentals of Educational Planning No.* 5 (Paris: UNESCO, 1967).

school than what is done inside. Dodd sees success of agricultural experiences in school directly related to what is happening in the adult world of agricultural development.[16] His criterion for measurement of success in agricultural education is what the school leavers do.

The curriculum, then, needs to develop a study of the environment and how to maximize the possibilities in primary and secondary education. Much attention should be given to observation and deductions. Primary education should include the basic notions of technology, and secondary education should include a practical bias. Pre-vocational education must be accompanied by a humanistic and artistic education to achieve the various goals of Ujamaa-ism.

9) It is recommended that pre-service and in-service training of teachers receive careful attention for their role as examples of Ujamaa, as teachers, and as part of a community coordinating team:

The great faith placed in teachers by President Nyerere and educators is not all misplaced, for they will probably play an effective role in socialization; 86 per cent of primary and 177 per cent of secondary-student respondents were willing to trust teachers, according to Koff and Von der Muhll's study.[17] Students spend hours with the teacher and perceive his true attitudes and values; Spindler contends that the teacher conveys his conflicts over traditional and emergent values into the classroom.[18] So the teacher, who spends much time with students, influences them toward or away from the goals of Ujamaa-ism.

Teachers tend to teach in the manner they were taught. Is it, therefore, possible for teachers to adopt new attitudes and initiative not heretofore a part of their experience? Time will reveal how much can be accomplished. This whole area of communication of attitudes, values, and behavior needs research for greater understanding in dealing with the problem. Margaret Mead's "total" rather than "selected" change is impossible in a situation

---

16. Wm. Dodd, 'Education for Self-Reliance': A Study of its Vocational Aspects (New York: Teachers College Press, 1969), p. 26.

17. Koff and Von der Muhll, op. cit., p. 23.

18. George D. Spindler, The Transmission of American Culture (Cambridge: Harvard University Press, 1959).

where the same teachers, same structure, and same population exist.

The younger, new brand of teacher has the greater possibility for success in attitudinal change. First of all, his youthful, adventurous spirit encourages change. Secondly, he himself experienced his former aspirations thwarted by the "failure" to rate a selection on to further schooling. Then he looked to National Service to provide for his frustration. After a period of National Service, he took a year of teacher training to combine pedagogical methods with his political education. He will probably be the more versatile teacher as well as one whose heart is set on successful teaching, for after three years he will be upgraded if he has done well. The teacher who is upward mobile is better able to teach for the future because his outlook is attuned to change, contends Mead in *The School in American Culture*, a 1950 Inglis lecture (Cambridge: Harvard University Press, 1951). More intensive training at that point in his experience would be more profitable to him than preservice training courses because of his own desire to teach and because of his experience in the classroom. He should be able to work vicariously with other P/S leavers and nonschool children in the community if his own position is not rewarded too greatly to set him off from them socially.

10) It is recommended that sociologists, psychologists, anthropologists, and consultants lend more aid through research, which can guide the education planners:

Educational change and social change are relative and reciprocal. Each needs periodical reevaluation. Some of the areas in which further research needs to be done are the following:

a) Child growth and development in the African setting;
b) Communication of attitudes, values, and behavior;
c) Attitudes and values of educated and uneducated to see the difference caused by education;
d) How to recruit for further education without unduly focusing away from terminal-type education at each level;
e) Control of inputs to postprimary education and tied bursaries without ignoring freedom of choice and human dignity;

   f) How far material rewards can be decreased without cutting
      off motivation;

   g) How far indoctrination or persuasion can be advanced and
      still accommodate and desire critical thinking.

   In summary, to reflect the times, schools will need to become
more community centered and preparatory for life in the local
rural areas. Revisions in the structure and content of education
must be made in order to implement the necessary changes. Cau-
tion must be given on one point. Any change suggested in isolation
will disrupt other aspects of education or social change. The
required revisions demand the sanction of a complete team of
educators, economists, sociologists, political scientists, and anthropologists as well as a total perspective of the ramifications of each
change.

GLOSSARY

African socialism as upheld by the Arusha Declaration, sometimes called "democratic socialism": According to President Nyerere, it is based on three main principles: 1) equality and respect for human dignity, 2) sharing of the resources that are produced by the efforts of the people, and 3) work by everyone and exploitation by none.

Arusha Declaration: The official statement of socialism adopted by TANU and delivered by President Nyerere at Arusha on January 27, 1967.

CNE: College of National Education. See TTCs.

Democratic one-part state: Tanzania's politics are based on a one-party democracy. "In the Tanzanian context, 'democracy' means above all the right of every citizen to participate in free political discussion. It includes free association, but only within the framework of the single national movement."[1]
"We call our Government democratic because we, the people, hold the power in the State. For practical reasons we choose a number of fellow citizens who are then charged with the work of the government. They represent us, the people, and fulfill our wishes."[2] Tanzania holds popular elections. The last one took place in 1970 when a number of politicians discovered, as had many of their counterparts in 1965, that they had divorced themselves from their constituencies and had not been voted in again.

Forms: Corresponding to high-school grades, or classes.
DEO: District Education Officer (Administration). See also PSI.

GEE (General Entrance Examination): Taken for recruitment to S/S. See PSLE.

LAs (Local Authorities): The new names for the NAs after 1961.

LEAs (Local Education Authorities): Correspond to NAEC after independence.

M/Ss (Middle Schools): Offered Standards V to VIII.

NAs (Native Authorities): The Governmental bodies of power on the local level.

NAEC (Native Authority Education Committee): Delegated power of responsibility over primary education on the local level.

P/Ss (Primary Schools): Offered elementary education; any part of the primary course with grades one to, and including, seven/eight.

---

1. William Tordoff, *Government and Politics in Tanzania* (Nairobi: East Africa Publishing House, 1967), p. 3.
2. Hildebrand Meienberg, *Tanzanian Citizen: A Civic Textbook* (Nairobi: Oxford University Press, 1966), p. 20.

215

PSI: Primary School Inspector; later changed to DEO Inspectorate.

PSLE: (*Primary-School Leavers Examination*): The new name for the (GEE since 1967.)

REO: Regional Education Officer.

Self-reliance: The *Arusha Declaration* defines it as follows: "From now on we shall stand upright and walk forward on our feet . . . Industries will come and money will come, but their foundation is THE PEOPLE and their HARD WORK, especially in AGRICULTURE."

S/Ss (*Secondary Schools*): Correspond to our high schools.

S.d./Stds.: Standards correspond to elementary grades.

Tanganyika and Tanzania: Tanganyika, under the Germans from 1885 to World War I, a mandated territory under the British between the wars, and a trusteeship territory of the United Nations with British administration from 1946 until it gained its independence in 1961, continued under the same name until it joined with Zanzibar, the island along the eastern coast. On October 24, 1964, the name of the union was changed to the United Republic of Tanzania. In this study the names Tanganyika and Tanzania are used as synonyms and refer to the mainland only, which was originally called Tanganyika.

TANU: an abbreviation for the Tanganyika African National Union, the sole political party.

TTCs: Teacher Training Centers later Teacher Training Colleges. Now (CNE, College of National Education.)

Ujamaa: The Swahili word given to socialism by Nyerere denoted more than the meaning usually given to the English socialism including all the subtle associations of bonds of kinships, tribal hospitality, and the welfare obligations of the extended family.

UTS: Unified Teaching Service.

VAs (*Voluntary Agencies*): Mostly mission groups that composed the second part of the dual system with Government for management and control of schools.

BIBLIOGRAPHY

A. *Sources from the Government of Tanganyika/Tanzania*

Great Britain. Colonial Office. *Education for Citizenship in Africa.* Col. No. 216. London: Her Majesty's Stationery Office, 1948.

    Education Policy in British Tropical Africa. Cmd. 2374. London: HMSO, 1925.

    Mass Education in African Society. Col. No. 186. London: HMSO, 1943.

    Memorandum on the Education of African Communities. Col. No. 103. London: HMSO, 1935.

    Report for the Year 1958. Col. No. 342. London: HMSO, 1959.

    Report for the Year 1960. Col. No. 349. London: HMSO, 1961.

Jamhuri ya Muungano wa Tanzania. *Hotuba ya Waziri wa Elimu ya Taifa, Mheshimiwa C.Y. Mgonja, Mbunge kwenye Kikao cha Makadirio ya Mapato na Matumizi ya Fedha, Juni,* 1970 (Budget Speech) Government Printer, Dar es Salaam, 1970.

Tanganyika African National Union. *The Arusha Declaration and TANU's Policy on Socialism and Self-Reliance* (Eng.) and *Azimio la Arusha na Siasa ya TANU juu ya Ujamaa na Kujitegemea* (Swah.) Dar: Government Printer, 1962.

Tanganyika Government. "Report of Education Conference 1925: Together with the Report of the Committee for the Standardization of the Swahili Language," *Report of the Proceedings of Conference between Government and Missions held* 5-12 *October,* 1925. Dar: Government Printer. 1925.

    "Report of the Committee on the Integration of Education 1959." Dar: Government Printer, 1960.

    Department of Agriculture. "Report on an Inquiry into Agricultural Extension at Primary and Middle Schools." Dar: Government Printer, 1956.

    Department of Education. *Annual Reports. (Triennial Survey of Education* for 1955-57.) Dar: Government Printer, 1956.

    Middle School Handbook No. 1. Dar: East Africa Literature Bureau, 1960.

    Muhtasari ya Mafundisho katika Middle Schools. Dar: Government Printer, 1955.

    "Non-African Education." *A Report by Donald Riddy and Leslie Tait.* Dar: Government Printer, 1955.

217

Primary School Handbook No. 1. Dar:East African Literature Bureau, 1960.

Provisional Syllabus of Instruction for Middle Schools. Dar: Government Printer, 1952.

Provisional Syllabus of Instruction for Secondary Schools. Dar: Government Printer, 1955.

Syllabus of Instruction for African Schools, Primary. Dar: Government Printer, 1947.

Syllabus of Instruction for African Schools, Secondary. Dar: Government Printer, 1947.

A Ten-Year Plan for the Development of African Education. Dar: Government Printer, 1947.

Trade Training: Technical and Commercial Education. Dar: Government Printer, 1954.

Legislative Council of Tanganyika. "Ten-Year Plan for African Education (Scheme for Revision)" Dar: Government Printer, 1950.

The Basis for an Integrated System of Education. Government Paper No. 1, 1960. Dar: Govermnent Printer, 1960.

Wizara ya Elimu. *Muhtasari ya General Science.* Dar: Tanganyika Standard, 1964.

Muhtasari ya Mafundisho ya Afya katika Shule za Primary. Dar: Government Printer, 1963.

Muhtasari ya Mafundisho ya Elimu ya Viumbe katika Shule za Primary. Dar: Government Printer, 1963.

Muhtasari ya Mafundisho ya Historia. Dar: Government Printer, 1963.

Muhtasari ya Mafundisho ya Kiswahili katika Shule za Primary. Dar: Government Printer, 1963.

Muhtasari ya Mafundisho ya Sanaa na Kazi za Mikono. Dar: Tanganyika Standard, 1963.

Muhtasari ya Shule za Primary Zenye Mafunzo kwa Kiswahili. Dar: Government Printer, 1963.

United Republic of Tanganyika and Zanzibar. *Five-Year Plan for Economic and Social Development, 1 July 1964 to 30 June 1969.* Vols. I and II. Dar: Government Printer, 1964.

The *Gazette* of the United Republic of Tanzania, *Bills, Acts,* and *Subsidiary Legislature.* (From 1960 to 1969, inclusive.)

United Republic of Tanzania. *Tanzania's Second Five-Year Plan for Economic and Social Development, 1 July 1969 to 30 June 1974.* Dar: Government Printer, 1969. (Vols. I, II, and IV.)

"United Republic of Tanzania: Educational Developments in 1966," by Mr. J. E. Mhina, *International Yearbook*. Vol. XXIX: No. 310 (1968), pp. 403-11.

"United Republic of Tanzania: Educational Developments in 1967/68" from Mr. Eliufoo's Budget Speech, June 1968, *International Yearbook*. Vol. XXX (1968), pp. 527-35.

Idara ya Habari. "Risala ya Rais, Mwalimu Julius K. Nyerere kwa Kuadhimisha Sikukuu ya Uhuru, Desemba 9, 1967." Dar: Government Printer, 1967.

Ministry of Economic Affairs and Development Planning. *Background to the Budget, Manpower and Education*. Dar: Government Printer, 1968, also 1969 year.

Ministry of Education. "Schools and Agriculture: It is the Responsibiilty of all Schools to Prepare Pupils for Agriculture," EDTT/SI/10/36 of 4 June, 1966.

Ministry of Information and Tourism. *Tanzania Today*. Nairobi: University Press of Africa, 1968.

Wizara ya Elimu. *Conference on the Role of the University College, Dar es Salaam, in a Socialist Tanzania, 11 March 1967*. Mimeographed.

Wizara ya Elimu ya Taifa. *Muhtasari za Shule za Msingi kwa Madarasa ya I-VII*. Dar: Government Printer, 1969.

Tanzania Education Journal. Vol. I to V, 1965 to 1969.

B.   *President Nyerere's Speeches and Writings*

Nyerere, Julius K. "Africa's Concept of Democracy." *Spearhead* (November 1961), p. 8.

Arusha Declaration Answers to Questions. Dar: Government Printers, 1967.

"Communitarian Socialism" in *Seeds of Liberation*, edited by Paul Goodman. New York: G. Braziller, 1964. pp. 184-91.

Education for Self-Reliance. Dar: Government Printers, 1967.

Freedom and Socialism/Uhuru na Ujamaa. Dar: Oxford University Press, 1968.

Freedom and Unity/Uhuru na Umoja. Dar: Oxford University Press, 1967.

"How Much Power for a Leader?" *Africa Report*, Vol. VII: No. 7 (July 1962), p. 5.

The President explains "The Arusha Declaration—Teach-In," August 5, 1967. Dar: Dar es Salaam Printers Ltd., 1967.

"Public Ownership of Property." February 2, 1967. Mimeographed.

"Socialism: An Attitude of Mind," *East Africa Journal*, Vol. IV: No. 2 (May 1967), pp. 24-30.

Socialism and Rural Development. Dar: Government Printer, 1967.

"Socialism is not Racialism." February 14, 1967. Mimeographed.

"Tanzania's Political Policies and their Economic Effects," *East Africa Journal*, Vol. III: No. 5 (August 1966), pp. 30-40.

Uhuru na Maendeleo. Dar: Government Printer, 1968.

"Ujamaa: the Basis of African Socialism" in *The Ideologies of Developing Nations*, edited by Paul E. Sigmund. New York: Prager, 1967. pp. 288-94.

Ujamaa: Essays on Socialism. New York: Oxford University Press, 1968.

"Walimu Wasaidie kuleta Mapinduzi ya kuondoa unyonge," *Tanzania Education Journal*, Vol V: No. 13 (June 1969), p. 9.

"We Cannot Afford to Fail," *Africa Report*, Vol. IV: No. 12 (December 1959), pp. 8-10.

"Will Democracy Work in Africa?" *Africa Report*, Vol. V: No. 2 (February 1960), pp. 3, 4.

C. *Articles, Reports and Speeches*

Allen, John. "The Case for Developing Swahili, " *East Africa Journal*, Vol. II: No. 2 (May 1965), pp. 29-34.

American Association of Colleges for Teacher Education. "Analysis of Teacher Education in East Africa, 1969." For AID. An unpublished report.

American Embassy, "Some Comments on the Achievements of Tanzania's Program of 'Education for Self-Reliance'" Memo A-248 of November 7, 1969.

Anderson, C. A. "The Social Context of Educational Planning," *Fundamentals of Educational Planning, No. 5*. Paris: UNESCO, 1967.

Arrighi, Giovanni, and John S. Saul. "Socialism and Economic Development in Tropical Africa," *The Journal of Modern African Studies*, Vol. VI: No. 2 (1968), pp. 141-69.

Awori, Aggrey S. "East African University Must be Africanized," *East Africa Journal*, Vol. IV: No. 8 (December 1967), pp. 16-22.

Balogh, Thomas. "Misconceived Educational Programmes in Africa," *Universities Quarterly*, Vol. XVI: No. 3 (June 1962), pp. 243-49.

Barkan, Joel D. "Elite Perceptions and Political Involvement of University Students in Ghana, Tanzania, and Uganda." Paper at the 11th Annual Meeting of ASA, October 18, 1968, at Los Angeles.

Bennett, George. "Kenya and Tanzania." *African Affairs*, Vol. LXVI: No. 264 (1967), pp. 329-35.

Bigelow, Karl W. "Problems and Prospects of Education in Africa," *Education and Foreign Aid.* (The Inglis Lecture, 1964). Cambridge, Mass.: Harvard University Press, 1965, pp. 43-74.

Brown, Irene. "Tanzania's Education Revolution." *Venture,* Vol. XIX: No. 6 (June 1967), pp. 13-17.

Cameron, John. "The Integration of Education in Tanganyika," *Comparative Education Review,* Vol. XI: No. 1 (February 1967), pp. 38-56.

"Wastage in Tanganyika with special reference to Primary Schools," *Teacher Education,* Vol. VI: No. 2 (November 1965), pp. 103-14.

Chagula, W. K. "The Role of the Elite, the Intelligentsia, and Educated East Africans, in the Development of Uganda, Kenya, and Tanzania," *East Africa Academy, the Second Foundation Lecture,* September 20, 1966, Kampala, Uganda.

Chukwukere, B. I. "African Culture and Modern African Education," *Africa Quarterly,* Vol. III: No. 2 (September 1963), pp. 92-100.

Cliff, Lionel. "Tanzania Socialism—New Emphasis," *Venture,* Vol. XIX: No. 6 (June 1967), pp. 4-8.

Collins, Sidney. "The Social and Economic Causes of Wastage in Schools and other Educational Institutions in Tanganyika," *Teacher Education,* Vol. V: No. 1 (May 1964), pp. 40-50.

Condon, John C. "Nation-Building and Image Building in the Tanzanian Press," *Journal of Modern African Studies,* Vol. V: No. 3 (November, 1967), pp. 335-54.

Dodd, William. "Centralization of Education in Mainland Tanzania," *Comparative Education Review,* Vol. XII: No. 3 (October 1968), pp. 268-80.

" 'Mobile Teachers' Colleges' in Tanzania," *Teacher Education,* Vol. VI: No. 3 (February 1966), pp. 232-36.

Edgington, D. W. "Tanzania," *The British Survey,* No. 230 (May 1968).

Eliufoo, S. N. "Education for Service-Men Only: Tanzania Government Policy for Higher Education." *East Africa Journal,* Vol. IV: No. 8 (December 1967), pp. 23, 24.

Evans, P. C. C. "American Teachers for East Africa," *Comparative Education Review,* Vol. VI: No. 1 (June 1962), pp. 69-77.

Fox, Lorene K. "Learning Ventures in East Africa," *Childhood Education,* Vol. LXI (March 1965), pp. 343-48.

Frost, Emma. "School Libraries in Tanzania," *UNESCO Bulletin for Libraries,* Vol. XXIII: No. 6 (November-December 1969), pp. 300-09.

Gappert, Gary. "An American on Science in East Africa," *Transition,* Vol. II: No. 5 (August 1962), pp. 28-30.

Geiss, Immanuel. "Nyerere's Political Philosophy—2," *Venture*, Vol. XIX: No. 6 (June 1967), pp. 11-13.

George, B. G. "Education for Africans in Tanganyika: a Preliminary Study," *Bulletin No. 19*. Washington: U.S. Department of Health, Education and Welfare, Office of Education, 1960.

"Information on Education around the World: Recent Educational Developments in Tanganyika," Vol. 54: Washington: U.S. Government Printing Office, 1961.

Gladden, E. N. "Adult Education in Tanganyika: The Story of Kivukoni," *International Journal of Adult and Youth Education*, Vol. XV: No. 4 (1963), p. 171-78.

Glitsch, R. E. "Report on Mission to Tanzania, 12-13 March 1969." Africa Sector, TER, UNESCO, 30 May 1969. Mimeographed.

Griffiths, V. L. "The Problems of Rural Education," *Fundamentals of Educational Planning No. 7*. Paris: UNESCO/IIEP, 1968.

Hapgood, David. "The Politics of Agriculture," *Africa Report*, Vol. XIII: No. 8 (November 1968), pp. 6-11.

Harbison, Frederick. "Educational Planning and Human Resource Development," *Fundamentals of Educational Planning No. 3*. Paris: UNESCO/IIEP, 1967.

Helleiner, G. K. "Tanzania's Second Plan: Socialism and Self-Reliance," *East Africa Journal*, Vol. V: No. 12 (December 1968), pp. 41-50.

Honeybone, R. C. "The African University and the Preparation of Teachers: Pre-Service Teacher Education, particularly at the Undergraduate Level." *Documents of the Conference on the African Univrsity and National Educational Development*, September 8-18, 1964. Columbia Teachers College. Mimeographed.

Hornsby, George. "German Educational Achievement in East Africa," *Tanganyika News and Records*, No. 62 (March 1964), pp. 83-90.

Hunter, Guy. "Manpower Employment and Education in the Rural Economy of Tanzania," *Africa Research Monograph No. 9*. Paris: UNESCO/IIEP, 1966.

International Bank for Reconstruction and Development. *The Economic Development of Tanganyika: Report of a Mission Organized by the International Bank for Reconstruction and Development*. Baltimore: John Hopkins Press, 1961.

International Labor Office. "Report to the Government of Tanzania on the Development of Vocational Training." from a January-February 1965 visit ILO/TAP/Tanz./ R.1. Geneva: ILO, 1965.

King, Jane, "Planning Non-formal Education in Tanzania," *Africa Research Monograph No. 16*. Paris: UNESCO/IIEP, 1966.

Kinunda, Michael J. "Certain Aspects of the Implementation of Reforms in Education," *IIEP Occasional Papers No. 14.* Paris:UNESCO/IIEP, April 1969.

Klinglehofer, E. L. "Occupational Preferences of Tanzanian Secondary School Pupils," *The Journal of Social Psychology,* Vol. LXXII (1967), pp. 149-59.

           "Performance of Tanzania Secondary Schools Pupils on the Raven Standard Progressive Matrices Test, *The Journal of Social Psychology,* Vol. LXXII (1967), pp. 205-15.

Knight, J. B. "The Costing and Financing of Educational Development in Tanzania," *Africa Research Monograph No. 4.* Paris: UNESCO/IIEP, 1966.

Koff, David, and George Von der Muhll. "Political Socialization in Kenya and Tanzania," *Journal of Modern African Studies,* Vol. V (May 1967), pp. 13-51.

Korner, Karl. "Education in the German Colonies," *Education Yearbook,* 1931, *International Institute of Teachers Colleges, Columbia University.* New York: Bureau of Publications, Teachers College, 1932, pp. 595-643.

Langa, A. "Socialism and Rural Revolution," *Africa Report,* Vol. III: No. 8 (November 1968), pp. 19, 20, 37, 38.

Legum, Colin and Margaret. "Nyerere's Political Philosophy—1," *Venture,* Vol. XIX: No. 6 (June 1967), pp. 9-11.

Lema, Anza Amen. "The Challenge of Teaching in our Secondary Schools Today," *The Tanzania Education Journal,* Vol. IV: No. 12 (May 1968), pp. 12, 13.

Lewis, Arthur J. "Education for Self-Reliance Must Underlie Curriculum Development in East Africa," *East Africa Journal,* Vol. V: No. 4 (April 1968), pp. 27-33.

Linton, Neville. "Nyerere's Road to Socialism," *Canadian Journal of African Studies,* Vol. II: No. 1 (Spring, 1968), pp. 1-6.

Lucas, Eric. "Education in Africa: A Panoramic View (A Review Article)," *East Africa Journal,* Vol. VII: No. 2 (February 1970), pp. 18-22.

Mazrui, Ali A. "Language and Politics in East Africa," *Africa Report,* Vol. XII: No. 6 (June 1967), pp. 59-61.

Mohiddin, Ahmed. "Ujamaa: A Commentary on President Nyerere's Vision of Tanzania Society," *African Affairs,* Vol. LXVII: No. 267 (April 1968), pp. 130-43.

Morrison, David. "Educating Citizens for Tanzania." Makerere Institute of Social Research Conference Paper, 1967. Kampala, Uganda.

Mwingira, A. C. "The Role of the University: Solving the High Level Manpower Problem in East Africa," *East Africa Journal,* Vol. II: No. 5 (August 1965), pp. 38-44.

Mwingira, A. C., and Simon Pratt. "The Process of Educational Planning in Tanzania," *African Research Monograph No.* 10. Paris: UNESCO/IIEP, 1966.

The *Nationalist,* for 1968-69.

Nour, M. A., and H. K. F. Hoffman. "Higher Agricultural Education," Serial No. 1105, March 1969, UNESCO.

Odhiambo, T. R. "The Crisis of Science in East Africa," *East Africa Journal,* Vol. III: No. 1 (April 1966), pp. 3-30.

Pratt, R. C. "East Africa's University Problem," *East Africa Journal,* Vol. I: No. 5 (August 1964), pp. 3-11.

Pratt, Simon. "Report on the Supply of Secondary Level Teachers in English-Speaking Africa," *Country Study No.* 8: *Tanzania.* Overseas Liaison Committee of the American Council of Education. East Lansing: Michigan State University, 1969.

Prosser, Roy. "Social Change and Adult Education," *East Africa Journal,* Vol. I: No. 2 (May 1964), pp. 13-17.

Ranger, T. O. "Students and the Nation," *East Africa Journal,* Vol. IV: No. 2 (May 1967), pp. 3-8.

Rivers-Smith, S. "Education in Tanganyika Territory." *Educational Year-book,* 1931, *International Institute of Teachers College, Columbia University.* New York: Bureau of Publications, 1932, pp. 141-97.

Schindler, Clayton M. "Tanzania Teacher Education," *Journal of Teacher Education,* Vol. XIX: No. 3 (Fall 1968), pp. 305-11.

"School Leaver Problems in Tanzania," *East Africa Journal,* Vol. III: No. 2 (May 1966), p. 27.

Shils, Edward. "Political Development in the New States," *Comparative Studies in Society and History,* Vol. II: No. 3 (April 1960), pp. 227-233.

Skorov, George. "Integration of Education and Economic Planning in Tanzania," *Africa Research Monograph No.* 9. Paris: UNESCO/IIEP, 1966.

Smith, Anthony. "The Missionary Contribution to Education (Tanganyika) to 1914," *Tanganyika Notes and Records, No.* 60 (March 1963), pp. 91-109.

Svendsen, K. E. "Socialist Problems after the Arusha Declaration," *East Africa Journal,* Vol. IV: No. 2 (May 1967), pp. 9-15.

University College. "Report on Research 1967-68." Mimeographed.

UNESCO. *Declaration of the Principles of International Culture Cooperation.* Paris: UNESCO, 1967.

The *Development of Higher Education in Africa, conclusions and recommendations of the Conference,* 1963. Paris: UNESCO, 1963.

225   Social Revolution in Tanzania

Final Report on the Conference on Education and Scientific and Technical Training in Relation to Development in Africa, Nairobi, 16-27 *July* 1968. Paris: UNESCO/OAU, 15 November 1968. Mimeographed.

"Work-Oriented Adult Literacy Pilot Project: Plan of Operation." Paris: UNESCO, 1967. Mimeographed.

"Working Party on Higher Education, 1967." Serial No. 1105, Annex 5, Page 4. Paris: UNESCO, 1967.

World Survey of Education, Vol. I: Educational Organization, 1954. Vol. II: Primary Education, 1958. Vol. III; Secondary Education, 1961. Vol. IV: Higher Education, 1964. Paris: UNESCO.

United Nations Visiting Mission to Trust Territories in East Africa. Report T/1345 and T/1550 of 1957 and 1960. New York: U.N. Publications.

"Vocational and Social Training of Primary School Leavers in the African Countries of the Commonwealth." Commonwealth Secretariat, London. Mimeographed.

Von der Muhll, George. "Education, Citizenship and Social Revolution in Tanzania." ASA Conference paper, November 1967, in New York. Mimeographed.

Wilson, John. "Education and Cultural Change in Africa," *Teachers College Record,* Vol. LXIII: No. 3 (December 1961), pp. 189-95.

Wright, Marcia. "Local Roots of Policy in German East Africa," *Journal of African History,* Vol. IX: No. 4 (1968), pp. 621-30.

D. *Books*

Adams, David, and Robert H. Bjork. *Education in Developing Areas.* New York: David McKay Co., Inc., 1969.

Almond, Gabriel, and Sideny Verba. *The Civic Culture.* Princeton: Princeton University Press, 1963.

Berelson, Bernard, and Gary A. Steiner. *Human Behavior: An Inventory of Scientific Findings.* New York: Harcourt, Brace & World, 1964.

Bienen, Henry. *Tanzania; Party Transformation and Economic Development.* Princeton: Princeton University Press, 1967.

Burke, Fred B. *Tanganyika: Preplanning.* (National Planning Series No. 3.) Syracuse: Syracuse University Press, 1965.

"Tanganyika: the Search for Ujamaa" in *African Socialism,* edited by William Friedland and Carl Rosberg. Stanford: Stanford University Press, 1964.

Burns, D. G. *African Education: An Introductory Survey of Education in the Commonwealth Countries.* London: Oxford University Press, 1965.

Cameron, Sir Donald. *My Tanganyika Service and Some Nigeria.* London: Allen & Unwin, 1939.

Cameron, John. *The Development of Education in East Africa.* New York: Columbia University Press, 1969.

Castle, E. B. *Growing Up in East Africa.* London: Oxford University Press, 1966.

Coombs, Philip H. *The World Educational Crisis: A Systems Analysis.* Paris: UNESCO/IIEP, 1967.

Cowan, L. Gray. *The Dilemmas of African Independence.* New York: Walker and Co., 1965.

Cowan, L. Gray, James O'Connell and David G. Scanlon, *Education and Nation-Building in Africa,* New York: Praeger, 1965.

Curle, Adam, *Educational Strategy for Developing Societies; A Study of Educational and Social Factors in Relation to Economic Growth.* London: Tavistock Publications, 1963.

DeCecco, John P. *The Psychology of Learning and Instruction: Educational Psychology.* Englewood Cliffs, N. J.: Prentice-Hall, Inc. 1968.

Diamond, Stanley (ed.) *The Transformation of East Africa: Studies in Political Anthropology.* New York: Basic Books, 1966.

Dodd, William A. *Education for Self-Reliance in Tanzania: A Study of its Vocational Aspect.* New York: Columbia University Press, 1969.

Dumont, Rene. *False Start in Africa.* Translated by Phyllis Nauts Ott. New York: Praeger, 1969.

Giles, H. Harry. *Education and Human Motivation.* New York: Philosophical Library, Inc., 1957.

Golan, Tamar. *Educating the Bureaucracy in a New Polity: A Case Study of L'Ecole Nationale de Droit et D'Administration (ENDA), Kinshasa, Congo.* New York: Teachers College Press, 1968.

Hanson, J. W., and Cole S. Brembeck. *Education and the Development of Nations.* New York: Holt, Rinehart and Winston, 1966.

Hanson, J. W., and Geoffrey W. Gibson. *African Education and Development since 1960: A select and annotated bibliography.* East Lansing: Michigan State University, 1966.

Harbison, Frederick, and Charles A. Myers. *Education, Manpower and Economic Growth.* New York: McGraw-Hill, 1964.

Heijnen, J. D. "Results of a Job Preference Test Administered to Pupils in Std. VII, Mwanza, Tanzania," in *Education, Employment, and Rural Development,* edited by James R. Sheffield. Nairobi: East Africa Publishing House, 1967, pp. 431-43.

Herrick, Allen Butler, et al. *Area Handbook for Tanzania*—1968. DA Pam. No. 550-62. Washington: U.S. Government Printing Office, 1968.

Honeybone, R. C., and J. K. Beattie. "Mainland Tanzania" in *Examinations*

(The World Yearbook of Education, 1969), edited by Joseph A. Lauwerys and David G. Scanlon. New York: Harcourt, Brace & World, Inc., 1969.

Hunter, Guy. *Education for a Developing Region: A Study of East Africa.* London: Allen and Unwin, 1963.

"Manpower and Educational Needs in the Traditional Sector with special reference to East Africa" in *Manpower Aspects of Educational Planning: Problems for the Future.* Paris: UNESCO/IIEP, 1968. pp. 161-80.

"Primary Education and Employment in the Rural Economy with special reference to East Africa" in *Educational Planning,* edited by Bereday and Lauwerys. (The World Year Book, 1967), New York: Harcourt, Brace & World, Inc., 1967, pp. 242-56.

Iliffe, John. *Tanganyika under German Rule, 1905-12.* Cambridge: The University Press, 1969.

Jones, Thomas Jesse. *Education in East Africa.* East Africa Commission for the Phelps-Stokes Fund. London: Edinburgh House Press, 1925.

Karefa-Smart, John. *Africa: Progress through Cooperation.* African Conference on Progress through Cooperation, Kampala, Uganda, 1965. Council on World Tensions. New York: Dodd, Mead, and Company, 1966.

Kazamias, Andreas M., and Byron G. Massiales. *Tradition and Change in Education.* Englewood Cliffs, N.J.: Prentice-Hall, 1965.

Kitchen, H. (ed.). *The Educated African: A Country-by-Country Survey of Educational Development in Africa,* Ch. 10, "Tanganyika." New York: Praeger, 1962, pp. 145-59.

Lewis, L. J. (ed.). *Phelps-Stokes Reports on Education in Africa.* London: Oxford University Press, 1962.

MacDonald, Alexander. *Tanzania: Young Nation in a Hurry.* New York: Hawthorn Books, Inc., 1966.

Macridis, Roy. *The Study of Comparative Government.* New York: Random House, 1964.

Malinowski, Bronislaw. *The Dynamics of Culture Change: An Inquiry into Race Relations in Africa.* New Haven: Yale University Press, 1958 (c. 1945).

Maluki, Eliud. "Development Priorities" in *The Challenge of Development* (Contemporary African Monograph No. 7) Nairobi: East African Publishing House, 1968, pp. 41-58.

Mason, R. J. *British Education in Africa.* London: Oxford University Press, 1959.

Mazrui, Ali A. *The Anglo-African Commonwelath: Political Friction and Cultural Fusion.* Oxford: Pergamon Press, 1967.

Mboya, Tom. "Vision of Africa" in James Duffy and Robert A. Manners (eds.), *Africa Speaks.* Princeton: D. Van Nostrand, 1961, pp. 13-27.

Mead, Margaret. *The School in American Culture*. The 1950 Inglis Lecture. Cambridge: Harvard University Press, 1951.

Meienberg, Hildebrand, *Tanzanian Citizen*. Nairobi: Oxford University Press, 1966.

Meister, Albert. *East Africa: The Past in Chains, the Future in Pawn*. Translated by Phyllis Nauts Ott. New York: Walker & Co., 1968c.

Moffett, J. P. *Handbook of Tanganyika*, 2nd edition. Dar: Tanganyika Government, 1958.

Mustafa, Sophia. *The Tanganyika Way*. London: Oxford University Press, 1962.

Mwingira, A. C. "Tanganyika's Educational Development" in *The Challenge of Development*. Nairobi: East African Publishing House, 1968, pp. 130-40.

Novack, David E., and Robert Lekachman. *Development and Society: The Dynamics of Economic Change*. New York: St. Martin's Press, Inc., 1964.

Nsekela, A. J. *Minara ya Historia ya Tanganyika: Tanganyika hadi Tanzania*. Arusha: Longmans of Tanzania, 1965.

Onuoha, Father Bede. *The Elements of African Socialism*. London: Andre Deutsch, 1965.

Pye, Lucian W. *Communications and Political Development*. Princeton: Princeton University Press, 1963.

Resnick, Idrian N. (ed.). *Tanzania: Revolution by Education*. Arusha: Longmans of Tanzania, 1968.

Roach, Penelope. *Political Socialization in the New Nations of Africa*. New York: Teachers College Press, 1967.

Scanlon, David G. *Traditions in African Education*, Classics in Education No. 16. New York: Bureau of Publications, 1964.

Schadler, Karl. *Crafts, Small-scale Industries and Industrial Education in Tanzania*. Series Africa-Studien, No. 34. Munchen: Weltforum Verlag, 1969.

Sigmund, Paul E., Jr. *The Ideologies of Developing Nations*. New York: Praeger, 1963.

Spindler, George (ed.). *Education and Culture: Anthropological Approaches*. New York: Holt, Rinehart and Winston, 1963.

The Transmission of American Culture. The Burton Lecture, 1957. Cambridge: Harvard University Press, 1959.

Stephens, Hugh W. *The Political Tranformation of Tanzania: 1920-1967*. New York: Praeger, 1968.

Thompson, A. R. "Ideas Underlying British Colonial Policy in Tanganyika" in Resnick (ed.). *Tanzania: Revolution by Education*. Arusha: Longmans of Tanzania, 1968, pp. 15-32.

Tordoff, William. *Government and Politics in Tanzania*: a collection of essays from September 1960 to July 1966. Nairobi: East Africa Publishing House, 1967.

E. *Masters' Theses and Doctoral Dissertations*

Chambati, Aristone M. "The Process of Transition from Colonial Rule to Independent Status in Tanzania." MPA thesis, New York University, 1968.

Chilivumbo, Alifeyo Bartholomew. "Tanganyika Mono-Party Regime: A Study in the Problems, Conditions and Processes of the Emergence and Development of the One-Party State on the Mainland of Tanzania." Unpublished Ph.D. dissertation, University of California, Los Angeles, 1968.

George, Ellen. "Education for Self-Reliance' in Tanzania: An Evaluation of Nyerere's Approach," Unpublished qualifying paper, Harvard University, 1968.

Hector, Henry J. "The Government's Role in African Post-primary Education in Tanganyika, 1919-1939." MA thesis, Teachers College, Columbia University, 1967.

Heyman, Richard David. "Manpower and Educational Planning in Kenya and Tanzania: A Comparative Study," MA thesis, Columbia Teachers College, 1967.

Hinkle, Rodney James. "Educational Problems and Policies in Post-Independent Tanzania." EdD Document, Teachers College, Columbia Univerversity, 1969.

Hodges, Norman E. "A Critical Evaluation of the Cambridge Examination System as it Applies to Contemporary Kenya." MA thesis, Columbia University, 1965.

Kayuza, Matthew Gordon. "An Analysis of and Recommendations for the Secondary Education in the East African Republic of Tanganyika." ME thesis, Cornell University, 1963.

Maluki, Eliud Ikusa. "The Influence of Traditionalism upon Nyerere's 'Ujamaa-ism.' " Unpublished PhD dissertation, University of Denver, 1965.

Mamuya, Matthew Salim. "Relgiion and Society in Tanganyika: An Encounter of Western Civilization with Traditional Culture." MA thesis, University of Pennsylvania, 1965.

Martin, Robert M. "An Analytic Survey of Tanganyikan Educational System during 1961-1964 Period." MA thesis, San Francisco State College, 1966.

Mbirika, Abukuwe V. E. P. "An Examination of the Functions of the University of East Africa in Relation to the Needs of the People." Unpublished Ph.D dissertation, New York University, 1970.

Miller, Richard I. "United Nations' Trusteeship System and Educational Advancement: A Report of a Type C Project." EdD document, Columbia Teachers College, 1958. Ch 5, "Tanganyika under the United Kingdom Administration."

Ramos, Sr. Regina V. "A Study of Some Factors Influencing Trends in the Philosophy of Education in East Africa." MA thesis, Catholic University of America, Washington, D.C., 1967.

Rweyemamu, Anthony Hubert. "Nation-Building and the Planning Processes of Tanzania." Unpublished Ph.D dissertation, Syracuse University, 1966.

INDEX

accountancy, 156
acquisitiveness, 87, 90, 109
activity method, 76, 159, 179
adaptation, 29, 30, 32, 56, 66, 67, 79, 80, 168, 197, 202; of African culture, 202, philosophy of 29, 30; principles of, 32; to local community, 56, 66-68 79, 80, 197, 199.
Addis Ababa, Conference at, 135
administration, 46, 67-68, 140-141, 158, 168-70, 175, 183; see also District Education Officer
administrators, 146
admission to schools, 129-31; to primary education, 121, 139; to secondary education, 75, 117, 129, 139; to teacher education, 129; to higher education, 150, 202
ADU Commission, 196; report of, 152
adult education, 142, 151, 155, 169-70, 173, 184, 201; in colonial days, 42, 50, 59, 74; from 1961-66, 141, 152, 161, 184; since 1966, 117, 169, 173, 185, 188, 190; definition of, 150; educational institutions and, 171; Institute of, 151; Nyerere and, 111; under Ministry of National Education, 169, 173, 186, 191, 199; in Phelps Stoke Report, 30, 36; and rural development, 190; and social change, 111, 207, 208
Advisory Committee on African Education, 46, 49, 129
Advisory Committee on Native Education in British East Africa, 29, 31, 36, 37
aesthetics: Nyerere and, 105; versus vocational values, 138, 158, 159
Africanization: of civil servants, 95, 116, 127, 135, 141, 147, 177, 193, 199, 210; of the curriculum, 198, 199; see also localization
L'Afrique Peut-Elle Partir? 97
Afya, 38
African personality, 8, 83
African School Supervisor, 59, 64, 66-68, 77
African socialism, 83, 84, 95
agricultural assistants, Nyerere on, 111, 120
agricultural change, 90
agricultural production, 21
agricultural versus industrial development, 98
agriculture, 14, 52, 92, 146, 206, 209, 210, 212; Department of, 35; education and training in, 31, 32, 38, 61, 71, 72, 79, 152, 176, 212; in Primary Schools, 38, 42, 76, 158-60, 178, 180, 197, 211; in Middle Schools, 44, 60, 65, 75, 76, 158, 159; in Secondary Schools, 145, 158, 159, 171, 211; seminars for Primary School Inspectors, 175; government and, 47, 109, 179, 187; Ministry of, 126; Nyerere on, 111, 119, 120, 122; in Ujamaa villages, 119
aims of education, 75; of primary education, 35, 68; of secondary education, 66, 68. See also goals; objectives
akidas, 20, 26

allowances in teacher education, 147, 161, 184
Anderson, C. A., 211
Annual Reports, on education: of 1923, 28; of 1924, 39; of 1936, 41; of 1944, 51, 52; of 1953, 62; of 1954, 62. See also Trienniel Survey of Education
Anthropologists, 209, 213-14
Arabic, 19
Arabs, 13, 14 See also Koranic Schools; Moslems, education of
Arithmetic, 105
Arrighi, Giovanni, 11, 92, 98, 102
Art, 39
Arts, 79, 156, 158, 182, 184, 187; versus science, 144, 160, 176
Artisan, 22, 28, 38, 146
Arusha Declaration, 9, 10, 11, 13, 96, 110, 123, 124, 139, 166, 167, 173, 180, 193
Asian education, 57; See also Goans: Indian education; Non-native education
Asian vernaculars, 193
Asians, 13, 91, 133, 144
Assistant Chief Education Officer, 135
attendance, 21, 28, 37, 154. See also Wastage
attitude of mind, 84, 85 n, 91-93, 104, 122, 165
attitudes, 106, 108, 109, 119, 125, 167, 168, 172, 179, 206; communication of, 203, 208, 212; institutions and, 93, 95, 117; negative, 10, 21, 28, 44, 50, 52, 65, 69, 122, 158, 210; of equality, 102, 110, 202, 203; of inferiority, 125; of parents, 21, 28; towards agriculture, 209, 210; towards education, 50, 52, 56, 65, 69, 80; towards girls' education, 69; towards money, 91, towards rural life, 44, 121, 209, 210; towards work, 58, 87, 101, 209; traditional, 90, 123
attitudinal change, 14, 112, 121, 150, 172, 203, 207, 209, 212, 213

bands in school, 21
Barkan, Joel W., 11, 211
bee-keeping, 171
Bennett, George, 94
Binns Mission, 133
Binns Study Report, 61
blind, education of, 174
Board of Governors, 130, 131, 133, 141, 161, 169, 191, 192, 199
boarding schools, 191; Central Schools, 37; District Schools, 68; elimination of, 42, 170, 176, 189; Middle Schools, 65, 69, 142; 144,153; Secondary Schools, 70, 117, 120, 178, 194; Upper Primary Schools, 153, 154, 170
bootmaking, 38
Boy Scouts, 39, 51
British Colonial Development Act of 1929, 44
British Colonial Development and Welfare Act: of 1940, 44; of 1945, 45, 74

232

budget, the, 142, 170 n, 183
building course, 71, 72, 78
buildings, 68, 135, 180, 194; relevancy of, 36, 37, 118, 185, 194; self-
help projects, 153, 194; use of, 153, 154, 187,194
Burke, Fred B., 10, 87, 92, 97, 151
bursaries, 113, 148, 150, 155, 156, 161, 176, 177, 186-88, 195, 200, 213
bush schools, 34, 47, 59, 62, 64, 67; see also Schools, Part II
Bwiru Girls Secondary School, 145, 159
Byatt, Sir Horace, 25

Cambridge Overseas School Certificate Examination, 67, 70, 75, 76,
129, 147, 153, 160, 175
Cambridge Mock Examination, 155, 177
Cameron, John, 11, 56, 154
Cameron, Sir Donald, 26, 27, 32, 43
capitalism, 84-87, 89-91, 97
Capuchin Sisters, 37
*Careers for Nation Building: A Career Guide Book for Secondary
School Students,* 155
carpentry, 38, 71, 75, 87, 121, 123, 158, 159
Castle, E. B., 149, 207
cattle raising, 13, 14, 47, 60, 94, 121, 128
Central Inspectorate, 134
Central Schools, 26, 34, 35, 37, 38, 40, 46-49
Centralization: of colonial government, 55; of education system, 127, 187,
190, 206; of vocational training, 48; versus decentralization,
192, 193
change: in traditional society, 26, 122; school's role in social change,
42, 146, 158, 185, 209, 212, 213
See also, Attitudinal change; Social change; Cultural change
character: assessment of, 121; development, 21, 30, 32, 33, 38, 77, 105;
recommendation of, 177, 185, 196; training, 61, 79, 108, 182
chemistry, 179
Chief Education Officer, 130, 141, 169
Chief Inspector for Indian Schools, 46
chiefs, 46, 52, 56, 96; education of, 36, 60
Chiefs Ordinance of 1954, 62
child development, 177, 208, 213
Christian Council of Tanzania, 141
citizenship: duties of, 33; education for, 59, 60, 68, 77, 151, 188, 206;
national, 114; rights of, 88, 103, 113, world, 115; 116
civic responsibility: objectives of, 113-16; policies for, 188
civics, 105, 124, 181, 188
clerical education, 72, 78
climate, 12, 20
co-educational institutions, 63, 68-70
coercion, 92, 97, 119
coffee, 18, 128
College of Business Education, 171

233

College of Commerce, 72
College of National Education, 172; tutors of, 189
colonialism, 157; effects of, 18-19, 90-91; opposition to, 89, 115
Colonial Office Advisory Committee, 42
commercial education, 49, 60, 63, 72, 145, 156, 159, 171, 189
Committee on the Integration of Education in Tanganyika, 129
Common course, 175
communication, 116, 125, 160, 207, 213
communism, 84-86, 113
community development, 60, 66, 151, 168, 171, 180, 187, 204, 205; see
    also rural education
Community Development Training Centre, 151
competition, 81, 87, 107-08, 170, 177, 185, 186, 202
compulsory education, 21
concept learning, 208-09
Condon, John C., 182
consultants, 213
contract, 186, 188, 195
cooperation, 84, 86-89, 101, 102, 107-09, 121, 181, 186; with other
    agencies, 190, 199
cooperatives, 93, 186, 203, 205
coordinators, of subjects, 179
correspondence courses, 60, 149, 152, 172
cottage industries, 111
Cox, Christopher, 58
Cox Commission, 58
crafts, 111, 145, 158, 159, 169, 171, 179, 184
craftsmen, 71-72
creative arts, 77, 162
critical judgment, 113-14
critical thinking, 105, 121, 125, 162, 165, 214
cultural change, 30, 158
culture: adaptation of, 202; African, 8, 14, 105, 123-24, 182, 203, 204;
    education and, 79, 124, 174, 179; revival of, 182-84, 210; West-
    ern, 24, 204
current affairs, 160
curriculum, 158, 166, 199, 211; adaptations in, 30, 36, 210; Africaniza-
    tion of, 198, 210; content, 38, 49, 79, 81, 124, 160, 178, 197,
    198, 200, 208; development, 74, 124, 125, 177, 179; of primary
    education, 38, 49, 160, 180, 183; relevancy of, 69, 79, 185, 191,
    212; revisions 168, 175, 176, 182; unification of, 187; of voca-
    tional education, 145
Curriculum Development and Examinations, 169

Dar es Salaam Technical College, 145,171
deaf, education of, 174
decentralization: of authority for schools, 8, 44, 67, 93, 132, 161, 187,
    192; of authority for curriculum development, 179; versus central-
    ization, 132, 192-93

degrees, 73, 122, 143, 148, 160, 208
De la Warr Commission, 43, 49
democratic, 88, 93, 100, 204
democracy, 104; one-party, 14, 83, 93, 96; in traditional society, 84, 89, 90
Department of Agriculture, 35
Department of Education, 35, 66; see also Ministry of Education; Ministry of National Education
Depression, the, 39, 42, 48, 79
Development Plan for Tanganyika, 1961-64, *The,* 100, 101, 128, 141, 142, 147, 171, 189, 194
diploma, 73, 143, 148, 151
Director of Education, 26, 33, 35, 37, 63, 66
Director of National Education, 169, 173, 182, 183, 191
discipline, 18, 21, 62, 93, 126, 158, 191
disease, 110
District Commissioner, 55, 67
District Education Committees, 59
District Education Officers, (A) and (1), 134, 141, 175, 178, 192; see also Primary School Inspector
District Schools, 59, 67-69
District Training Centres, 151, 152
Dodd, Wm. A., 11, 131, 132, 192, 212
Domestic Science, 69, 71, 72, 75, 143, 158, 159, 171
Doob, Leonard, 207
"double streaming", 194
Dumont, Rene, 11, 207, 211

East Africa Examination Council, 175
East African Muslim Welfare Society, 141
East African Certificate of Education, the, 175
eccentric, 93, 94, 114; see also opposition
economic development, 45, 55, 102, 138
economic efficiency, 109-112, 145, 201; policies for, 186-88
economic goals, 26, 125, 126, 138-40, 145, 152, 159, 195, 201, 203
economic rights, 88
economy, 39
economy measures, 152-54, 172, 194-96
Education Act of 1969, 132, 169, 183, 190, 191, 199
Education Act Supplement No. 62, 169, 191
Education Assistant, 65, 67, 77
Education Conference of 1925, 29, 32
Education, courses in university, 160
Education for Citizenship in East Africa, 59
Education for Self-Reliance, 96, 104, 108, 120, 167, 180, 191
Education Integration Committee, 64
Education Officer, 146, 148
Education Ordinance: of 1927, 33, 41; of 1933, 47; amendments to, of 1954, 62, 63; of 1961, 130-32, 140, 144, 169, 190; amendments

to, of 1965, 32
Education Planning Unit, 128, 135, 139, 161, 187, 195, 200
education policies: of 1920-31, 29-34; of 1932-45, 41-46; of 1946-61, 58-66; of 1961-66, 128-141; after 1966, 166-168
Education Policy in British Tropical Africa, 31
Education Secretary, 74, 141, 161, 167, 169, 193
Education Secretary General, 141, 169, 191, 192
egalitarianism, 84, 90, 104, 109, 111, 117, 140, 166, 203, 204, 210
elementary education; see bush schools; district schools;
    Extended Primary Schools; Lower Primary Schools; Middle Schools;
    primary education; Primary School course; Primary Schools;
    Upper Primary Schools; Village Schools.
elite, 13, 93, 118, 125, 167, 174, 183, 185, 211
employment, 60, 142, 168, 171, 187, 191, 200, 201, 210, 211
Enemy Property, 43
engineering, see technical education
England: 73
English: Course, 35.38; as a medium of instruction, 13, 24 n. 31, 50, 61, 75, 132, 153, 154, 160, 174, 184, 185, 192, 193, 199; status of, 46, 147, 199; teachers of, 50, 63; teaching of, 34, 68, 77, 105-06, 174, 194
enrollment, in primary education, 13, 22, 28, 34, 41, 51, 57, 63, 73, 136, 139, 142, 170 n, 190; in secondary education, 13, 57, 58, 73, 136, 137, 139, 170 n, 190; in higher education, 13, 150; in non-formal education, 151-52; of Africans, 57; of Asians, 57; of Europeans, 57, 144; of girls, 34, 57, 69; of Indians, 37
equality, 24 n. 84-86, 88-90, 92, 101, 104, 110, 116, 117, 121, 145, 152, 182, 186, 187; attitudes of, 102, 110, 202, 203
ethic, National, 14, 83, 88-89, 113, 159, 165
European Education Authority, 60, 67, 129
Europeans: population of, 13, 91; education of, 22, 34, 37, 57, 60, 70, 144
Evan, P. C., 145
examinations, 20, 40, 81, 106, 121, 132, 159, 161, 162, 169, 170, 177, 184, 190, 197, 199; of Standard IV, 67, 75; for Secondary School entrance, 50, 129; G.E.E., 75; Territorial Std. VIII Examination, 67, 75; Territorial Std. X Examination, 67, 69, 70, 78, 148, 149, 155; Cambridge Overseas Certificate Examination, 67, 70, 75, 76, 160, 175; Cambridge Mock Examination, 155, 196; for clerical entrance, 50; English Qualfiying Examination, 149; in teacher education, 36, 48, 50, 172
expansion: of adult education, 161; of the education system, 59, 80, 127, 127, 148, 161, 165, 192, 198; of higher education, 142, 189; of post primary education, 50, 135, 142, 158, 170, 171, 183, 188, 189, 195; of primary education, 68, 71, 77, 111, 117, 141, 142, 148, 168, 170, 172, 184, 189, 196, 200; of secondary education, 47, 50, 62, 137, 142, 145, 147, 154, 170; of teacher education, 50, 62, 148, 172; of technical education, 62; patterns, 189-90
expatriates, 71, 81, 98, 122, 128, 143, 144, 152, 167, 171, 177, 183, 197
experimentation, 36-37, 44, 47, 52, 61, 79, 80, 122, 166, 168, 202, 203,

205, 208
exploitation, 87, 88, 90, 93, 108, 125, 181
Extended Primary Schools, 142, 147

farming, 119, 146, 158, 191, 205, 210, 211
fees, 21, 65, 147, 154, 161, 178, 187; remission of, 154
Five-Year-Plan, of 1956-61, 56, 58, 62, 71
Five-Year Plan for Economic and Social Development, 1964-69, *The,*
    101, 102, 110, 128, 137, 138, 141, 148, 151, 154, 166, 167, 167,
    171, 194, 200
flexibility, 121, 169
folk tales, 182
foreign aid, 128, 187
foremanship, 72
forestry training, 72
Form E.F. 65, 177, 196
Fox, Lorene K., 162
freedom, 84, 89, 115, 116, 126, 140; personal, 85-88, 104, 110, 125, 213,
    group, 88, 93, 104, 125; a principal of Ujamaa-ism, 84, 90, 93,
    101, 103, 117
Freedom and Socialism, 100, 113, 114
Freedom and Unity, 94, 114
French, 160, 186, 198
frugality, 112, 187, 188, 194, 200, 203
Full Primary Schools, 142, 159

Geiss, Immanuel, 84
General Entrance Examination (GEE), 75
General Knowledge, 77
General Science, 75
geography, 105, 160, 198
George, Ellen, 11
German administration; Anglo-German agreement, 17; education in,
    17-24; German-Portuguese Agreement, 17; Helgoland Treaty, 17;
    language policy of, 19, 20, 23
German Colonial Society, 20
German East Africa Company, 17
Ghana, 84
Girl Guides, 51
girls' education, 31, 33, 41, 46-48, 59, 75, 207; aim of, 51; attitudes
    toward, 69; homecraft courses in, 75, 78; in mission schools, 23,
    34, 48; percentage enrolled, 57, 69; in post-primary education,
    48, 59, 69, 72, 78; in village schools, 34, 69; wastage in, 56, 57,
    68-70
goals: cultural, 185, 195, 201; economic, 26, 140, 195, 201, 203;
    national, 175, 202; social, 10, 80, 140, 195, 201, vocational, 10,
    80, 201; ultimate, 100-103; see also Nyerere, Objectives
Goans, 37, 60
Government Paper No. 1 of 1960, 129

237

governor, 25

Grades of teacher education: I, 34-36, 40-42, 50, 70, 78; II, 35, 40, 59, 70, 71, 75, 78; III, 59, 70; A, 135, 143, 146-49, 155, 159, 172, 189, 196; B, 148, 149; C, 143, 147-49, 172, 178, 189; C special, 172, 189; D, 172, 189; Education Officer, 146, 148

graduates, 149, 191, 195; Education Officers, 146; of industrial education, 40; of Kivukoni College, 151; of secondary education, 143, 155, 160, 162, 168, 176; salary of, 152, 161; of teacher education, 71, 135, 143, 148; of trade schools, 156; of university, 58, 87, 120, 122, 137, 156, 160

grants-in-aid, 20, 31, 33, 34, 37, 40, 64, 66, 118, 121, 129, 131, 141, 194; see also Schools, assisted

group, 85, 110; versus individuals, 86, 87, 103, 104, 182

handicraft education, 31, 42, 49, 71, 75, 143, 158
handymen, 49
Hapgood, David, 205
harmony, 87, 88, 109
health education, 30-32, 38, 45, 77, 79, 105, 112, 158
Hector, Henry J. 11, 39, 158
Heijnen, J. D., 210
Higher School Certificate, 70; course, 129, 155, 176, 195
higher education, 38, 47, 72, 73, 80, 118, 141, 142, 146, 149, 160, 169, 181, 182, 185, 187, 188, 200; courses, 202; entrance to, 150, 185, 195, 201; institutions of, 31, 32, 191-93; role of, 118, 137, 138; student of, 208; university education, 150, 160, 172, 173, 186, 194; see also university
Hinkle, Rodney James, 11, 132, 157
H. H. the Aga Khan's Education Department, 141
history, 105, 123, 124, 160, 181, 183, 198
homecrafts, 60; see also Domestic Science
human relationships, policies for, 185-186
Hunter, Guy, 138, 139, 211
hygiene, 31, 33, 38, 56, 101

identity, 125
idleness, 87
ignorance, 110
Ifunda Trade School, 72, 145, 159
illiteracy, 10, 38, 50, 87, 117, 142, 191, 196, 205, 207
Imperial German Government, 17
imperialism, 113
improvement: of society, 90, 101; approach, 204
India, 73
Indian education, 22, 34, 37, 46, 48, 51, 60, 61, 70
Indian Education Authority, 60, 67, 129
indirect rule, 26, 27, 36, 38, 41, 47
individual, 32, 33, 81, 85-88, 100, 103, 113, 123, 125, 201, 209; versus group, 85-87, 89, 103, 104, 109

industrial development vs. agricultural development, 98
industrial education, 31, 32, 35, 38, 40, 72, 152; see also technical education; vocational education
industries; cottage, 111; nationalization of, 9, 14, 93, 174
inegalitarianism, 166, 177, 183, 192
inequalities, 56, 65, 80, 86, 90, 102, 128, 165
inferiority, 91, 108
informal education 191
inservice training, 98, 141, 151, 152, 154, 155, 160, 161, 172, 175, 187, 196, 208, 212; see also refresher courses
inspection, 40, 46, 50, 66, 68; Chief Inspector, 46; Inspector for Indian Schools, 46; see also supervision; African School Supervisor
inspectorate, 66, 134, 161, 169, 175; reform of 1963, 134, 161, 191; see also Primary School Inspector
Institute of Adult Education, 151, 173
Institute of Education, 149, 160, 175, 181, 198
Institute of Public Administration, 151
institutions, 92, 95; educational, 46-48, 67-74, 92, 95, 141-152, 170-74
integration: of government and mission schools, 169, 174, 190; of knowledge, 209; of multi-racial systems, 8, 64, 108, 127, 130, 132, 133, 144, 159, 161, 184, 186, 188, 199; of schools and community, 120, 131, 167, 173, 176, 178, 183, 191-92, 198, 199, 202; of schools and nation-building, 172, 175, 178; of values, 204
International Development Association, 178
Ireland, 73
Islam, 19, 123; see also Moslem, education of; Koranic schools
itinerant educators, 177

Jeanes School, 60
Junior Secondary Schools, 44, 47, 49
justice, 113

Kaayk, Jan, 205
Kenya, 9, 37, 84, 146
kindergarten, 22
King, Jane, 151, 152
Kitchen, Helen, 77
Kivukoni College, 150-53, 173
Klinglehofer, E. L., 11, 159
Koff, David, 11, 211, 212
Koranic schools, 19, 20, 56, 57, 68
laboratory assistants, 143

Labourism: Christian, 84; Fabian, 84; Welfare, 84
Langa, A., 207
language: official, 13, 168, 174, 199; policy, 193-94; as a subject, 77, 193; use of English, 61, 152-53, 159-60, 174, 192-94, 199; use of Swahili, 18-20, 24 n, 38, 124, 133, 152-53, 159-60, 168, 174, 183, 192-94, 199; vernacular, 31, 38, 56, 61, 193

239

Laubach, Frank, 50
law, 39, 93, 114, 156
leaders, 32, 90, 93, 94, 98, 113, 114, 116, 147, 205, 206
leadership, 97, 165, 167, 201; changes in requirements of, 8; and Five-Year Plan (1964), 167, 184; in traditional society, 27, 55, 89, 206; training for, 173-74, 188-90, 198, 200
LeVine, Robert, 96, 97
library services, 183
life expectancy, 13, 137
lingua france, 18
literacy, 10, 23, 34, 35, 46, 50, 53, 60, 68, 79, 105, 143, 207, 211; of adults, 59, 74, 150, 151, 171, 173, 185, 190; rate, 13, 58, 205
local: adaptation, 122, 197, 203; decisions, 114; initiative, 112, 189
Local Authorities, 65, 131, 187, 190, 194
Local Education Authorities, 8, 46, 131, 140-42, 153, 161, 169, 176, 189, 192
localization, 95, 116, 127, 159, 172
Lower Primary Schools, 142
Lugard, 27
luxury, 109

Makerere, 44, 47, 50, 58, 59, 69, 72, 143, 148
Malangali, 36, 37, 40
Mali, 84
Malinowski, Bronislaw, 46
malnutrition, 106
Maluki, Eliud I., 12, 94, 96, 97
Mamuya, Matthew S., 12, 18, 204
man: purpose of, 84, 85, 103; well-being of, 85
manpower, 135, 155, 167, 180, 195; goals, 26, 102, 140, 161, 176, 195, 201, 203; highly-skilled, 9, 66, 118, 137, 138, 150, 176, 186, 198, 201; over-development of, 168, 190, 195, 200; Planning Unit, 110, 161, 195; requirements of, 127, 137, 147, 149-51, 154, 160, 166, 185-86, 188; self-sufficiency in, 25, 137, 166, 171, 193, 195, 201; surveys, 145, 195; targets, 110, 137, 156; see also Overproduction, dangers of
Marham, AEO, 211 n
Martin, Robert M., 12
Mass Education in the African Society, 45, 52
masonry, 71, 72, 123
mathematics, 179
Maxwell, John Francis, 97
Mazrui, Ali A., 204
Mboya, Tom, 17
Mead, Margaret, 212, 213
Meister, Albert, 26, 83, 93, 96, 97, 146, 147, 211
Memorandum in the Education of African Communities, 42
Mgonja, C. Y., 182
micro-teaching, 182

240

241

Natural Resources School, 70, 72
nature study, 158
needlework, 78; see also Domestic Science
non-citizens, 113, 154, 188
non-native education, 61, 65
Non-native Education Authority, 67, 129
Non-native Education Ordinance, 60, 130
Non-native Education Tax Ordinance, 60, 67, 130
Nuffield, 179
nursing education, 75
Nyerere, Julius K.: on adult education, 111; on agricultural assistants, 111, 120; on attitudes, 87, 111; on character, 105, 106, 108, 114, 121, 125; on colonialism, 18-19, 90-91; on critical thinking, 105, 125; on curriculum, 105-06, 124; on democracy, 104; on examinations, 106, 121; on freedom, 84-89, 93, 101, 103, 104, 110, 115-17, 125, 126; on leadership, 89, 90, 93, 94, 97, 98, 113, 114, 116; life of, 8-10, 94, 95; on local versus overseas' education, 120, 123; on nationalization, 96; objectives of, 4, 103-16; philosophy of, 83-99; on religion, 85, 88, 106; on role of schools, 108, 109, 118, 120; on social change, 102, 121; on teachers, 118-19, 126; on traditional society, 89-92; on Ujamaa villages, 119; and university student protest, 157; see also coercion; eccentric; *Education for Self-Reliance;* improvement approach; transformation approach; workers

objectives, Nyerere's: for civic responsibility, 113-16; for economic efficiency, 109-12; for human relationships, 106-09; for self-realization, 103-06; see also aims; goals
one-party system, 14, 83, 93, 96
opposition, 87, 102, 105; see also eccentric
overproduction, dangers of, 28, 37, 43, 156
overseas' education, 23; scholarships, 59, 156, 176, 188, 195; versus African oriented, 123, 150

parasitism, 87, 110, 165
participation, 101, 104, 111, 125, 162, 205, 207
Peace Corps, 76, 144, 155, 159, 180, 193
pension, 133
Percival, 49
Phelps-Stoke Commission to East Africa, 29, 31, 32, 34, 37, 41, 47, 55, 61
physical education, 51, 77, 158, 182
'Plant More Crops' campaign, 40
political: awareness, 45, 172, 182; education, 170, 174, 175, 182, 183, 187, 188, 191, 196-99, 213
population, 12-14, 29, 142, 165, 179
postprimary education: cost of, 202; emphasis on, 38, 171, 183, 188, 190, 200; institutions, 131, 141, 161; opportunities, 121, 166, 178, 190, 195, 206, 213; relevancy of, 160

242

243

244

245

Swynnerton, 60, 76
syllabuses, 39, 42, 74, 130, 131, 158, 159, 161, 182, 188, 190, 196; of
     1935, 51; of 1947, 49, 51; of 1963, 134, 178, 197, 198; of
     1968, 180, 197, 198; for girls, 51, 78; for Indian education, 51;
     for Middle Schools, 76, 159, 180; for Secondary Schools, 76; re-
     vision of, 51, 132, 145, 154, 158, 160

Tabora: Central School, 47; Clerical course, 50; Girls' Secondary
     Schools, 171, Junior Secondary School, 49, 72; Secondary School,
     50, 70
tailoring, 38, 71
Tait and Riddy Report, 60
Tananarive, Conference at, 135, 138
Tanganyika African National Union (TANU), 9, 14, 56, 67, 91, 96,
     100, 131, 151, 157, 166, 175, 188, 203, 205
Tanganyika African Parents Association (TAPA), 56, 67, 141
Tanganyika Broadcasting Company (TBC), 77, 207
Tanganyika Episcopal Church, 141
Tanga School, 19, 20, 23, 35
TANU na Raia, 96
TANU Youth League, 175, 181, 186, 190, 191, 199
Tanzania Elimu Supplies, Ltd., 174
taxation, 122
teacher education: in German times, 23; of 1920-31, 31, 34-36, 38; of
     1932-45, 44, 48, 50; of 1946-61, 59, 62, 70, 75, 77, 78; of 1961-
     66, 129, 135, 141, 147-49, 154, 160-61; after 1966, 168, 172, 175,
     184, 189, 196, 212-13; in agriculture, 71; alliances in, 48, 50; in
     Domestic Science, 71; in Handwork, 71; heads of, 167, 175, 177,
     193; Nyerere on, 118; studies on, 11; see also allowances in
     teacher education; grades of teacher education; graduates of teach-
     er education; inservice training; quality, in teacher education;
     refresher courses
Teachers for East Africa (TEA), 144, 193
Technical Advisor Component, 172
technical assistants, 146
technical education: of 1920-31, 38; of 1932-45, 48; of 1946-61, 59,
     62, 63, 71; of 1961-66, 141, 145-47, 155, 159, 161, 162; after
     1966, 169, 171, 182, 185, 187, 189, 200; engineering, 72, 78;
     staff in, 146, 193; see also Dar es Salaam Technical College;
     Royal Technical College
Technical Institute, 60, 64, 72, 78
Ten-Year Development Plan, 51, 56, 58, 60, 67; revision of, 56, 58, 60,
     72
Territorial Standard VIII Examination, 67, 75, 76, 129
Territorial Standard X Examination, 67, 69, 70, 75, 78, 148, 155, 161
textbooks, 63, 81, 112, 122, 174, 180, 181, 188
Thomas, Robert L., 145, 195
Three-Year Plan, the: of 1959, 65; of 1961-64; see *The Development
     Plan for Tanganyika*, 1961-64

Tobias, George, 145, 195
trade, 17, 18, 29, 49
trade schools, 22, 58, 60, 64, 171; policy for, 71; training in, 72, 75, 78, 124, 145; see also Ifunda Trade School; Moshi Trade School
traditional society, 38, 89, 203, 206; arts, 182, 184; and change, 26, 90, 91, 96, 210; democracy in, 84, 89, 90; education in, 79, 199; inadequacies in, 90; institutions of, 92, 210; methods of, 122, 209; values of, 12, 83, 91, 94, 97, 140, 204, 209, 210, 212
transformation approach, 101, 102, 125, 189, 201, 204
tribe, environment of, 36, 38, 39
Triennial Survey, 68, 71

Uganda, 9
Ujamaa, 89, 92, 101, 168, 172, 178
Ujamaa-ism, 8, 9, 84, 86, 87, 210; aims of, 212; criticisms of, 93-98; freedoms in, 116-17; principles of, 109; versus communism and capitalism, 84, 86, 91, 92
Ujamaa: the Basis of African Socialism, 93, 95
Ujamaa villages, 102, 110, 114, 119, 125, 201, 203, 204
Unified Teaching Service, 8, 130, 133, 152, 169, 174, 186, 191
Unified Teaching Service Board, 133
UNESCO, 172, 173, 194, 195
United Nations, 94, 115
UN Visiting Missions, 55: of 1948, 41; of 1957, 57, 64
United States, 73
unity, 87, 90, 101, 108, 109, 117; African, 89, 115
Universal Declaration of Rights, 113
universal primary education, 10, 65, 111, 117, 118, 166, 170, 183, 184, 189, 195, 200
university, 43, 70, 73, 78, 87, 113, 123, 150, 156, 161, 162, 194, 211; cost of, 202; enrollment, 13, 150; entrance to, 208; evaluation committee of, 173, 182; Faculty of Agriculture, 172; Faculty of Arts and Social Sciences, 150; Faculty of Commerce, 172-73; Faculty of Engineering, 150, 173, 195; Faculty of Law, 150; Faculty of Medicine, 172; Faculty of Science, 150; graduates of, 58, 122, 156; nationalization of, 186, 188, 191; role of, 118, 120; student protest, 89, 96, 105, 137, 139, 156-57, 163, 180; see also bursaries; Institute of Education; overseas' education versus African oriented
University College, 137, 148, 150, 151, 155, 160, 175, 182, 189, 190, 194, 198
University of Dar es Salaam, 73, 200, 202, 208
University of East Africa, 141, 143, 150, 173, 186, 190
upgrading courses, 37, 78, 148, 149, 154, 161, 172, 175, 187, 196, 213
Upper Primary Schools, 142, 147, 153, 154, 180
urban, 28, 89, 95, 96, 210; education, 118, 144, 173, 184; immigration to, 39, 146, 191, 205; versus rural, 13, 49, 66

vernacular language, 31, 38, 61

247

veterinary training, 72
village schools, 34, 35, 38, 44, 53, 59, 67, 68
visual aids, 134
vocational: goals, 10, 51, 80, 168, 207; education and training, 33, 35; 37, 38, 48 49, 71, 72, 78, 141, 145, 147, 158, 162, 171, 178-80, 183, 185, 187, 192, 197, 199, 200, 211
vocational-guidance counseling, 150, 176, 177, 188, 195
Volksschule, 23
Voluntary Agencies (VAs), 47, 51, 63, 66, 130, 133, 144, 161, 169, 174, 183, 188, 190, 199; see also mission schools
von der Muhll, George, 11, 211, 212

wages, 8, 41, 121-22, 142, 152, 172, 174, 176; see also salaries
Wallerstein, I., 96
wastage in enrollment, 80, 127, 161; causes of, 52, 154, 187; of girls, 56, 57, 68-70; in primary education, 52, 56, 58, 68, 142, 154, 178; in teacher education, 70, 71
wealth, 105
weaving, 38
welding, 38
women; education of, 33, 48, 50, 57, 152, 207; rights of, 90; see girls' education
Women's Education Officer, 46, 66
Working Party of Higher Education, 64, 72
workers, 85, 101, 105, 108, 111, 112, 116, 121, 152, 166
work-study projects, 122, 126, 171, 179, 185, 206
World Bank Mission, 61, 69, 195
World War I, 25
Warld War II, 40-42, 44-46, 48, 51, 55, 80, 81